Tuomas M. S. Lehtonen
FORTUNA, MONEY, AND THE SUBLUNAR WORLD

Tuomas M. S. Lehtonen

Fortuna, Money, and the Sublunar World

Twelfth-century Ethical Poetics and the Satirical
Poetry of the *Carmina Burana*

Finnish Historical Society ■ Helsinki

Coverpicture: Carmina Burana clm 4660

ISSN 1238-3503

ISBN 951-710-027-2

Gummerus Kirjapaino Oy,
Saarijärvi 1995

■ Contents

■ Acknowledgements

To complete this study, the help of a number of teachers, friends and relatives has been crucial. I now have the pleasure of thanking them for their learning, correction, and support. Many greater and lesser points are to their credit but I alone am responsible for all flaws and errors.

It is sad that my thanks will not reach the teacher who had the most profound impact on my scholarly career and intellectual orientation, namely the late Professor Matti Viikari from the Department of History, University of Helsinki. I cannot exaggerate his influence on my work or the significance of his friendship and encouragement. Under his guidance I acquired a commitment to study and an emphasis on rational argument, discussion, and came to understand the minor importance of formal qualifications.

I am very grateful for the guidance and help which Professor Matti Klinge has offered me especially during the final phase of my work. He has taught me that a real humanist aspires both to the *vita contemplativa* and *activa*, and thus reaches beyond his own cell - and out towards society at large.

I am indebted to Professor Simo Knuuttila for his teachings in medieval (and ancient) philosophy. He has made many valuable suggestions on earlier stages of my work, and has had a decisive impact on its final version as an official referee. His remarks have undoubtedly saved me from many mistakes and lapses. Likewise I wish to thank my other referee the Director General of the Finnish National Archives, Docent Veikko Litzen, for his remarks.

The director of the Finnish Institute in Rome, Docent Päivi Setälä has also been an important guide and supporter from the very beginning of my scholarly career.

During these years I have used my senior and junior colleagues unscrupulously, asking them advice or to read my work. I owe a special debt of gratitude to several literary scholars. First, I wish to thank Päivi Mehtonen who has generously offered me her knowledge of medieval poetics and theories of narration. Similarly, Docent Pirjo Lyytikäinen has read my work several times, revealing some of its blind spots by making numerous important comments. I hope that I have not left all the reciprocal obligations unfulfilled. Hannu K. Riikonen, acting Professor of comparative literature, also kindly agreed to go into my study, emended some of my mistakes and made important suggestions for changes.

My colleagues in the field of history have not only helped my work with their comments but equally with their friendship, example and by accepting me as a member of a lively scholarly community. They are so many that I cannot name them all here. Among those to whom I feel the deepest gratitude is Docent Juha Sihvola who has always been a sharp commentator and a good friend, and in his company I have had the pleasure of acquainting myself with ancient philosophy and modern good life. Dr. Heikki Mikkeli adviced me in the preliminary stages and since then has helped and has encouraged me to trust my own judgement. In its various stages my work has been also read by scholars in medieval history and philology, including Derek Fewster, Mika Hakkarainen, Anja-Inkeri Lehtinen, Jarmo Pankamaa and Leena Talvio to whom I owe my gratitude. Tapani Hietaniemi has been an important friend and colleage in various scholarly pursuits.

Dr. Rod McConchie from the Department of English in the University of Helsinki has corrected the English in this work for which I am deeply grateful. I want to emphasize that I am alone responsible for what mistakes remain.

Rauno Endén from the Finnish Historical Society has been a pleasant collaborator, and had offered his advice long before the decision to publish my study in the prestigious Finnish Historical Society series was made.

Sources of financial support have been many, and those who had made the decisions even more numerous. I wish to thank them all through the institutions they represent. My doctoral studies were enabled by receiving the grant bearing the name of the late Professor of general history, Jaakko Suolahti, in 1988. Later on I enjoyed for the privileged position of associate reseacher of the Academy of Finland four years (during 1989-93). These funds made my postgraduate studies and research in Paris possible. The Finnish Cultural Fund helped me to finish my work with its grants in 1994 and 1995, and the last two months were secured by a grant of the University of Helsinki.

Without libraries and their helpful staff this study would not have been possible. I wish to thank two of them especially, namely the University of Helsinki Library and Bibliothèque Nationale in Paris, both of which are most generous and beautiful establishments. Nor is serious study easy without a place to do it in. For this I am grateful to the Renvall Institute of the University of Helsinki and its most helpful and kindly staff. The Institute has become an important scholarly community where I have pestered my colleagues Seppo Aalto, Christer Bruun, Markku Peltonen and Johannes Remy with my questions through the years. I wish to thank them for their forbearance and obliging answers. Without the people of the Doku-laitos and later on the Renttu-instituutti I would have lacked not only practical facilities and positive working community but also a place for seminars, study-groups and workshops.

I am thankful to my parents Elina and Samuel Lehtonen who prompted me very early in independent thought, scholarly work and the pursuit of wisdom and have supported my acquisitions of scholarly literature.

Perhaps my deepest gratitude of all is to my wife Dr. Kirsi Saarikangas who knows my debt to her only too well. We have grown into intellectual life together, she has always encouraged me to go on and has also offered me a model of successful academic work. To her and our son Elias I am grateful for their love, which has given meaning to this endeavour.

I wish to dedicate this work to my late Professor Matti Viikari - *ibi nullus timet mortem*.

Vuorikatu, Helsinki, November 1995
Tuomas M. S. Lehtonen

■ Introduction

Points of departure: Latin poetry, clerical culture, and ethical poetics

The period from the eleventh to the thirteenth century is widely considered an age of social, political and cultural transition in Western Europe. In the field of literary and learned culture the middle of this period is usually called "the twelfth-century renaissance", referring to a cultural movement which took place especially in the most important school centres of Northern France, i.e. Laon, Chartres, Orléans, Le Mans and Paris, etc. where the new scholarly and literary achievements exceeded the achievements of Western Christianity in the Early Middle Ages both in quality and quantity.[1]

In the Church the new orientation towards secular society surpassed the earlier monastic trend which had dominated institutionally, doctrinally and in the forms and contents of religious practices until the twelfth century.[2] Economically and socially strengthened towns functioned as motors of this change. In ecclesiastical life this meant that the locus of activity moved from the monasteries and cloister schools to the urban episcopal sees and cathedral schools under their control.[3] The expansion of urban lay society led to growth in the importance of secular clergy and to the emergence of a new learned clerical order.[4]

---

1   The notion of the "twelfth-century renaissance" was introduced by Charles H. Haskins in his classic study *The Renaissance of the Twelfth Century* (1928). As a study it is already outdated - mainly because of wide-ranging research and discussion it has itself inspired. See e.g. Chenu 1957, 19-51; Clanchy 1983, 162-179; Stock 1990, 72-73; de Gandillac 1992, 138-148. A lot of literature complementary to Haskins' work has been published, among others a large collection of articles *Renaissance and Renewal in the Twelfth Century* (ed. by R.L. Benson & G. Constable, 1982). However, manuscript tradition demonstrates that there was never a total rupture in the study of the literature of antiquity. The renewal of learning in the twelfth century nevertheless meant a "renaissance" which differed from the earlier medieval scholarly pursuits. M.T. Clanchy writes: "Drawing on the best of classical tradition and at the same time adapting it to their own needs, the men of the twelfth century created a new art which developed from Romanesque to Gothic, a new literature in both Latin and vernaculars (notably the *Carmina Burana* and the romances of Chrétien de Troyes), and a new system of education centred on the teaching of theology and law at universities." (1983, 162.) For "traditionalistic" cultural movements as motors of transformations and "renaissances" in the Middle Ages, see Stock 1990, 159-171.
2   Chenu 1957, 225-251, 343-350; Southern 1970/1983, 34-44, 230-299; Ehlers 1974, 58-79; Little 1978/1983, 97f. and *passim*.
3   See e.g. Delhaye 1947, 211-268; Little 1978/1983, 197-217 and *passim*; Murray 1978/1990, 50-58, 213-233; Barthélemy 1990, 146-153, 159-197; Baldwin 1982, 97-98, 138-172.
4   See Le Goff 1957/1985; Baldwin 1970; Murray 1978/1990; Stock 1983; Rüegg 1993; Boureau 1993. See also notes 2 and 3.

In this study I will concentrate on the new cultural situation by examining some of the intellectual products of clergy, both secular and regular, acting in secular urban society, i.e. the moral-satirical poems of the *Carmina Burana* which I will analyse as attempts to describe and conceptualize the preconditions of human action and some contingent historical forces influencing them. This material is mostly anonymous and has been filtered through several intermediaries, its connections being first of all textual. For this reason the search for and analysis of textual connections are central to this study. My interpretation will however be built on those general socio-cultural features which the texts analysed reflect and react to. To achieve this goal it is necessary to examine twelfth-century characterization, definition and placement of poetry in the system of disciplines and knowledge to construct an interpretative background for the historical study of the poetry itself.[5] Instead of interpreting the *Fortuna*-poems and money-satires of the *Carmina Burana* simply as literary artefacts, I will read them as efforts to conceptualize the change going on in its contemporary society. In other words they can be regarded as attempts to construct notions with which to describe the nature of human action in the sublunar world and as descriptions of what was thought to be the primary historical cause for moral and social disturbance.

Secular Latin poetry played a central role in learned clerical culture in the High Middle Ages, but it has rarely been an object of intellectual or cultural historical study, even if such studies of the time do refer to it.[6] On the other hand, the literary studies of Latin secular poetry do connect it with its intellectual and socio-cultural context.[7] Serious attempts to use Latin poetry as a document of historical study are nevertheless rare, if not non-existent.[8]

---

5 The theme of this study is however outlined by the materials themselves. Originally, I began my study with the nature of the *Carmina Burana* collection and its role in its own historical and intellectual context. My goal was to get a grip on the social and intellectual tumult of the High Middle Ages by using materials earlier regarded marginal when similar questions have been posed. The 228 poems recorded in the manuscript in the first half of the thirteenth century proved to be simultaneously an ideal and, from the point of view of a single scholar, exhaustive source. This can be demonstrated by the fact that the commentaries on the modern critical edition remain unfinished still, and the fact that editing and publishing the texts took over forty years from 1930 to 1971.

   I have published parts as independent studies; see Lehtonen 1989, 1990, 1991, 1992 and 1996. Some earlier articles I have included in this study in modified form (i.e. Lehtonen 1993 and 1994).

6 E.g. Le Goff 1957/1985; Morris 1972, 122-133; Clanchy 1983, 162; Murray 1978/1990, 241, 273-274; Horowitz & Menache 1994, 37.

7 This is naturally the case in the almost all literary studies. Among the best historically oriented studies are e.g. Yunck 1963; Schüppert 1972; Rigg 1977a; *idem* 1977b; Cairns 1980, 87-161; Robertson 1980, 131-150. Great classics of the scholarship of this area are among others Lehmann 1922-23/1963; Manitius 1931; Raby 1934; Curtius 1948; Auerbach 1958; and also the entire *oeuvre* of Peter Dronke (e.g. 1965-66). See also Szövérffy 1992-1994.

8 There are some exceptions, e.g. Yunck 1961 (in some respects also *idem* 1963); Schüppert 1972; Stock 1972; Wetherbee 1972; Murray 1978/1990. Vernacular poetry seems to have been used for this purpose more often (and more explicitly in a wider social, cultural and historical perspective), cf. e.g. Bloch 1939-40/1980, 143f.; Gurevitch 1970/1979; *idem* 1972/1983; Duby 1988; and, especially Vance 1986; *idem* 1987; Bloch 1983/1986.

I will read poems mostly from the first section of the *Carmina Burana* side by side with the abundant medieval poetical, rhetorical, grammatical, philosophical and theological literature. One can justifiably argue that the learned clerics of the time whose poetry the *Carmina Burana* was used Latin as their literary language and formed a culturally coherent social group which shared a common literary framework.[9] The Latin poetry, then, can be read as the ideological articulation of certain strata in this group.

The learned in twelfth- and thirteenth century regarded themselves as "dwarfs on the shoulders of giants". They thought they could see further than their predecessors, but only on the doctrinal and intellectual basis already built.[10] The *auctores antiqui* were authoritative models, their writings being either taken as literally true or at least incorporating beneath their figurative surface deeper meanings which articulated truths. All authors accepted in the scholarly canon were in some sense authors *(auctores)* and authorities *(auctoritates)*.[11]

"Moderns", or writers of the time *(moderni)*, were not considered as serious or comprehensive as the "ancients" *(antiqui)*, although some writers of the time may have risen to the position of an authority, especially if their formal or institutional standing backed them, and sometimes even without it, because of the sharpness of their arguments or efficacy of their persuasion.[12] The contemporary writings were, however, regarded as worthy of commentary usually only when they were doctrinally especially important. Theological, philosophical and legal writers were commented on quickly but poets of the time rarely attracted brief introductions, let alone comprehensive explanations. Naturally, there were exceptions such as Alan of Lille and Walter of Châtillon

---

9   Delhaye 1947, 211-251; Chenu 1957, 225-251; Grundmann 1958, 1-65; Murray 1978/1990, 234-244, 263-265; Baldwin 1982, 138-172.

10 The comparison was put into the mouth of Bernard of Chartres, master of the cathedral school of Chartres (d. ca. 1126/30). Until recently there were no writings reliably attributed to him. Now there is an edition of his commentary on Plato *(The Glosae super Platonem of Bernard of Chartres*. Studies and Texts 107. Toronto: Pontifical Institute of Medieval Studies 1991). His maxim was repeatedly quoted e.g. by William of Conches (ca. 1080-1154) in *Glosae super Priscianum* (cit. Stieffel 1985, 106-107), and John of Salisbury (ca. 1115/20-1180) in *Metalogicon* (III.4, p. 136). It was also quoted without reference to Bernard, e.g. by Alan of Lille (1116-1202/1203) in *Anticlaudianus* (prol., p. 55-56), Ralph of Longchamp (ca. 1150- ca. 1220) in *In Anticlaudianum Alani commentum* (I.lxx, p. 65), and by the anonymous author of *Distinctionum monasticorum et moralium* (II.112, p. 467-468). See also Gössmann 1974; Stock 1979; de Gandillac 1992, 138-148.

11 See e.g. Raban Maur (776-856), *De institutione clericorum*, prol., p. 3; Conrad of Hirsau (ca. 1070-ca. 1150), *Dialogus super auctores*, p. 72-76. Also Curtius 1948, 56-62; Chenu 1957, 352-357; Häring 1982, 173-200; Minnis 1984, 1-8; 10-12.
    Ralph of Longchamp gave the following definition of an *auctor*:
    Auctoris ab authentim. Licet enim quilibet tractatores dicantur auctores quidam tamen specialiter dicuntur auctores qui augent scilicet rem secundum poesim. Quidam ab 'authentim' id est ab auctoritate, qui scilicet sub exteriori verborum superficie aliquid occultant et claudunt misticum et spiritualis intelligentiae et de talibus hic loquitur. *(In Anticl. Al. comm.*, Rec. I dist., p. 67.)

12 See e.g. Chenu 1957, 351-365; Häring 1982, 173-200. See also *Antiqui und Moderni. Traditionbewußtsein und Fortsschrittsbewußtsein im späten Mittelalter*. Miscellanea medievalia Bd. 9. Hrsg. von A. Zimmermann, 1974.

whose works were commented on early. However, this is a field not thoroughly examined, and thus it is possible that still unedited and unpublished manuscripts may change the present view.[13]

Nevertheless, Latin secular poetry occupied a central cultural position in the twelfth and early thirteenth century, forming a problematic and in its own context seemingly anomalous phemomenon in several senses. Firstly, secular Latin poetry was commonly practised among learned clerics and had an important position in ecclesiastical culture. Secondly, as poetry of the ecclesiastical learned, a major part of it seems to be very difficult in fit into the framework of Christian thought. Anti-clerical and anti-papal satires are common, as are openly erotic love-poems and gambling and drinking songs. Modern interpreters have had grave difficulties in explaining the nature and status of such poetry written, read, and performed among the clergy.[14] Thirdly, its ideological anomalies are further underscored by the fact that medieval learned did not recognize any category for "poetry as such" or *"belles lettres"*. On the contrary, poetry was a part of philosophy or a system of knowledge, and was as such regarded first of all as ethical discourse.[15] The anomaly of seemingly "unchristian" poems becomes even more glaring. It seems obvious that a historical analysis of the poems should depart from the status ascribed to poetry in clerical *curricula*.

However, earlier research on medieval Latin poetry has not been very much interested in medieval notions of poetry and poetics as a framework for historical interpretation. With the exception of prescriptive poetics, medieval notions of poetry have rarely been studied thoroughly.[16] Until recently there has been no more than occasional interest in understanding the specific

13 See the commentaries on Alan of Lille: Bossuat 1955; Ralph of Longchamp, *In Anticlaudianum Alani commentum*; on Walter of Châtillon: Chatillon 1951, 151-152.
14 See e.g. Jackson 1960, 225-241; Wilhelm 1965, 105-139; Morris 1972, 128. Cf. Lehtonen 1996. The Latin language alone attaches the poetry to the world of the ecclesiastical learned. In addition, several identified authors themselves held ecclesiastical offices, e.g. Peter of Blois (ca. 1135-ca. 1204), Philip the Chancellor (chancellor of the University of Paris 1218, d. 1236) and Marbod of Rennes (ca. 1035-1123) (Schumann 1930/1961, 86*; Dronke 1965-66; *idem* 1976; Bischoff 1970b; Bernt 1975, 446-451; Parlett 1986/1988, 41-45; Wolff 1995, 16-18) or belonged to circles close to ecclesiastical courts or cathedral schools, e.g. Archipoeta (active during the latter half of the 12th c., esp. 1162-1164), Hugh Primas (ca. 1093-ca. 1160) and Walter of Châtillon (ca. 1135-ca. 1179) (for the first, see on Schumann 1930/1961, 87*; Watenpuhl & Krefeld 1958, 19-45; for the second McDonough 1984, 1-6; for the third Pepin 1988, 89-115). In two early autobiographical texts the authors, who belonged to the ecclesiastical learned, confessed to having written earthly love-lyrics in the style of Ovid or so-called goliardic poetry (Guibert of Nogent ca. 1055-ca. 1125, *De vita sua sive Monodiae* XVII, p. 134-138; Peter Abelard 1079-1142, *Historia calamitatum* 347-362, p. 73).
15 See Allen 1982; Zumthor 1986; Lehtonen 1996; and part I in this study.
16 On prescriptive poetics see e.g. Faral 1924; Delhaye 1949/1988; *idem* 1958/1988; Bagni 1968; Murphy 1974/1981; Klopsch 1980; Mehtonen 1992; *idem* 1996. On medieval genre-theory see Kindermann 1978; *idem* 1982; Kelly 1993.
    I have left prescriptive poetics outside this study because their perspective is compositional, and they do not offer any direct characterisations of poetry's place in the medieval system of discursive sciences. Furthermore my emphasis is on the interpretation which is also outside the scope of medieval prescriptive poetics. Hence I concentrate on the commentary tradition and classificatory texts (cf. also Minnis & Scott 1988/1991).

concepts of poetics and poetry in the 12th and early 13th century. However, in the last thirty years it has been increasingly asked whether modern concepts of literature and fiction are compatible with medieval poetry, and whether one should consider the textual categories used in clerical circles more closely. Recent scholarship has been increasingly interested in definitions given in the commentary tradition and the place of poetry in the system of disciplines and branches of knowledge.[17] Nevertheless, systematic studies to the position of poetry in the scholarly system have been incomplete and fragmentary. I will attempt to fill this gap in the first part of the present study, in which I will discuss poetry as a part of the system of knowledge in the twelfth and early thirteenth century. Further, the essential point in this study is to adapt these discussions on the interpretation of poetry itself. The status of poetry is a fundamental element in the discursive field in which medieval poets worked, and it outlined the ways of conceptualisation, the "way to seize the world", which was proper to clerical poetry. As far as I know, the earlier scholarship has not touched upon this feature in interpreting either the poetry of the *Carmina Burana*, or medieval Latin poetry in general.

As mentioned already above, the *Carmina Burana* was composed at a time when Western European society was in the midst of a change from a feudal, agrarian, non-monetary and monastic society to more centralised, urban and commercial, monetarised and secular Christian one. The clerical order was the focal point of this change. Bureaucratisation and monetarisation occurred first in western ecclesiastical hierarchy as did their reverse the disintegration of reciprocal obligations.[18] During this process, poetry formed a central tool in cognitively outlining and criticizing this change. The importance of poetical conceptualisation was grounded on several facts. Firstly, the authoritative model offered by ancient Roman satirists was, in the discursive and cultural landscape of the High Middle Ages, extremely influential. For instance Alexander Murray has not only pointed out their authoritative influence but has also drawn parallels between the early imperial Roman poets and their medieval successors as well as their conservative reaction against the new social mobility based on a monetary economy.[19] Moreover, where the ongoing social tumult was regarded as a challenge to individual morals, the discursive genre (i.e. poetry) which by definition dealt with individual morals naturally became especially important. Further, traditional monastic introspective or normative moral encyclopedias, e.g. the anomymous *Distinctionum monasticorum et moralium* and *Moralium dogma philosophorum*, did not seem to offer means considered valid for dealing conceptually with a new situation where vigorous monetarisation and bureaucratisation were

---

17 See note 11 in part I p. 40; also Lehtonen 1996.
18 Baldwin 1970, 117-130; Duby 1973/1985, 60-69; *idem* 1978, *passim*; Le Goff 1957/1985, 104-108; *idem* 1977/1984, 253-257; Little 1978/1983, 3-41 and *passim*; Murray 1978/1990, *passim*; Southern 1970/1983, 151-152; Yunck 1963, 47-92.
19 Murray 1978/1990, 75.

challenging the earlier reciprocal system of lordship *(Herrschaft, seigneurie)*.[20] And, finally, scholarly speculation was either developing logical tools and their adaptation to theological issues or, when concerned of morals, was more or less introspective and interested in the inner structure of human mind and volition.[21] Thus poetry with sermon literature and other less philosophically systematic genres bore the burden of solving moral problems caused by contemporary tumults.[22]

The *Carmina Burana* and its moral-satirical poetry

The origins and the breadth of the contents of the *Carmina Burana* make it a unique document of the clerical culture of its time. A scrutiny of its overall contents and organization, as well as its internal and external relationship to the central topics of clerical discussions, show that despite the fact that it was compiled in a rather peripherial region, it is firmly rooted in the very core of the clerical culture of Western Europe. It is a large, perhaps the largest known, collection of secular Latin clerical poetry.[23] The modern critical edition contains 228 numbered pieces, and there are 26 later medieval additions scattered here and there on the blank spaces – mostly on the blank leaves at the end of the manuscript. Modern scholars generally agree that the manuscript was originally written in one go following an overall plan around 1225/30 somewhere in the border regions of modern Austria and Italy, perhaps in the episcopal court of Seckau in Steiermark, or in South Tyrol in the Augustinian house of Neustift (Novacella) near the town of Brixen (Bressanone) or in the cathedral school of the town itself.[24] The original work

---

20 See also Honorius Augustodunensis, *Speculum Ecclesiae*; Chenu 1957; Baldwin 1970; Little 1978/1983.

21 See Lottin 1942/1957, *passim*; Luscombe 1971, xv-xxxvii; Delhaye 1949/1988, 59-81.

22 Cf. Murray 1978/1990, 71-80.

23 The *Carmina Burana* was found in 1803 in the Bavarian monastery of Benediktbeuern and was removed to the Bayerische Staatsbibliothek in Munich. In 1847 Johann Andreas Schmeller published it for the first time in printed form. Wilhelm Meyer started his wide-ranging research on the manuscript in the 1880's but it was not until 1930 that Alfons Hilka and Otto Schumann published the first volume of critical edition with commentaries (Schumann 1930/1961, 3*-5*; see also Schmeller 1847). The edition was continued alone by Otto Schumann, who published the second volume in 1941. The third volume was published in 1971 after Schumann's death, and the edition was finished by Bernhard Bischoff. Bischoff also published a facsimile edition in 1967 (see CB I.1-3; Bischoff 1970a; *idem* 1970b; Schaller 1975, 106-115).

   The manuscript consists of 112 vellum folios to which is added seven folios of *Fragmenta Burana*. The modern annotated edition contains three volumes which cover alltogether 665 pages (excluding the 216 pages of the commentary volume). See also Schumann 1930/1961, 82*-86*.

24 Most of the recent studies agree that the manuscript was written during the first half of the thirteenth century somewhere in the Carinthia, Steiermark or Tyrol. Among others Bernhard Bischoff dates the collection to 1225/30. He asserts that it may have been composed in the court of bishops of Seckau (1970b, XI-XII). Recently Georg Steer has strongly argued on the behalf of Augustian house of Neustift (Novacella) near Brixen (Bressanone) in Southern Tyrol (1983). However, Walther Lipphardt had already discarded this hypothesis before the

was done by three scribes who may also have composed some of the poems themselves.[25] The greater part of the poems is however anonymous, mostly originating from the twelfth century. Rare attributions and similarities in the manuscript point to the school centres in Northern France, whereas the final German stanzas in several erotic poems connect them to the southern parts of the Bavarian linguistic region.[26]

The dating of the *Carmina Burana* is no longer controversial and, in practice, all recent scholars put its compilation around 1225/30 (see note 24). The collection is unique in its breadth and conistency but its contents are not really exceptional since similar Latin secular poetry was quite popular and widespread among learned clerics in the latter half of the twelfth century. Its nature as an anthology however makes it problematical for close historical analysis. It seems that most of its poems, especially its satires, were composed sometime in the late twelfth century (see note 14 and part III in this study). This fact has certain consequences in my approach. I will consider these poems first of all through their intellectual, idea-historical and literary network, and I will relate this analysis to those socio-cultural changes which influenced on their background only at a rather general level. On the other hand, it seems that their hypothetical connections with contemporary historical events are of secondary importance, lying beyond the scope of this study. My primary concern is the general status of poetry in the clerical and ecclesiastical world and its effect on the way the individual poems treat general contemporary changes, abstractly define the nature of events in the sublunar world and, finally, the reaction caused by monetarisation and new social relations. The standing of this poetry as a part of ethics makes this reaction especially interesting for intellectual and cultural history.

As I have already mentioned above, the *Carmina Burana* has not been studied from the standpoint of cultural history. In point of fact, the manuscript has not been examined as a whole from any other viewpoints with the exception of some general introductions and the very recent study by Olive Sayce on its plurilingualism and setting at the crossroads of cultural influences.[27] Sayce puts forward strong evidence for dating the *Carmina*

---

publication of Steer's article by putting forward arguments to support Bischoff's view of the provenance of the *Carmina Burana* either from the See of Seckau or its Augustinian collegiate (1982, 209-223).

Most recently Olive Sayce has provided further support for Steer's localisation of the manuscript in Brixen (Bressanone) but she regards the cathedral school or episcopal court as a more probable provenance than the Augustinian house (Sayce 1992, 198-203). See also Schieffer 1974, 412-418; Dronke 1962, 173-183; *idem* 1975, 116-137.

25 About scribes and their probable compilation methods, see Schumann 1930/1961; Bischoff 1970b; Dronke 1975; Walsh 1976, 1-8; Sayce 1992, 25-38 and *passim*.

26 Schumann 1930/1961, 68*f.; Bischoff 1970b, 27-28; Beatie 1967, 16-24; Schieffer 1974, 412-418; Sayce 1992, 189f. and *passim*.

27 See the introductions to various editions and translations of the collection as well as encyclopaedic articles dealing with it (Schumann 1930/1961; Bischoff 1970a; Bernt 1975; *idem* 1978; Walsh 1976; Parlett 1986/1988; Wolff 1995). Otherwise it has been used as a store of medieval Latin clerical poetry (e.g. in Manitius 1931; Raby 1934; Dronke 1965-66; Szövérffy 1994) Sayce 1992 being in my knowledge the only monograph on the *Carmina*

Burana about 1225/30, its localisation in Brixen (Bressanone) in Southern Tirol in the border region between German and Italian cultures, and its linguistical and stylistical associations with romance languages (both *langue d'oc* and *langue d'oïl*) despite the fact that it was composed in a German (or Bavarian) speaking area and that it included a significant number of German strophes.[28] Furthermore both internal and external features attest its relations to the clerical world and cathedral schools (especially in the case of its satires), with special reference to the Augustinian order.[29] All these connections seem to put it into the intellectual context of the clerical scholarly environments of Northern France.[30]

The modern edition of the *Carmina Burana* contains three volumes of poetry (I.1. 112 p., I.2. 315 p., I.3. 238 p.), a few short prose passages and a couple of religious plays. The shortest texts have just a few words, and the longest one, a Christmas play, CB 227, takes fourteen printed pages (a later addition, a Passion play CB 16* is a couple of pages longer). The contents of the manuscript are mostly in Latin. However, it includes some poems or stanzas in German, and some single lines in German, French or Greek. The texts can roughly be grouped into the four main parts according to which the manuscript is organised (and which the structure of modern edition follows). The sections are moral-satirical poems, love-songs, drinking and gambling songs and religious plays.[31] The original manuscript was not an accidental compilation, but was organised consistently.

The manuscript, especially the moral-satirical part, is structured into small groups of *rhythmus* and *versus* poems. Otto Schumann has distinguished 23 groups in the first two parts of the collection. The final part (the third volume of the modern edition) cannot be divided as unambiguously into these groups.

Burana.

28 Sayce 1992, 36-38, 189f. and *passim*.
29 E.g. CB 39.7 (CB I.1, 63); see part III; also Sayce 1992, 143-144; 193, 196, 201.
30 Olive Sayce argues that the second main scribe, h², came from a linguistically French area (langue d'oïl), probably from the crossroads of German and French cultures, perhaps from Trier or Alsace to which CB 199 and 200 refer (CB I.3, 40-41, 49-50; Sayce 1992, 63-117, esp. 78-79). The first scribe, h¹, was probably an Italian speaker (Sayce 1992, 39-62). On other evidence of the relations of the manuscript to Northern France see Sayce 1992, 9, 14-16, 22-24, 88, 96, 117, 189; see also Lipphardt 1982; Dronke 1965, 564.
31 Schumann 1930/1961, 41*-54*; Bischoff 1970a, 21-23.
    The *codex Buranus* has not quite survived as the manuscript was written down around 1225-30. From the beginning an unknown number of leaves, which probably included mostly moral-satirical texts disappeared. Furthermore, some leaves are missing from the middle of the love-songs. On the other hand, some texts have been slightly altered after the three scribes (h¹ and h² being the main scribes) but not so as to radically change their contents. Likewise, some of the miniatures are later additions although most were included in the original manuscript version. The 26 additions at the end of the modern edition were written in the blank leaves or lesser spaces scattered here and there in the manuscript and in the so-called *Fragmenta Burana* by several different scribes. The later additions clearly differ in their handwriting from the original manuscript, and they have been dated from the 1250's until the late fourteenth century. Excluding the religious plays, the later additions contain the only expressly spiritual poems in the collection. Cf. Schumann 1930/1961, 31*-39*, 46*, 54*-63*, 66*-67*; Bischoff 1970a, 19-20; Steer 1982, 195; *idem* 1983, 14-15; see also Sayce 1992.

However, Schumann does divide it into nine groups and two religious plays which are separate from the group structure.[32]

In the present collection there are 55 moral-satirical poems which are divided into 14 *rhythmus-versus* groups. The first (CB 1-2, incomplete) and the second one (CB 3-5) deal with *avaritia*, especially the purchasable nature of justice, the power of money, the disappearance of honesty and the corruption of this world.[33] The stress in the third group (CB 6-7) is on the depravity of learned men and the lack of true nobility.[34] The fourth group (CB 8-11) deals with simony and again the power of money, the fifth (CB 12-13) with the sins of hatred and envy.[35]

The sixth group concentrates on *Fortuna* and transience and the virtue of constancy (CB 14-18). The next group (CB 19-20) turns again to *avaritia* and disappearance of *largitas*. The eighth group (CB 21-25) guides the reader towards faith and simultaneously criticises prelates.[36] The ninth group (CB 26-28) is the first with a title of its own, *De correctione hominum*, the earlier groups being headed only with the word *item* or *item unde* if they had a title at all. It aims to strengthen faith and offers precepts for the correct practice of religion.[37] The next group is entitled *De conuersione hominum* and warns about the attractions of Venus, discusses the flourishing of youth, offers guidance to the right path and deals with the problem of temptation.[38] The eleventh group (CB 33-38) is titled *De ammonitione prelatorum* and it is addressed to bishops, dealing with their obligations.[39] The next, i.e. the twelfth group (CB 39-40), returns to the general degeneration of the sublunar world and gives, suprisingly, detailed precepts for a priest *(sacerdos)* on how to perform a mass correctly with a purified heart.[40] The second last group (CB 41-45) of the moral-satirical part deals once again with *avaritia* and *simonia*.[41] The moral-satirical part finishes with a larger group (CB 46-55) of crusade poems titled *De cruce signatis*. This group is the only one in the whole *Carmina Burana* which is openly related to contemporary historical events with the names of places and persons and exact indications of time. The group curiously ends with two poems of exorcism.[42]

The second volume of the modern edition, *Die Liebeslieder*, begins with CB 56, a poem dealing with the turn of the year and beginning of springtime. This volume is the largest of the three volumes of the *Carmina Burana*.

---

32 Schumann 1930/1961, 31*, 41*-54*.
33 CB I.1, 1-7; Schumann 1930/1961, 41*-42*.
34 CB I.1, 7-10; Schumann 1930/1961, 42*.
35 CB I.1, 10-30; Schumann 1930/1961, 42*.
36 CB I.1, 31-45; Schumann 1930/1961, 42*-43*.
37 CB I.1, 45-49; Schumann 1930/1961, 43*; see also CB facs., fol. 3[r/v].
38 CB I.1, 49-54; Schumann 1930/1961, 43*.
39 CB I.1, 54-62; Schumann 1930/1961, 43*-44*.
40 CB I.1, 64.
41 CB I.1, 65-89; Schumann 1930/1961, 44*.
42 CB I.1, 90-110; Schumann 1930/1961, 44*; Hilka & Schumann 1930/1961, 97-116 (datings span from 1149 to 1188).

However, Otto Schumann finds only nine groups of love-poems which means that the groups are much larger than in the first part.[43] The victory of spring and summer opens most of the texts, which then turn to the subject of erotic love. Miscellaneous themes connected with studies and learning appear here and there, as well as reflective poems about poetry and role of a poet and even some satires and elegies. Among the love-poems, there is a group (no. 18, CB 126-131) of openly parodic and satirical poems which have as their subject-matter the complaint of a pregnant girl, a swan being roasted, and attacks on the papal curia.[44]

In the grouping of the love-poems another principle, than that presented by Schumann, which has been interpreted as a vestige of the compilation and collection's international and local background has also been detected. Peter Dronke writes:

> The love-songs seem to fall into two groups. In the first group (56-121) the compilers of the Carmina Burana drew considerably on an international repertoire (Saint Martial, Notre Dame, possibly England), in the second (135-186) they collected a local repertoire, usually adding German stanzas. It is noteworthy that ... only two of the Latin pieces in the entire group are found elsewhere: the epigram 154 ... and the song 178 .... Between them comes the curious mélange 122-134, which includes songs of Walter of Châtillon and Philip the Chancellor, even lines of Marbod, and only one song (126) that has anything to do with love. One might suppose that the copyists had to return some borrowed non-German manuscript(s) at this stage, and wanted to include all they could before returning it, even if it meant disturbing the overall pattern of the love-songs in their own collection. They had already begun do so a little earlier, to seize the chance of copying such famous pieces as 'Sacerdotes mementote' (91) and 'Pergama flere volo' (101).[45]

The group distinguished by Dronke (CB 126-134) is almost the same as the one that Schumann thinks is a later addition by scribe h^2 (CB 126-131/131a as well as CB 91).[46] However, it is possible that the anomaly does not originate from practical necessities but is connected to an ironic and parodic structural principle which can be found in the poetry of the *Carmina Burana* and generally in Latin secular poetry.[47] Such an attitude was not strange for love-poetry in general - some of the seemingly plain love-poems appear on closer scrutiny to be parodies, or at least strongly ironic[48] and, of course, the complaint of a pregnant girl (CB 126) or a swan being roasted (CB 130) are

---

43   Cf. CB I,2, *passim*; Schumann 1930/1961, 45*-51*.
44   CB I.2, 209-220; Schumann 1930/1961, 47*-48*.
45   Dronke 1965, 564.
46   Schumann 1930/1961, 45*-55*.
47   Cf. Lehmann 1922-23/1963; Mann 1980; Cairns 1980; Elliott 1982; Smolak 1986; *idem* 1988; also Lehtonen 1996.
48   Cf. Robertson 1980, 131-138, 150 (Robertson's article concerns the CB 62 *Dum Diane vitrea* which has also been discussed by Dronke 1975 and Jackson 1980b); Elliott 1982, 353-368; Pelen 1988.

apparently ironic parodies.[49] Why would not the irony and parody utilised so sophisticatedly also appear in the composition. The elegies (CB 122-134), whether parodic or not, follow the complaints of unhappy love, turn to "sublime" subject-matters such as the deaths of kings, and then to absurd and comical exaggerations with lower themes.[50] However, whether this hypothesis is right or wrong, the emphasis on the international background of the collection is more important here. The only larger apparent local deviation in the whole collection is expressly among the erotic poems (groups nos. 20, 22 and 23; CB 135-155, 162-176 and 177-186),[51] and the earlier moral-satirical part seems to be drawn mostly from international sources.[52] This fact is relevant to the interpretation of the poetry of the first part.

The last volume titled by the editor(s) *Die Trink- und Spielerlieder - Die geistlichen Dramen und Nachträge* includes poems nos. 187-228 and the later additions 1*-26*. The volume is thus noticeably shorter than the preceding one even comparing the moral-satirical part if one concentrates on the contents of the original manuscript and not on the later additions. The two religious plays are much longer than most of the other texts in the collection. The third part begins with complaints about the wordly care *(curas hominum)* to which the papal curia is attached, and these are followed by other satirical poems, once again directed towards the avaricious *caput mundi*, i.e. the papal see.[53] The last part also contains the famous and in its own time well-known poem *Estuans intrinsecus ira vehementi* (CB 191) by the Archipoeta which is a parodic confession.[54] This is followed by various more or less parodic drinking and gambling songs (also parodying earlier love-poems!).[55] Then comes a very famous drinking-song *In taberna quando sumus* (CB 196) and other praises of the tavern and Bacchus. In a certain sense the opening words of CB 203 *In hiemali tempore* set up drinking as a wintry contrast to the spring and summertime eroticism.[56]

In the continuation, the drinking themes are relegated to background when "royal Trier" is praised (CB 204), although drinking does still have a place in it. Different kind of games are given poems of their own: both chess, backgammon and dice are presented, and are also depicted in miniatures.[57]

---

49 CB I.2, 209-211, 215. For the term ironic parody see pages 39, 67-69, 131-134; cf. also Green 1975; Knox 1989.
50 CB I.2, 209-227.
51 They include Latin poems which end with a German stanza. The vernacular endings are interpreted either as directed to (female) participants who did not understand Latin, or as indications of the melody (i.e. the German stanzas would have been picked from well-known songs on whose melody the Latin poem was adapted). See Wolff 1995, 34-36. On this "macaronic" or plurilingual poetry see Beatie 1967, 16-24; Sayce 1992.
52 Schumann 1930/1961, 86*f., Bernt 1975, 436-438, 446-450; Sayce 1992, 200.
53 CB I.3, 1-5; Schumann 1930/1961, 51*.
54 CB I.3, 6-21. A thorough and convincing analysis of the poem has been presented by Francis Cairns (1980).
55 The poem CB 195 *Si quis Deciorum* seems to be a travesty of the earlier CB 61 *Si quem Pieridum* (CB I.3, 31-35, see esp. 34; CB I.2, 14-19).
56 CB I.3, 35-47.
57 CB 207-210; CB I.3, 54-59; CB facs., 91^r/v-92^r; Schumann 1930/1961, 52*.

After the games Epicurus arrives on the stage (CB 211): love-games, poetry, drinking and gambling are not enough; eating gets its turn as well. However, the poem is followed by a request for moderation.[58] From moderation the poems turn to a mass-parody entitled *Incipit officium lusorum* (CB 215).[59] This gambler's mass is followed by a couple of feast-poems, a trilingual poem against stinginess, and the famous parody *Cum 'In orbem universum' decantur 'ite'* (CB 219) which has caused speculation about an order of goliards, but which is an obvious parody of monastic *regula*.[60] Finally there are some begging poems which appeal to the charity and learning of the clergy, and a poem which laments the degradation of morals in this world, and especially the disappearance of *largitas* (CB 224-226).[61]

The original version of the manuscript finishes with two religious plays. CB 227 is a Christmas play which begins with a disputation between Augustine and *Archisynagogus* about the Immaculate Conception, and then step by step proceeds to the events of Christmas.[62] The latter play continues the previous one in that Mary and Joseph have escaped to Egypt in CB 227, and CB 228 starts with a description of the court of the king of Egypt where people are practising the joys of love in the same way as in the erotic poems of the *Carmina Burana* a little bit earlier. The court worships idols, and indeed, the play is a *ludus de Antichristo*, actually part of a play found in its complete version from the monastery of Tegernsee.[63] In contrast to the king of Egypt, the king of Babylon, who appears on the stage, is studying the seven liberal arts and respects the wisdom of ancient Greece. He conquers Egypt and is presented as an Antichrist who goes into the last battle against Christianity. In the *Carmina Burana* version it remains unclear who returns from the battle the winner. Such an ending leaves the somehow ambiguous

---

58   CB I.3, 59-62; Schumann 1930/1961, 52*-53*.
59   CB I.3, 64-68.
60   CB I.3, 71-77.
    Golias, goliardus, familia Goliae, ordo goliardorum or *vagorum* appear all in medieval sources. Until recently, their medieval meaning has remained obscure. The original expression was mixed up in medieval myths and romantic scholarly fancies from which ideas of either a pre-protestant or hedonistic rebellious clerical order (or in more recent versions, a "subculture") of goliards or wandering scholars *(clerici vagantes)* and their goliardic poetry *(Vagantendichtung)* emerged in the 19th century (see e.g. Waddell 1927/1955; Dobiache-Rojdestvensky 1931; Bechtum 1941; Garcia-Villoslada 1975; Marks 1975). The myth has proved tenacious even in the modern scholarship (e.g. Le Goff 1957/1985, 29-35; cf. Moulin 1991, 107-110) despite the fact that by the early 1920s Paul Lehmann demonstrated that CB 219 and other similar poems are textual parodies without any reference to some real order of wandering scholars (Lehmann1922-23/1963, 158-161; see also Hanford 1926, 38; Mann 1980). The originally pejorative label *Golias* (alluding to Goliath, i.e. a personification of the devil, and to *gula*, i.e. throat) and its variants seems to have been transformed to denote ironically the authors of Latin satire becoming a generic term for satire - sometimes even for all rhythmic and rhyming Latin poetry as it is used now in scholarship (see Jackson 1960, 228-229; Fichtner 1967; Rigg 1977a; *idem* 1977b; Walsh 1983, 1-7; on the *Carmina Burana* and goliards Bernt 1975, 445-446; Parlett 1986/1988, 42-43; Wolff 1995, 19-22).
61   CB I.3, 83-86.
62   CB I.3, 86-104.
63   CB I.3, 104-111; Bischoff 1970a, 22; Langosch 1963/1975, 11-12; *idem* 1964, 145, 161-162.

feeling that the play – and perhaps the entirety of the *Carmina Burana* - might condemn the learned pursuits, that is, the very basis of the identity of the clerics active in secular society (whether they were regular canons or secular clerics). Whether this is correct or not, it is a question which lies outside the scope of this study.

The *Carmina Burana* is a rather full anthology of typical medieval Latin secular poetry, so called goliardic poetry. The partial musical notation in the manuscript indicates that it was intended as a song-book.[64] On the other hand, it is evident that its compilation is guided by a thematic "plot" from moral satires to erotic poetry and drinking songs which are in their turn mixed up with satirical themes. The whole finishes with two scholarly and spiritual plays. In a way, the collection makes a wide detour through the landscape of the sublunar world as perceived by learned clerics. In the following, I will concentrate on moral-satirical texts and on their relation to ethical dogma and notions of poetry. These texts form a framework for the rest of the collection, into which the love poems for example are *mise en abyme*. Despite the abundant scholarship, the collection as an entirety – let alone the role of any of its parts in the entirety – has remained a largely untouched question (see note 27). However, one way to move towards the riddle of the *Carmina Burana* is to draw up a textual and contextual analysis section by section. An analysis of contextually less ambiguous satires and an explication of their structures, allusions, ironies and intellectual and historical connections also offers a means of interpretating of the erotic poems which were more problematic in their cultural context.

The clerical order, twelfth-century schools, and the *Carmina Burana*

The poetry of the *Carmina Burana* seems to vacillate between the monastic Benedictine view and that of the urban secular clerical orders and regular Augustinian canons, with an inclination towards the latter groups. In the late eleventh and early twelfth century it was the Augustinian order which first turned strongly towards secular society and "this world" and influenced the deepening lay piety. Both secular clergy and regular canons were defined by their function of preaching and moral instruction as against monks whose task it was to pray.[65] The emphasis on the instructive function was the very

---

64 E.g. P.G. Walsh asserts that "all the lyrics were composed to be sung, and in the manuscript nine of the songs (i.e. 98, 99, 108, 109, 119, 128, 131a, 187, 189) as well as one play (227) have the neumes inserted by the same scribes who copied the words. Other hands have inserted melodies for other poems, so that musicologists have now recovered thirty of the tunes. ... In short, the *Carmina Burana* is a scholars' song-book." (1976, 2). Nevertheless, there is no general agreement on this thesis, Étienne Wolff among others having criticised it in his very recent French translation of the *Carmina Burana* (1995, 9).

65 Heimbucher 1933, 398-496; Le Bras 1959, 10, 150-178, 179-195; Little 1978/1983, 97-112, 171-217; Rapp 1993, 9-25; Boureau 1993, 35-43; Foulon 1993, 45-60.

core of the new inclination towards the lay society. However, Latin poetry was not directed to laymen but to clerics and scholars preparing to instruct or already instructing them. The poetry thus touched upon the clerical learned (whether secular or regular) acting in lay society (and not withdrawing into monasteries). Among the different *scientiae* it belonged to a branch treating their own morals.

The ecclesiastical orders, both members of secular and regular clergy *(clerici)* in schools, cathedral chapters, collegial churches and towns, were the actual motor of the twelfth century renaissance. These ecclesiastical orders were in charge of the new learning and scholarly activity, and were often more or less antagonistic to the earlier ideologically dominant group, the Benedictine (and Cistercian) orders of monks *(monachi)* who withdrew to monasteries and cloisters.[66] The appearance of urban life, both clerical and lay, came as a shock to the former elites, the landed military feudal aristocracy and Benedictine monks, mostly recruited from the ranks of the first. The new urban ecclasiastical orders were close to urban lay groups, the urban aristocracy (especially in Italy and Southern France), merchants and artisans. The self-definitions and moral discourse of clerical orders were related to this situation. It gave new importance to an old, somewhat negelected ecclesiastical division into monks as prayers (i.e. those who took care of the relation between God and mankind) and clerics as teachers and preachers (i.e. those who taught Christian doctrine and morals) which was actively propagated from the late eleventh century both by reformating popes and by clerics themselves.[67] The division also reflected the relation to learning. Monks studied mostly *sacra pagina* and applied a ritualistic and contemplative approach when clerical learning was governed by rationalistic argument and discursive persuasion. This led to more emphasis on the discursive arts (the *trivium,* that is, *grammatica, rhetorica* and *dialectica*). Thus the turn to "secular" society meant a new concern for the Christian teaching among the whole of society – monastic withdrawal was no longer the only way to see to the salvation of the soul. Indeed, the "secular" turn meant deepening Christianisation among the lay orders as well (not of course, "secularisation" in the modern sense).[68]

The available ideological approaches were not applicable in the new situation. At the beginning of the twelfth century there were two central systems for dividing society into groups. Neither was wholly compatible with twelfth-century society in central Western Europe nor were they in accordance with the actual internal structure of the church.

The more recent one of these divisions was the tenth-century doctrine of the three orders, *oratores, bellatores* and *laboratores.* Originally this doctrine was formulated in Northern France on the vestiges of the Carolingian order

---

66 Chenu 1957, 225-251; Le Bras 1959, *passim*; Little 1978/1983, 59-96, 97-169, 173-183.
67 Chenu 1957, 225-251; Boureau 1993, 35-43.
68 See Boureau 1993; Foulon 1993; also notes 66 and 67 above.

and, at the time, had some correspondence with the structure of the so-called first feudal society.[69] There were three kinds of Christians in the world. First, there were true Christians, i.e. those who prayed and communicated with God. They were most distant from this world and closest to the world beyond. The most perfect way to fulfil the task of prayer was to withdraw into a monastery isolated from the secular world where the monks concentrated on ritualistic and contemplative religious practice. Often it seems that a monk was equated with the concept of true Christian.[70] The two lay groups, that is, those who fought and those who worked were considered to exist for the up-keep of the *oratores*.

This ideology was rediscovered during the twelfth century as a conservative reaction to social changes related to the emerging towns. Monastic Christianity and its latest revival, the Cistercian order, was hostile towards the new mercantile towns. Thus the system of three orders offered the opprtunity to articulate an alternative ideology which leaned on feudal aristocracy, lordship and agrarian production. This same aristocracy was an important supporter of the monastic way of life.[71] This ideology left no proper place for urban groups, be they lay or clerical orders. Lester K. Little has given a pertinent description of this new urban world in contrast to this ideology:

> The dominant members of the urban sector of society were merchants, bankers, lawyers, school masters and certain of the landlords who organized production on their lands for the market. They did not make their living by praying, or by fighting, or by 'working', not at least with their hands. They talked; they argued; they negotiated; they wrote; they entertained; above all they tried to persuade other people.[72]

In the mercantile, urban world of Northern France, Southern England, Flanders, the Rhine Valley, and Northern Italy a new learned group flourished which had emerged from the numbers of secular clergy and, according to some modern scholars, distinguished itself as a wholly separate intellectual "class".[73] This emergent new social group had to solve ideological and moral dilemmas which had never been problematical for the earlier Benedictine learned elite. It is their articulation and formulation of self-awareness that Latin secular poetry in the twelfth and early thirteenth century reflects and, as I try to demonstrate later, this poetry had a special position in the treatment of such themes not possible in the other discursive genres.

The new urban society made actual many older conceptions and literary genres. Ancient literary classics had wintered in monasteries but from the

---

69   See Duby 1978; Bloch 1939-40/1980; Little 1978/1983, 197-199.
70   Chenu 1957, 225-271; Le Bras 1959, 171-177; Foulon 1993, 49.
71   Little 1978/1983, 3-18, 61-96; also Southern 1970/1983, 214f.; Lawrence 1984, 97-124.
72   Little 1978/1983, 197.
73   Le Goff 1957/1985; Murray 1978/1990, 130, 219-229.

perspective of the urban, mercantile and learned world they probably seemed to deal with topics of new current interest. Similarly among the Christian authors of late antiquity the writers of the urban world rose to prominence. If the Early Middle Ages was dominated by Gregory the Great and Benedict of Nursia, in the twelfth century Augustine and Boethius, and the pagan Martianus Capella, Plato (his *Timaeus*), Cicero and increasingly Aristotle not to mention the Roman poets Virgil, Horace, Juveval, Persius and Ovid, were the most-read authors.[74]

In this respect it is not paradoxical that the early threefold Christian division to *laici*, *clerici seculares* and *religiosi* in its approximate character corresponded to the social reality better, at least in the view of the ecclesiastical learned.[75] The division of ecclesiastical orders not included (at least explicitly) in the late carolingian division was essential since those who withdrew themselves into monasteries for prayer could be distinguished from those who were active in the (urban) secular society and were preaching.

On the other hand, this division was interpreted anew by some twelfth century authors. In reality the ecclesiastical orders at the time were no longer simply divisible into secular and regular clergy, at least not that regular clergy could be identified with the contemplative Benedictine and Cistercian orders. During the twelfth century the clergy's activities in secular society had become more complex. In many cathedral chapters the clergy was following the so-called Augustinian order or its variants and, further, the same order had established its own collegial churches. They both belonged to orders, and thus to the regular clergy, although they were involved in lay society and did not shut themselves in monasteries. Furthermore the schools run by the Augustinians were often open to those who did not belong to their order (quite contrary to the situation in monastic schools from the eleventh century onwards).[76]

The social and intellectual change in the eleventh and twelfth centuries in the central areas of Western Europe meant that the separate social enclaves (monasteries, castles, villages, cf. *oratores*, *bellatores*, *laboratores*) broke down and society was increasingly structured on continuous scales which were not only vertical but also horizontal. In the ecclesiastical sphere this meant that the definition of clergy and monks as a whole whose task was to pray did not correspond either with reality or ideological conceptions. First this change altered the organisation of the world of secular clerics and regular canons, and with the appearance of new orders, as Premonstratensians (or Norbertins), Cistercians and mendicants it gradually affected monastic system

---

74 Delhaye 1947, 232-238; also *idem* 1949/1988; *idem* 1958/1988; Curtius 1948, 56-65; Chenu 1957, 108-158, 323-350; Glauche 1970; Ehlers 1974; cf. Stock 1972; *idem* 1983; *A History of Twelfth-Century Western Philosophy*, ed. by P. Dronke, Cambridge 1988/1992; see also Conrad of Hirsau, *Dialogus super auctores*; anon. *Accessus ad auctores*.
75 Isidore, *Etym.* VII.12. 13 (ed. Lindsay 1911/1987); Raban Maur, *De inst. cler.* I c. 6-9; Le Bras 1959, 149; Boureau 1993, 38.
76 Delhaye 1947, 231-234, 241-246; Little 1978/1983, 197-199.

itself. Actually, the notion of *clerici seculares* was a product of the early twelfth century while earlier the difference between *clericus* and *monachus* was sufficient.[77] The situation became complicated with the emergence of regular canons and various Augustinian orders.[78] The difference between a secular and regular cleric did not mean that they differed according to whether they functioned and lived in secular society and the towns.[79] Now the learned clerical orders in the towns, that is, those groups which were defined by their intellectual education and task to preach and teach *(cura animarum)* became the ideological leaders in the church while monks were left on the marginal with their task of prayer.[80]

The idealogists of the learned secular clergy started to emphasize the difference between *litteratus* and *illitteratus* by giving it significant new dimensions. In the Early Middle Ages this distinction had meant simply the difference of those who were able to read and write Latin (and thus were clerics or monks) and those who could not. In the High Middle Ages the title of *litteratus* became a more demanding term and it started to denote a more deeply learned person. The word was identified with *clericus*, and some authors even argued that a learned layman – that is, unordained – could be called *clericus* if he was a real *litteratus* rather than a monk *(monachus)* without proper learning.[81] This was probably an exaggeration meant to irritate unlearned monks but, in the other hand, it reveals the new clerical pride on their own learning. In the *Carmina Burana* a few strophes, originally probably a part of a poem by Archipoeta (in the 1160s), depict this attachement to learning:

> *1. Sepe de miseria mee paupertatis / conqueror in carmine viris litteratis; / laici non sapiunt ea que sunt vatis / et nil michi tribuunt, quod est notum satis.*
>
> *2. Poeta pauperior omnibus poetis / nichil prorsus habeo nisi quod videtis, / unde sepe lugeo, quando vos ridetis; / nec me meo vitio pauperem putetis.*
>
> *3. Fodere non debeo, quia sum scolaris / ortus ex militibus preliandi gnaris; / sed quia me terruit labor militaris, / malui Virgilium sequi quam te, Paris.*
>
> *4. Mendicare pudor est, mendicare nolo; / fures multa possident, sed non absque dolo. / quid ergo iam faciam, qui nec agros colo / nec mendicus fieri nec fur esse volo?*[82]

---

77 Boureau 1993, 35-43.
78 Little 1978/1983, 102-112; see also Heimbucher 1933, 398-496; Southern 1970/1983, 241-250; Lawrence 1984, 137-142.
79 Boureau 1993, 35-43.
80 See Foulon 1993.
81 Delhaye 1947, 211-213; Grundmann 1958, 44-54 and *passim*; Boureau 1993, 38.
82 CB 220, CB I.3., 77-78; see also Archipoeta, IV.17-20, p. 59. I have followed the ortography of the latter edition (in CB 220.1.3 *capiunt pro sapiunt* in AP IV.17.3). The order of stanzas is from CB-version (CB 220.1 = AP IV.20, CB 220.2 = AP IV.17, CB 220.3 = AP IV.18, CB 220.4 = AP IV.19).

Often I complain in my verse, to men of learning, / of the great distress that my poverty is causing; / laymen just don't know the situation of a poet, / and (the fact's quite evident) they give me nothing for it. // As a poet poorer than all the poets, I / don't own anything at all apart from what you see; / which is why I'm often lamenting when you're laughing; / you should not imagine I'm poor through my own doing. // Digging isn't right for me, because I am a scholar, / born of knightly family, skilled in arts of warfare; / but because I had no heart for military labour / I chose Vergil rather than Paris as my mentor. // Begging is a shameful thing, I will not go begging; / thieves possess a lot, but they get it by deceiving. / Therefore what am I to do, with no fields to till, / and no willingness to go begging or to steal? (Tr. Adcock)[83]

Archipoeta distinguishes a learned poet and his literate audience from laymen. He also presents himself as unfit for both warfare and agricultural labour because he is a scholar.[84] At the same time, he is cleverly flattering his mentors and appealing to their reciprocal obligations: the poet's gift is his poem, the patron should offer his protection and material aid in return.

Both the compilation and contents of the *Carmina Burana* attach it first of all to the urban learned world in the environments of cathedral and collegial schools. Although there is some who reached rather high positions in the ecclesiastical hierarchy among the writers identified (see note 14), it seems that the moral hortatory message is often directed from below to the upper grades of the hierarchy – the lower clergy seems to criticize its superiors up to bishops and popes. We know from other sources that similar so-called goliardic poetry was related to carnivalistic feasts celebrated by the lower clergy turning the world hierarchy upside down.[85] Thus the viewpoint of the poems – and supposedly their versifiers and their immediate public - were very close to the perspective of the lower clergy.

In the late twelfth century the clergy of the urban churches, especially of the cathedrals, had grown very numerous in Western Europe and included several hierarchical degrees. The clerical order included in practice all teachers and students functioning near the churches. According to Gabriel Le Bras the question of *status vitae* became especially important in the twelfth century when various ecclesiastical groups were vigorously competing with each other (clerics and laymen, monks and canons and various religious and

---

83 *Hugh Primas and the Archpoet.* Cambridge Medieval Classics. Ed. & transl. by F. Adcock, Cambridge 1994, 90-93 (AP IV.17-20).
84 Archipoeta was the court-poet of Reinald of Dassel (d. 1167), the Archbishop of Cologne and the chancellor of Frederick Barbarossa. The quotation is in the *Carmina Burana* combined with another poem not by him (CB I.3, 77-80). Originally it belonged to a longer poem in which the poet declares that he is unable to compose an epic poem of the heroic deeds of Emperor's Italian campaign (probably in 1163). He alludes to a passage from Luke (16:3: *fodere non valeo, mendicare erubesco*) which seem to have been rather popular scholarly allusion at the time (see Watenpuhl & Krefeld 1958, 108-109).
85 Baldwin 1970, 131-133, 198; Schmidt 1974/1990, 39-56; Hood 1994, 195-216; see also Schüppert 1970 1972.

monastic orders).[86] Traces of this competition and antagonism can also be found from the poetry of the *Carmina Burana*.[87] The clerical order as a whole formed one social order which was defined in legal terms.[88] A tonsured cleric belonged to the sphere of canon law, was protected by ecclesiastical authorities and was of course under their jurisdiction. The tonsure was the visible sign of being a member of ecclesiastical orders and, in the case of clerics, it was the local bishop who admitted a candidate. In itself, taking the tonsure meant the taking of lowest consecration which required less than the full sacerdotal consecration (hence the important distinction between *clericus* and *sacerdos*). The status of a *sacerdos* proper, that is a full priest, was achieved by climbing up through the intermediate ranks. Within the clergy the most important distinction was between those who had access to the Christian mysteries and had a right to preach and administer sacraments, that is, between subdeacons (and lower ranks) and deacons (and upper ranks). One step above a deacon was a priest, *sacerdos* – between the rank of a priest and a bishop there was no such distinction. The controversy about the right to preach was thus crucial in the relations between pope and various lay movements in the late twelfth century and the emerging Franciscans in the early thirteenth century.[89]

From my point of view, it is significant that in the twelfth and early thirteenth century sources the *festa stultorum* and suchlike were mentioned as the feasts of subdeacons and other lower clerics.[90] It was the perspective of this group that probably dominated the majority of secular Latin lyrics.

The education of the secular clergy started to change greatly from the late eleventh century. Popes and ecclesiastical councils, e.g. Gregory VII (1073-1085), Alexander III (1159-1181) and Innocent III (1198-1216), focused on the secular clergy and its education, emphasizing its task in *cura animarum* or teaching and preaching and tried to further the development of cathedral schools under episcopal control.[91]

The secular clergy received its education mainly in the cathedral and collegial schools and often during the twelfth century from independent masters holding teaching licences *(licentia docendi)* conferred by episcopal chancellors. At the beginning of the next century the numerous highly reputed schools functioning in various towns especially in Northern France were marginalised, first of all by the scholarly centres formed in Paris and Bologne and later on elsewhere in Western Christendom. These centres were called *studium generale* (i.e. university) and their own governing bodies freed from

---

86   Le Bras 1959, 149; Little 1978/1983, 106-107 and *passim*; Boureau 1993.
87   E.g. CB 8 (CB I.1, 10-13); CB 37 (CB I.1, 60-62); CB 39.7 (CB I.1, 63); CB 82 (CB I.2, 64-66); CB 92 (CB I.2, 94-119); CB 138 (CB I.2, 233-234); CB 215a (CB I.3, 67); CB 218.4 (CB I.3, 70); CB 219 (CB I.3, 71-77) CB 220 (CB I.3, 77-78).
88   Rapp 1993, 20; cf. also Brunner 1958/1984; Le Bras 1959.
89   Little 1978/1983, 113-145, 146-169.
90   Baldwin 1970, 131-133.
91   Delhaye 1947; Boureau 1993; Foulon 1993; see also Le Bras 1959; Little 1978/1983.

episcopal control, achieved the right of granting general teaching licences (*licentia ubique docendi*) which were to be accepted everywhere in Western Christendom.[92]

In Northern France during the twelfth century there were mainly three kinds of urban ecclesiastical schools: the cathedral or chapter schools directly under episcopal control, collegial schools run by Augustinian houses and the schools of the independent masters holding episcopal *licentia docendi*.[93] Among the students there were three main groups: canons who had *prebendae* and other income, internal clerics who lived at the canons and compensated it with payments or service, and finally external clerics who lived elsewhere and often served in other churches. The tensions between wealthy canons and other lower clergy and students is well depicted in the poems of Hugh Primas of Orléans (ca. 1093- ca. 1160).[94] Documents also seem to indicate that the school-towns soon attracted students whose position and income was even more insecure than that of external clerics.[95]

The schools concentrated on teaching the *trivium* (and for advanced students *quadrivium*). The first included *grammatica*, *rhetorica* and *dialectica*, that is, discursive arts.[96] The reading-lists varied from school to school and from master to master but the main *corpus* was more or less similar – the variation was in the emphasis on the different branches of this basic educational system.[97] In general, the schools offered basic verbal competence in Latin language and literature and produced clerics who knew the classical and Christian literature and the elements of logic well. These clerics were recruited to traditional ecclesiastical tasks but also both to ecclesiastical and secular administration.

The *Carmina Burana* manuscript was not, of course, compiled by the lower (and in many cases poor) clergy, but had to be funded by someone with means – perhaps a learned bishop who favoured scholars and learned poets or a wealthy canon or even the head of an Augustinian establishment. However, the viewpoint of its poetry – as I try to show later – was very close to the lower clergy and students who were well educated and capable of using all their classical, Christian and poetical learning. The more exact historical context for individual poems remains uncertain in most cases. As a cultural historical source it seems to tell very little of topical interest but more importantly, it articulates some reactions to rather general changes in its contemporary society and especially certain ways of thought and moral argument. It seems that the collection as a whole and especially its

---

92 Delhaye 1947, 253-268; see also *Geschichte der Universität in Europa: Bd. I Mittelalter.* Hrsg. von W. Rüegg. München 1993.
93 Delhaye 1947, 238-250.
94 Delhaye 1947, 250; about Hugh Primas see *idem* (ed. Adcock); McDonough 1984; Latzke 1968.
95 Baldwin 1970, 63-72, 117-149.
96 Delhaye 1947, 250-252; Wagner 1983/1986, 1-31.
97 Glauche 1970 (see note 74 above).

moral-satirical poems limits their treatment in the clerical world and discusses features important to it. Further, it seems that this clerical world corresponds first of all with the world of cathedral and collegial schools and that its ideological background suggests the schools of Northern France in the late twelfth century. The literary elements strengthen this impression with their abundant allusions to classical and Christian authors which were familiar from the canonical reading lists of these schools, not to mention the mocking remarks on monastic orders.[98] References to Gratian however the main authority for Northern Italian law schools, are rather hostile.[99] Thus the historical perspective of this study remains at the level of ideas and texts reflecting, reacting to and reformulating the general change in clerical culture and its contemporary society.

Intertextuality, socio-cultural context and cultural history

The historical analysis of the moral-satirical poems naturally requires placing them in their own literary and socio-cultural context; that is, they have to be read in accordance with medieval clerical understanding. However, this is not sufficient alone. A comprehensive scrutiny of their textual and intertextual nature is also required. Finally, to arrive at a properly historical interpretation, one has to transcend the contemporary horizon by setting the texts against the social change which was only partly visible to the medievals themselves. The twelfth-century notion of poetry already suggests lines for cultural historical analysis which approach the poetry as a voice of the (lower) clerical orders.

In principle, this kind of study is a combination of literary scholarship and historical research. This combination is not unproblematic since there is a tension between literary and historical approaches. In a radically simplified

---

98   E.g. CB 39 (CB I.1, 62-63); CB 219 (CB I.3, 71-77)
  Rather suprisingly, references to the intellectual and cultural history of the early thirteenth century are rare despite the fact that some of its poems have been attributed to poets active at the time and despite its two main scribes probably composing some of its poems during its compilation in ca. 1225/30 (see e.g. Philip the Chancellor; see note 14; Sayce 1992, 25-38 and *passim*). When there are identifiable references they relate mostly to the twelfth century Norbertin establishment (i.e. Premonstratensians, est. in 1121; CB 39.7; CB I.1, 63; Hilka & Schumann 1930/1961, 68) and disputes around the monastery of Grandmont (1185-88; CB 37.2.2; CB I.1, 60-61; Hilka & Schumann 1930/1961, 59-64; see also Schüppert 1972, 128-129, 175-176), Pope Alexander III and Frederick Barbarossa (CB 41, see part III; CB 53; CB I.1, 106-108; Hilka & Schumann 1930/1961, 115-116), and the second and third crusade (CB 46, 47, 50, 51a; Hilka & Schumann 1930/1961, 93-112; see also note 42). Further, Saladin (CB 50), Greek Emperor (CB 51a), Richard the Lionheart (CB 122), Philip of Swabia (CB 124) and Louis VII (CB 226) are mentioned. Even if the manuscript was compiled at a point of contact between German and Italian cultures the events of the turn of the twelfth and thirteenth centuries are not apparent. There is no mention of various Christian lay-movements or heretics and what is even more important, the collection does not know mendicant orders at all, only Benedictines *(monachi nigri)*, Augustinians and its filials the Norbertins and the monastery of Grandmont.
99   E.g. CB 41 (CB I.1, 65-74; Elredge 1970, 59-69.

perspective, the primary object of study is, in the first case, the literary work or text itself, and its more or less generally accepted goal is an interpretation of it.[100] On the other hand, historical research treats the texts only as sources or traces of the reality behind them and tries to reach the society or individual from which they originate.[101] On the other hand, both disciplines seem to have been intermingling recently with each other in that cultural studies and so-called "new historicism" have emerged among literary studies, and historians have become more aware of the textual or discursive intermediation of their materials (and their own expression).[102] A historian, especially a historian of culture, can not longer avoid the fact that "the vestiges of the past" are not simple traces of a reality caused by them but are complex signs and sign-systems which certainly do not speak directly about the rest of the socio-cultural environment they arise from. Furthermore, it is possible to perceive tendencies in literary studies which try to expunge hermetic textualism and set the texts in their wider non-textual context – even, in some cases, in their original historical context.

In medieval studies the situation is paradoxical in so far as the most emphatically unhistorical approaches never really touched medieval literary scholarship. The discipline remained more or less dominated by the philological approach. However, even if texts were reconstructed and interpreted in their historical context, more thorough attempts to set such things as Latin secular poetry in its contemporary society and even intellectual history have been until recently rather rare.[103] Thus my approach sets my study at the confluence of two more or less separate scholarly traditions, that is, the philological literary study of medieval Latin poetry and medieval intellectual and cultural history. In this attempt the impulses coming from literary studies and philology for textual analysis are important, and an approach proper for historical scholarship to stretch itself beyond the texts to reach the contemporary society even if only on a rather general level.

---

100 Cf. Jonathan Culler's critique of this kind of approach (1981/1983, 4-6); also Lehtonen 1989, 51-53. Of course this is a simplification and such tendencies in literary scholarship as structural poetics, reception aesthetics and cultural studies do not enter into this description.

101 Naturally, in practice, literary interpretation may lead "behind the text" or at least is often grounded on a reconstruction of socio-cultural context, and correspondingly, the historian may concentrate "only" on textual analysis. It is trivially true that the level of the historian's interpretation is always in a wide sense textual, i.e. his sources are (in most cases) cultural objects which can be understood as "texts" (cf. Stock 1990). The main difference in the emphasis of the disciplines is which texts and how one can legitimately put them together and which questions are considered as valid. (Cf. Culler 1981/1983; Lehtonen 1989.)

102 Cf. Vance 1986; idem 1987, esp. xx-xxxiii; Stock 1990, 16-29, 75-94; Nichols 1991, 1-26.

103 At the beginning of 1980's W.T.H. Jackson could still write: "Not very many years ago, it would have been perfectly possible to argue that interpretation of medieval lyric poetry, in the sense in which the term is used of post-Renaissance poetry, simply did not exist. There were, of course, books and articles about the lyric, but they were not concerned with the interpretation or evaluation of individual lyrics nor with the question of how good evaluation might be achieved. Still less did they attempt to propose any theory of interpretation or creation which might be of general use in studying poetry. ... The last ten years have seen remarkable changes..." (1980a, 1.) See also notes 7 and 8 above.

For the analysis of the moral-satirical poems of the *Carmina Burana* this means that they are understood as a discourse which is constructed on the basis of a textual network, and which reacts to the socio-cultural change in its social environment. My focus is on cultural production in a period when all levels of society from material modes of production, relations of lordship, social institutions to ideological representations and self-awareness were being transformed.

This study will concentrate only on some fragments of this complex process and thus does not attempt any description of the totality of culture and society. Firstly, it will concentrate on interpretation and representation presented by the urban and learned clerical order. The point of view thus limits itself to a new and emerging part of the dominant ideological elite expressing itself in Latin. Secondly, I have been content with limited themes and materials, primarily to discursive self-definitions (poetry as moral science, i.e. "ethical poetics"), outlines of the preconditions of human action (based on the *Fortuna*-poems) and reactions to actual threat to moral order (the money-satires, *Nummus*). Nevertheless, this demarcation also widens the perspective: a collection whose contents are mostly anonymous, and which originates from different sources and is filtered by several intermediaries, opens up a viewpoint on the poetical articulation of (lower) clerical orders.

Because I am dealing with complex cultural objects or "second-degree sign-systems" in my study,[104] the materials cannot be thus taken as simple sources or traces of the past as such. I must first carefully consider the medieval views of poetry and its interpretation. These analyses have an integral – and also independent – place in this study. Secondly, I will apply recent dicussions about intertextuality to the analysis of poems themselves. This theory about texts as textual networks not only provides means for analysis and interpretation of single poems but is connected to the ideas proposed above about the analysis of the socio-cultural totality. Utilised in a cultural historical viewpoint intertextuality can be understood as a description of a certain culture's discursive network.

From this perspective it is crucial that medieval Latin secular poetry was *par excellence* intertextual, the texts being interwoven conciously and apparently with other texts and devices pointing to (often authoritative) sources. The medieval writing was not, in this sense, guided by the mimetic but rather the semiotic principle of not to create a persuasive impression by a "realistic" description but by a tuning a textual network which ultimately seemed to lend more authoritative weight to what was said. Furthermore, the paradigm of writing emphasized the secondary significance of the author and, for accidental reasons, the poetry has remained mostly anonymous. Finally, the poetry was regarded as more or less circulating "common property", and the individual texts were changed, quoted and combined rather freely.

---

104 Cf. Lotman 1971, 281-299.

In the case of anthologies like the *Carmina Burana*, anonymity, intertextuality and collectivity are emphasized. Single poems are a part of a collection which compilers made of texts picked up from different sources, perhaps writing some themselves, to compose an anthology following their own principles.[105] Thus we have two interpenetrating intentional layers: the one of (mostly anonymous) authors and the other of (also anonymous) compilers. In addition, texts are handed down to the collection through different intermediaries.[106] Thus it is justifiable to argue that the poetry in the collection has gone through multiple collective control. However, we have to pay attention to the fact that this control was not necessarily systematic by ecclesiastical authorities or censors but was based on the conceptions of learned clerics. Obviously, it is highly probable that ultimately a higher ecclesiastical authority has participated in the composition of the collection, because otherwise it would be very difficult to explain how such an expensive, laborious and consistently composed manuscript would ever have been compiled. Eventually the "collective" nature of the *Carmina Burana* emerges from of its underlying textual paradigm and of its possible process of composition.

Some scholars have developed methods which would make possible a more refined analysis of structures of intertextuality and intertextual allusions as a counterpart to the more theoretical and abstract intertextual theory of culture.[107] This kind of pragmatic methodology offers tools for historical

---

105 Cf. Schumann 1930/1961; Bischoff 1970a; *idem* 1970b; Dronke 1975, 116-137; Walsh 1976, 1-7; Parlett 1986/1988, 45; Wolff 1995. Cf. Sayce 1992.
106 Schumann 1930/1961; Bischoff 1970a; Lipphardt 1982; Sayce 1992.
107 E.g. Mikhail Bakhtin; Gérard Genette (1982).
    According to modern intertextual theory the literary works have to be understood as texts which are not governed by an author's centralising intentional meaning but by diverse dispersive textual allusions, "a mosaic of texts" or "an ensemble of textual recollection" (see e.g. Kristeva 1969/1978, 85 (generally 82-112); Riffaterre 1978, 1-3, 19, and *passim*; *idem* 1981, 4-7; *idem* 1991, 29-45; Pfister 1985, 4-8, 11-15; Lehtonen 1989, 60-64). Such a theoretical approach underrates the role of the intentional author and emphasizes the collective and uncontrollable process of forming meanings. It can be viewed as analogous to the famous dictum paraphrasing Karl Marx that "people make their history and yet they do not make it". (Although the dictum does not seem to appear as such in Marx but is a reformulation of a passage in the preface of *Zur Kritik de politische Ökonomie* 1859/1903, XI, cf. Viikari 1985; *idem* 1995; on earlier formulations of this principle as the invisible hand see Funkenstein 1986, 202-205). An individual agent acts at the intersection of different forces influencing him and does not have the opportunity to see all dimensions and meanings of his deeds. This kind of view is for a historian simultaneously fruitful and problematic. The emphasis of anonymity opens the analytical possibility for history of mentalities pursuing the collective level of human mind(s) which includes both conscious and unconcscious ideas and beliefs governing human understanding and action. However, several scholars have remarked that the term "mentality" is fluid and unsatisfactory (e.g. Duby 1988). Nevertheless, it seems that social and cultural historians operate with such notions whether they mention it or not (cf. Stock 1983; *idem* 1990). The difference between the history of ideas (or intellectual history) and history of mentalities does not lie in the mere difference between concentrating on elites and the popular masses but on the fact that the first enquires, usually literally, into articulated conceptions while the latter one interprets various materials to get a grip of notions, beliefs and mental structures beyond the articulated surface (whether textual or functional). These "mentalities" are something which are commonly shared, changing slowly and remaining unarticulated. As such, they form

analysis. On the other hand, we should remember that the basis for an analysis of textual relations is traditional philological method as it had already been developed in the nineteenth century.[108] From the point of view of historical analysis, the novelty in the theory of intertextuality lies in the combination of conceptualisation of textuality at the ontological and meaningful level, the examination of the transformation of textual allusions, taking reception as a factor as important as the writing, and finally in the systematic analysis and typology of intertextuality instead of simple recognition of allusions.

Even if medieval Latin secular poetry was markedly intertextual and mostly anonymous, we would still know its socio-cultural "address", i.e. the learned clerical orders which actually emerged along with economic, social and cultural changes during the eleventh and twelfth centuries.

Indeed, the medieval ethical poetics outlined the ways for poetical discourse to get a grip of surrounding reality. The poetry's function as a "mirror of clerical order", a *speculum clericorum*, in which the changes in socio-cultural context were reflected and various strategies of reacting the change were constructed and the change was finally conceptualized, emerges from this. Thus poetry participated actively in the discursive formation of its socio-cultural environments. Clerical poetry can be read not only as a mere reflection, but as a projection in its own context (and into its own context) and as an interpretation of clerical order about the forces changing the sublunar world and their significance for their own moral strategy.

In this respect my study will also deviate from most earlier intellectual and cultural history which has not (with some exceptions) taken medieval poetry into account in its studies. I will read Latin materials as those of cultural history which open up a privileged viewpoint on the self-awareness of the clerical order at the turning point of the monastic and secular Christian world. The intertextual structure and intentional stratification makes it opportune to consider them as an articulation of more or less commonly shared attitudes and suppositions. Moreover, one can claim that poetry gives at least in some

---

conceptual preconditions of action which more or less govern and motivate human action and choice.

The theory of intertextuality can be understood as one analytical model for scrutinising such conceptions and structures. From this point of departure, the human action and culture can be understood as analogous to textuality (cf. Stock 1990, 16-29, 95-112; also Ricoeur 1986, 183-212 and *passim*). The "textual recollection" or "memory" activating the intertextual process and governing the formation of signification (Riffaterre 1981, 4-7; *idem* 1991, 29-45), can then be taken as parallel to what is called "mentality", ideology and such like. Riffaterre writes: "Since intertextuality is a dialectical, two-way relationship, the sociolectic fragment carved out or privileged by the text in turn valorizes or modifies the functions and especially the interpretation of that part of the text of which this fragment is now the mnemonic correlate." (1991, 34.)

Hence one task of cultural history can be understood as the reconstruction of this recollection - which, contrary to Riffaterre's view, is not independent of the surrounding historical and socio-cultural reality but is an integral part of it. Further, Gérerd Genette's taxonomical intertextual typologies can be utilised as a tool for reaching the cultural intertextuality (and "mentalities") with the analysis of the relations of hyper- and hypotexts (Genette 1982, 7-40).

108 Riffaterre 1981, 5-6; cf. Cerquiglini 1989; Auerbach 1958.

cases a perspective from *sub cathedra* when most other discursive genres are *ex cathedra*. Thus, from the basis of poetry it is possible to construct a clerical conception of certain characters of its contemporaneous society, which is not articulated as clearly in other kinds of source materials.

To summarize, in this study I will concentrate on the ethical poetics, i.e. a conception of poetry as moral discourse, ethical-poetical persuasion and argumentation, use of intertextual allusions as an integral part of it, and conceptions of satire as its paradigmatic case. From this viewpoint I will scrutinize the moral-satirical poetry, particularly the *Fortuna* poems and money satires of the first part of the *Carmina Burana*. The *Fortuna* poems open a window on the general preconditions of human action in respect to *divina providentia*, free choice or will, and chance. This window offers insight into the preconditions of human action in the sublunar world which is reconstructable with the help of textual allusions. In this regard, the money satires are a commentary on an actual and contingent historical event; that is, the breakthrough of the monetary economy into the purview of the clerical order. They conceptualize the distortion caused by money especially among the ecclesiastical hierarchy and the breakdown of idealised reciprocal order.

These elements comprise a textual mirror, *speculum clericorum*, which not only reflects but actively projects concepts outlining reality, and as such functions as an element of socio-cultural process. In the words of St. Paul:

> *Videmus nunc per speculum in aenigmate; tunc autem facie ad faciem.*
> *Nunc cognosco ex parte; tunc autem cognoscam, sicut et cognitus sum.*
> *Nunc autem manent fides, spes, charitas; tria haec; major autem est*
> *charitas. (I.Cor. 13:12-13.)*

> For now we see through a glass, darkly; but then face to face: now I know in part; but then shall I know even as also I am known. And now abideth faith, hope, charity, these three; but the greatest of these is charity.

To distort the words of St. Paul slightly, one can take them as guiding principles of the present research. The historian also sees the past through an enigmatic mirror, but in a certain sense he also sees better and is able to extend the view of past agents. He sees their actions in a context of historical forces, consequences and meaningful contexts that are out of the sight of contemporaries. But, he has to remember that when examining the human beings of the past, the most important principle is charity.

Note on translations

All translations from Latin to English are mine if not otherwise mentioned.

Part I

Poetry, the systems of knowledge and satire

Ethics and the *Art of Love*

An anonymous writer in the early twelfth century composed a series of introductions mainly on ancient pagan and Christian authors, including the following passage:

> *<Accessus> Ovidii de Amatoria Arte. Intentio sua est in hoc opere iuvenes ad amorem instruere, quo modo debeant se in amore habere circa ipsas puellas, materia sua est ipsi iuvenes et puellae et ipsa precepta amoris, quae ipse iuvenibus intendit dare. Modus istius operis talis est, ostendere quo modo puella possit inveniri, inventa exorari, exorata retineri. Finalis causa est ut perlecto libro in mandatis suis, quid tenendum sit in amore ipsis iuvenibus enucleatum sit. Ethicae subponitur, quia de moribus puellarum loquitur, id est quos mores habeant, quibus modis retineri valeant. Videndum etiam est quia morem recte scribentium sequitur: proponit, invocat, narrat.*

> Introduction to the *Art of Love* by Ovid
> His purpose in this work is to instruct young men in the art of love, and how they should behave towards girls when having a love-affair. The young men and girls, and the advice in love which it is his intention to give the young men, form his subject-matter. The way he proceeds *(modus)* in this work is to show how a girl may be picked up, how when picked up she may be won over, and, once won over, how her love may be retained. His ultimate objective *(finalis causa)* is that, when the book with the instructions he gives in it has been read thoroughly, the course they should follow in a love-affair should be made clear to young men. It pertains to ethics, because it speaks of the behaviour of young girls, that is, the sort of morals they should have, and how they may be kept faithful. One should also observe that Ovid follows the custom of correct writers. He puts forward his case, he makes an appeal, and he narrates. (Tr. Minnis & Scott.)[1]

The author composed the introduction for schools using a conventional formula established in commentaries and introductions to *artes*.[2] In the same

---

1   Anonymous, *Accessus ad auctores*, 1-11, p. 33; translation Minnis & Scott 1988/1991, 24.
2   Huygens 1970, 1-3.
       Formally this introduction follows the so-called "philosophical" type. Its model was the formula used by Boethius in his work *In Porphyrii Isagogen*. Medieval commentators variated the six questions, which in Boethius were *intentio, utilitas, ordo, nomen auctoris,*

accessus collection he also presented introductions to other works by Ovid.[3] His manner of interpreting Ovid is typical of the Early and High Middle Ages when Ovid was adapted to Christian ethics and was interpreted as *Ovidius moralizatus* - one can see this more clearly in the same author's other introductions to Ovid.[4]

However, at first sight the interpretation of the *Art of Love* as an ethical work is puzzling. Our author himself understood the *Art of Love* as a work encouraging adulterous behaviour,[5] but explicitly states that "it pertains to ethics" *(ethicae subponitur)*. It seems that there are two complementary ways of resolving this dilemma. The first is proposed explicitly by our author, and the second one is a contextual reconstruction which at the same time gives a key to the understanding of contemporary medieval poetry, and, of course, the moral-satirical poetry of the *Carmina Burana*.

The anonymous author puts the *Art of Love* into the context of Ovid's other works and his life history. He claims that Ovid changed his opinion after seeing the indignation his work aroused, and he composed several works to reconciliation. Among these were the *On the Remedy for Love* and the *Book without a Title* (i.e. *Amores*).[6] Thus a prudent student can see that the advice found in the *Art of Love* is not to be taken literally. This leads us to the second resolution which is connected to biblical exegesis, rhetorical theories on irony, and the notion of satire.

Biblical exegesis ascribed to the Holy Scriptures several complementary levels of meaning from the literal-historical level to spiritual-allegorical understanding, tropological-moral meaning and eschatological anagogical

---

titulus, and *cui parti philosophiae supponitur* (Hunt 1948/1980, 125-128; Chadwick 1981/1990, 145-146). The anonymous author of this passage has divided the *intentio* question into three parts *(intentio auctoris, materia, finalis causa)*. He also has changed the question of the place of the work in the school curriculum and its way of treatment *(ordo)* to concern only the latter. Further, he has dropped the questions about the name of author and title of the work which the title of the introduction already answers. The author has finally added a question about the approach of the text *(proponit, invocat, narrat)*. Some of these changes are common to commentaries concerning *artes*, and some became prevalent in twelfth-century commentaries on poetry (especially the last question which was later known as a generic question about *carminis qualitas*) (Quain 1945/1986, 3-47; Hunt 1948/1980, 117-144; Minnis & Scott 1988/1991, 12-36).

3 E.g. *Heroides, Remedia amoris, Ex Ponto, Tristia*, and *Fasti* (Anon., *Accessus*, 29-38).
4 Anon., *Accessus*, 35-37; see also Minnis & Scott 1988/1991, 28.
   About *Ovidius moralizatus* see Quian 1945/1986, 8-9; Curtius 1948, 209-210; McGregor 1978, 29-51; Allen 1982, 138-140; Sowell 1991, 4-8.
   The acceptance of Ovid was not unanimous among medieval commentators. For instance, Conrad of Hirsau doubted whether Ovid was useful reading at all. However, he then admits that "one can find gold from filth" *(in quibus etsi potest aurum in stercore inveniri*; in *Dialogus super auctores*, 114). Nevertheless, Ovid was among the most popular authors in monastic and cathedral schools. He also served as a model for imitators. For example abbot Guibert of Nogent says in his autobiography that he was inspired to write poetry after Ovid, which he later regretted and disapproved of *(De vita sua, sive Monodiae* XVII, 134-138). Most of Ovid's commentators regarded him however as an acceptable ethical poet who simply had to be read in the correct way (e.g. Allen 1982, *passim*). About Ovid in the schools see McGregor 1978, 29-52.
5 Anon., *Accessus*, 33; see also Minnis & Scott 1988/1991, 24-28.
6 Anon., *Accessus*, 36-37.

meaning.[7] The tropological meaning was the one most often applied to authoritative pagan authors. For a text to be ethical meant that it contained a moral meaning – if it was not presented openly on the literal surface one had to seek it in the hidden depth. While one understood that the *Art of Love* could not be taken literally either because it is contrary to Christian moral teachings or because of Ovid's own life and other works (or, probably because of both), the work had to be interpreted anew according to tropological understanding. In rhetorical and poetical terms one has to read it as an ironic satire; that is, to understand the praise of illicit love as praise in order to blame.[8] The true meaning is not on the literal level but hidden in its irony.[9]

This kind of procedure may seem artificial but commentaries on various pagan poets, and among them commentaries on Ovid, together with widespread conceptions of irony and allegorical reading, suggest that it was considered as an obvious way of reading. Such an interpretation connected authors and their texts to preconditions constitutive of their authoritative status and place in the Christian *curriculum*. Our anonymous author also states another fundamental conceptual view. In placing the work of Ovid, or indeed most works of the pagan authors, among works of ethics, he implies that authoritative poetry in general is a part of philosophy. It seems that there was no category for literature as a separate intellectual activity, but that it was considered as a *scientia*, a branch among other philosophical activities.

The *accessus* I quoted belongs to a collection which is one of the earliest known examples of introductions to poetry according to the *accessus* formula originally developed for works dealing with *artes* or philosophical subjects. Later on this formula became a commonplace in commentaries and

---

7   According to the exegetic allegorical interpretation, the Scriptures usually had three or four levels of meaning, which were the historico-literal sense, the allegorical sense or a kind of code revealing the spiritual truth which was formed by the moral message (the third level, or tropological sense), and the anagogical sense, i.e. the eschatological meaning of the fourth level. The historical level told what had happened (when the text was not a historical narrative, the first level was to be understood in its literal sense in general), the allegorical how to understand, the tropological how to behave to reach salvation, and the anagogic revealed the eschatological *telos*. The Christian fourfold allegory has its background in the Neoplatonic, Hebrew and Stoic theories of interpretation, and was further developed from St. Paul, Clemens of Alexandria and Origen to the Latin Church Fathers Jerome and Augustine. The fourfold scheme was formulated in the fifth century by John Cassien and Eucher, bishop of Lyon, and was later strongly promoted by Pope Gregory the Great. See de Lubac 1959-1964/1993; Chydenius 1960; Coulter 1976; Brinkmann 1980; Pépin 1987; Rollinson 1981; Whitman 1987.
    In the twelfth century, many scholars were opposed to the earlier, almost limitless allegorization, and stressed the literal and tropological (i.e. moral) meanings - the eschatological allegory, i.e. anagogy was left aside. See Hugh of St. Victor, *Didasc.* V.ii, p. 95-96; also Smalley 1952/1984, 83-97; de Lubac 1959-64/1993 II, 287-435; Sicard 1991, 74-77.
8   E.g. Quintilian, *Inst. or.* IX.ii; Diomedes, *Ars grammatica*, 456-462; Augustine *De doctrina christiana* III.xxix.41; Bede, *De arte metrica et de schematibus et de tropis* II.ii.12. Knox 1989 provides a concise study of medieval notions of irony (see especially 7-18); see also Green 1975, 119-159.
9   Bernard of Utrecht wrote: ... satirici enim yronice laudant vituperanda et vituperant laudanda. (*Comm. in Theod.* 99-108, p. 62.) See also *Accessus ab auctore incerto*, 90; Knox 1989, 16.

introductions to authoritative poetical works. The question *cui parti philosophiae subponitur* was regularly posed, and the most usual answer was *ethicae*. Thus poetry was considered to pertain to the general system of *scientiae*, and as such pertaining to philosophy. The most common definition was that poetry pertained to practical philosophy and especially to ethics.[10] The implications of this definition can be seen from at least three points of view: what were the systems of knowledge and categories of writing in which this kind of definition was made; what kind of ethics was it that included a great part of the works of authoritative poets of antiquity and even some works of contemporary poets; and, finally, which were the interpretative consequences for medieval Latin clerical poetry especially when it was identified as an ethical branch of knowledge?

In the following pages I will examine some of the twelfth- and thirteenth-century discussions on the system of philosophy and sciences, and its relation to poetry.[11] The historical analysis and interpretation of the learned literature

---

10 See Anon., *Accesus ad auctores*; Minnis & Scott 1988/1991; Allen 1982.
 With few exceptions, the habit of regarding all authoritative works (that is, those worthy of reading) as philosophy continued at least until the late fourteenth century (Minnis & Scott 1988/1991, 460-462, 476-491; Clogan 1990, 193-204; see also McKeon 1945, 217-234; Dahan 1980, 171-189; Kelly 1993, 132).

11 This topic has raised suprisingly little interest in spite of abundant scholarship on medieval poetry, poetics and philosophy. E.R. Curtius directed his attention to this in his classic study *Europäische Literatur und lateinisches Mittelalter* but he ended regreting the lack of understanding of poetry of the medieval learned. Indeed Curtius projected the romantic and post-romantic paradigm of art and literature as *belles-lettres* onto the medieval context (cf. Curtius 1948, 223-229, 475-478). Nevertheless, these views are still widespread among modern scholars.
 Recently the existence of the modern category of art and literature in the Middle Ages has been questioned (Allen 1982, *passim*; Zumthor 1986; also Wirth 1989, 11-12).
 Philippe Delhaye already demonstrated in his articles originally published in 1947-1958 that poetry had an important place in the twelfth-century school *curriculum* as a tool for moral teaching (see Delhaye 1949/1988; *idem* 1958/1988). More recently Paolo Bagni (1968, esp. 16-43) and Paul Klopsch (1980, 171-190) have made remarks on the place of poetics in the classification of sciences. Their focus is however poetics, not poetry itself. Gilbert Dahan has been working mainly on poetics although he draws an attention to the vague medieval notions which do not clearly separate poetics and poetry from each other. He elucidates interestingly the position of poetics and poetry as a propedeutic discipline and as a part of the discursive arts and, on the other hand, poetry as a special "moral logic" (the notion is from Roger Bacon and John Buridan) (Dahan 1980, 171-190, esp. 181-183). The topic has also been touched by Paul Clogan (1990, 193-204) and Anja-Inkeri Lehtinen (1993, 123-148). The most comprehensive recent work in this field is by A.J. Minnis alone (1984), and with A.B. Scott (1988/1990), in which he, seems to defend the slightly anachronistic way of taking the medieval commentaries as "literary theory and criticism" (Minnis & Scott 1988/1991, 1-11). Even more recently Päivi Mehtonen has analysed lucidly medieval Latin poetics and conceptions of veracity, fiction and narration (1991; 1992; 1996).
 Judson B. Allen (1982) has also worked on the assumptions made in commentaries on classical authors concerning the nature of poetry and its place in a general medieval intellectual framework. He takes a historicist and anti-anachronistic position and denies the possibility of taking medieval poetry as literature in a modern post-romantic sense. However, Allen does not place commentaries in the context of discussions on philosophy and branches of knowledge. Thus his remarkable study does not give a full picture of twelfth-century conceptions.
 These studies have not yet had any profound impact on scholarship of medieval Latin poetry itself. Only the surveys of satire has been done according to medieval ethical poetics (Witke 1970, 11-15; on the genre of satire: Kindermann 1978, see e.g. 41).

---

and poetry of the time must remain inadequate as long the meaning of words such as *philosophia, scientia,* and *poetria* (or *poetica, poesia,* and *carmina poetarum*) is not clarified. It is also important to examine what their mutual relations were. I will then proceed to the definitions of satire – how it formed a paradigmatic case for ethical poetics, and how its semantic nature deviated from the general nature of poetry.

The place of poetry in the classifications of disciplines

The system of knowledge: two traditions

The system of the branches of knowledge was a compilation from different sources of antiquity. Medieval scholars worked them up in different contexts and provided several new versions of them. Before the translation of the *Organon* of Aristotle the main sources for classification of sciences were the treatises of Anicius Manlius Severinus Boethius (ca. 475-524) and some remarks made by Aurelius Augustinus, or St. Augustine (354-430). Even after the corpus of Aristotle was brought into Latin these traditions remained vigorous. Indeed, the Boethian system was an adaptation of the Aristotelian classification, nor was the originally Stoic classification of Augustine totally incompatible with it.[12]

Indeed, a general survey is still lacking, as are wider adaptations of the analysis of medieval poetry itself.

12 Weisheipl 1965, 54-90; *idem* 1978, 461-482; Dahan 1980, 171-239; *idem* 1990, 5-27; Chadwick 1981/1990, 108-111.

In his *In Isagogen Porphyrii commentum* and *De Trinitate* Boethius divided philosophy into theoretical *(theorica* or *speculativa)* and practical *(practica* or *actualis)* philosophy of which the first included *scientia naturalis, mathematica,* and *theologia* as sub-branches. The latter also included three sciences called *moralia sive ethica, dispensativa sive domestica,* and *civilis sive politica* (Boethius, *De Trin.* II; *idem, De Isag. Porh. comm.* I.3, cit. Weisheipl 1965, 59-61; Dahan 1990, 11, 15-16). The first of the sub-branches of practical philosophy was ethics, which was concerned with the morals of individuals. The second was concerned with the management of the household *(oikos* or *domus),* and the third with government *(politeia* or *civitas).* The same classification was also given by an influential treatise on divine and secular learning, namely the *Institutiones divinarum et saecularum litterarum* (ca. 544/5) of Flavius Magnus Aurelius Cassiodorus (ca. 485-575/80) (II.3.iv-vii).

A divergent division was given by St. Augustine in his major work *De civitate Dei* (413-427). First, he gives a standard version of two major branches of *studium sapientiae* which are in his words *activa* and *contemplativa* - the first concerns human life or morals, and the second natural causes and pure truth. Then he turns to a Stoic tripartite division which he mistakenly attributes to Plato. This view divides philosophy into moral, natural and rational philosophy, that is ethics, physics and logic. Augustine did not try to join these two divisions in any tree-like system, stating baldly that ethics belongs mainly to active or practical philosophy and physics contemplative philosophy. However, he thought of logic as a method which belonged both to active and contemplative philosophy. This solution had an important impact in the High Middle Ages when there was a debate over the nature of discursive arts (that is the *trivium*) which was also related to the standing of poetry and poetics *(De civ. Dei* VIII.4; Weisheipl 1965, 63-64; Dahan 1980, 176-177; *idem* 1990). In another work Augustine defined *sapientia* (wisdom) as intellectual practice directed towards *aeterna res* (eternel things) while *scientia* (science or knowledge) was *rerum cognitio rationale* (rational knowing of things), see Gregory 1990, 11 (orig. in *De Trinitate* XII.xv.25;

Both of these classifications were also transmitted to the Middle Ages by Isidore of Seville (ca. 560-636) whose encyclopedic work *Etymologiae sive Origines* was disseminated all over Western Christendom and remained a standard work until the Late Middle Ages. Isidore proposed firstly the Stoic-Augustinian triad of *physica*, *ethica* and *logica*, which he did not relate to the twofold distinction as Augustine had done.[13]

Later in the same chapter Isidore presents the Boethian classification which he seems to have borrowed from Cassiodorus, and gives a more precise definition of theoretical and practical philosophy. I quote the general definition and the specification of practical philosophy:

> *Philosophia diuiditur in duas partes: prima inspectiua; secunda actualis. ... Inspectiua dividitur in tribus modis, id est prima in naturalem; secunda in doctrinalem; tertia in diuinam. Doctrinalis diuiditur in quattuor, id est, prima in arithmeticam, secunda in musicam, tertia in geometricam, quarta in astronomiam. Actualis diuiditur in tribus, id est prima in moralem, secunda in dispensatiuam, tertia in ciuilem. ...*
> *Porro actualis dicitur, quae res propositas operationibus suis explicare contendit. ... Moralis dicitur, per quam mos uiuendi honestus adpetitur, et instituta ad uirtutem tendentia praeparantur. Dispensatiua dicitur, cum domesticarum rerum sapienter ordo disponitur. Ciuilis dicitur, per quam totius ciuitatis utilitatis administratur.*

> Philosophy is divided into two parts: the first is speculative *(inspectiva)*, the second practical *(actualis)*. ... The speculative is divided into three divisions: the first is natural, the second theoretical *(doctrinalem)*, the third divine. The theoretical is divided into four, that is to say first arithmetic, second music, third geometry, fourth astronomy. The practical is divided into three parts, that is, first moral, second administrative *(dispensativam)*, third civil *(ciuilem)*. ...
> Moreover, the practical branch is that which attempts to explain suggested courses of action by examining the way they would work. This has three parts: moral, administrative and civil. That is called moral by which an honourable way of life is sought and habits tending to virtue fostered. It is called administrative, when the arrangement of domestic affairs is wisely administered. That is called civil through which the advantage of the whole state is secured. (Tr. P.K. Marshall).[14]

XIII.xix.24).

13 Philosophiae species tripertita est: una naturalis, quae Graece *physica* appellatur, in qua de naturae inquisitione disseritur; altera moralis, quae Graece *ethica* dicitur, in qua de moribus agitur; tertia rationalis, quae Graeco uocabulo *logica* appellatur, in qua disputatur quemadmodum in rerum causis uel uitae moribus ueritatis ipsa quaeratur. In *physica* igitur causa quaerendi, in *ethica* ordi uiuendi, in *logica* ratio intellegendi uersatur. *(Etym. II.xxiv.3,* ed. Marshall 1983, 103).

14 *Etym.* II.xxiv.10-11, xxiv.16, ed. Marshall 1983, p. 107, 111. I have changed from Marshall's translation the word *partes* (Marshall: sections) to 'parts' as he himself later translates the same word.

Isidore neither attempts to assimilate the two classifications nor comment on the differences between them. There is only a little hint in his vocabulary which might suggest

Aside from the division of philosophy and classification of *scientiae* was the system of *septem artes liberales*, that is, the liberal *curriculum* arts which included a sub-branch attributed either to mathematics (in Boethius's version) or to physics (in Augustine's version), namely, the *quadrivium (arithmetica, musica, geometria* and *astronomia)*. The other sub-branch was the *trivium (grammatica, rhetorica* and *dialectica)*.[15] The *trivium* or the discursive arts *(artes sermonicales* or *eloquentia)*[16] was an instrumental branch of knowledge which was not properly a part of philosophy in the Boethian system. In the Stoic-Augustinian version it was a proper part of philosophy under the heading *logica* – probably this use led to the widespread medieval use of *logica* as a general title for all discursive arts whereas *dialectica* meant what we would call formal logic.[17]

In the twelfth and thirteenth centuries several scholars attempted in different ways to synthesize these authoritative systems.[18] One can argue that the existence of two different authoritative traditions explains at least partly the various anomalies in the different medieval classifications of sciences. The classification of poetry and poetics sometimes as a part of practical philosophy and more specifically as a part of ethics, sometimes as a part of *logica* or as a parallel discipline to rhetorics is indeed an essential anomaly from our point of view.[19]

Poetry as a part of philosophy

Discussions on poetry's role in the Christian *curricula* and nature as a philosophical discipline appear first in early collections of introductions to

---

that they could somehow be assimilated: the first classification talks about the *species* of philosophy while the second divides philosophy in *partes*. There is however no further clarification of this difference.

15 Weisheipl 1965, 54, 63; Dahan 1990, 14-22.
16 All three notions were used to mean discursive or linguistic arts. E.g. Hugh of St. Victor, *Didascalicon* VI.xiv; Dominicus Gundissalinus, *De divisione philosophiae* prol., 5, 18; John of Salisbury, *Metalogicon* I.i.
17 Stump 1983/1986, 125-146; Dahan 1990, 21-22.
18 Gilbert Dahan has summarized the twelfth- and thirteenth-century divisions of sciences into four groups: 1) *trivium* and *quadrivium* which appear in this form as such or somewhat modified e.g. in Alan of Lille, Honorius Augustodunensis and Robert Grosseteste; 2) the Stoic-Augustinian division into logic, ethics and physics; 3) the Aristotelian-Boethian division into theoretical and practical philosophy and their sub-branches; and, 4) especially in the context of logical treatises, the division following the traditional order of Aristotle's *Organon* (this division reached Western Christendom from Arab philosophers by the twelfth century before the translation of the whole corpus of Aristotle into Latin (Dahan 1980, 176-178). Furthermore, in the twelfth century Gilbert Porreta (or de la Porrée, d. 1154) proposed a division different from all these, namely he divised *scientiae* to speculative and practical including however to speculative *scientiae* physics, ethics and logics of which the first one consisted of *naturalis scientia, mathematica* and *theologica* (Nielsen 1982, 87-98). He seems to have tried to combine the Aristotelian-Boethian system with the Stoic-Augustinian but at the meantime it was fundamentally original synthesis based on Gilbert's view that *scientiae* can be delimited and denominated either on the basis of their objects or the way in which they deal with objects (Nielsen 1982, 91).
19 Bagni 1968, 16, 23-32, 32-45; Klopsch 1980, 64-83; Dahan 1980, 171-189.

authoritative poetry. R.B.C. Huygens has edited three such introductory works, namely an anonymous late eleventh-century *accessus*-collection, Bernard of Utrecht's commentary on a tenth-century *Eglogus* by Theodulus, and Conrad of Hirsau's (ca. 1070-ca. 1150) *Dialogus super auctores* from the early twelfth century. They all use approximatively the same introductory model developed for works on arts, philosophy and theology. This model was later used with slight variations in almost all medieval commentaries on poetry.[20]

The *magister* in Conrad of Hirsau's dialogue explains to his pupil the way to write commentaries:

> *Nec te lateat, quod in libris explanandis VII antiqui requirebant: auctorem, titulum operis, carminis qualitatem, scribentis intentionem, ordinem, numerum librorum, explanationem. Sed moderni quatuor requirenda censuerunt, operis materiam, scribentis intentionem, finalem causam et cui parti philosophiae subponatur quod scribitur. ... De partibus philosophiae, quibus opus omne auctorum subponitur, in sequentibus docebimus, ubi disciplinarum liberalium nomina potius quam effectum earum indicabimus.*

> You must also be aware that in interpreting books the ancients asked seven questions: who the author was, the title of the work, the nature *(qualitas)* of the verse, the intention of the writer, the order and number of books, and the actual exposition [of the text]. But modern writers have laid down four questions that have to be asked: the subject matter, the intention of the writer, the final cause of the writing, and to what part of philosophy that which is written pertains. ... I will teach you about the parts of philosophy, to which every author's work pertains, later on in the book, when we shall set out the names of the liberal disciplines rather than their effects. (Tr. Minnis & Scott.)[21]

"Modern" *(moderni)* commentators especially do judge to which part of philosophy works commented on pertain. Conrad goes on to underline that *every author's* works pertain to philosophy, although it remains unclear if, for instance, all the pagan poets pertain to philosopy. Earlier in the dialogue Conrad's *magister* had made a distinction between author *(auctor)*, history writer *(historiografus)*, poet *(poeta)*, bard or seer *(vates)*, commentators *(commentatores)*, expositors *(expositores)*, and preachers *(sermonarii)*. The *auctor* writes about the deeds, sayings or thoughts of men of former times, when *poeta* is an inventor *(fictor)* or the one who gives shape to things *(formator)*. Instead of the truth the poet tells lies, or intermingles truth with falsehood.[22]

---

20 See e.g. Dominicus Gundissalinus, *De div. phil.*, 140; Ralph of Longchamp, I.1, p. 19; Allen 1982, 9-12; Minnis & Scott 1988/1991, 12-36; Friis-Jensen 1988, 81-147.
21 *Dial. sup. auct.*, 215f., p. 78-79; translation Minnis & Scott 1988/1991, 46. Conrad's model is nearly identical with the pattern proposed by Bernard of Utrecht in his commentary on Theodulus in the eleventh century *(Commentum in Theodulum*, 59).
22 Accipe: auctor ab augendo dicitur, eo quod stilo suo rerum gesta vel priorum dicta vel

The ambivalence in Conrad's dialogue recurs in some other systematical treatises on theology and philosophy but the tradition of commentary on ancient authors followed in the foot steps of the anonymous writer quoted at the beginning of this chapter. The works of pagan poets of antiquity were most usually considered as pertaining to ethics or sometimes exceptionally to other parts of philosophy, especially to natural philosophy or physics.[23]

Defining poetry and placing it in the system of disciplines and philosophy was not in any case a main issue during the twelfth and thirteenth centuries but rather a marginal problem which was discussed when the status of pagan poets in the comprehensive ecclesiastical school *curriculum* was in question. The question was also occasionally raised in the context of debates about similarities between poetry and the Scriptures. The nature and place of poetry was mostly treated in extensive commentaries on pagan poets, mainly in works like the commentaries on Virgil and Macrobius (whose work itself was an allegorical poem on the seven liberal arts) attributed to Bernard Silvester.[24]

Nevertheless, even as a minor issue, poetry remained problematical; it was accepted as a part of the system of knowledge, although its metaphorical and fabulous nature made it dubious. On the other hand, logic's position was similarly more or less anomalous since the Aristotelian-Boethian tradition had not seen it as an independent part of philosophy but as a mere instrumental skill or art, which was, however, an indispensable instrument of philosophy. Similarly, poetics was often understood as an instrumental discursive discipline and poetry itself as a means for moral-philosophical persuasion (and as such a discipline closely related to rhetoric).[25]

An influential overview of sacred and secular learning, *Didascalicon: de studio legendi* of Hugh of Saint Victor (1096-1141), composed probably in the late 1120s also mentioned the status of poetry in learning. The work was meant to be a kind of continuation or a new version of St. Augustine's *De*

---

dogmata adaugeat. Historia est res visa, res gesta: *historin* enim grece, latine visio dicitur, unde historiografus rei visae scriptor dicitur. Porro poeta fictor vel formator dicitur, eo quod vel pro veris falsa dicat, vel falsis interdum vera commisceat. Vates a vi mentis dicitur: magna enim vis mentis est perspicaciter futurorum intuitu presentia precurrere et ventura quasi pre oculis demonstrare. Commentatores sunt qui solent ex paucis multa cogitare et obscura dicta aliorum dilucidare. Expositores sunt qui mistica scripturae sacre dicta resolvunt, sermonarii qui ad edificationem auditorem sermones exhortatorios de diversa materia componunt. *(Dial. sup. auct.,* 75-76; see Minnis & Scott 1988/1991, 43-44.)

23 See *Accessus ad auctores*, 19-54; Allen 1982, *passim*; Minnis & Scott 1988/1991, *passim*. On poetry as a source of natural philosophical knowledge see e.g. William of Conches, *Glos. in Iuv.*, 96; Ralph of Longchamp, *In Anticl. Al. comm.* I.1, p. 20. Also Stock 1972.

    The views about the evaluation of poetry did not follow the lines of philosophical and religious thought. Peter Abelard (1079-1142) for example did not include poetics (and poetry) in the system of knowledge, while his ardent opponent Bernard of Clairvaux (1091-1153) claimed poetry as a worthy pursuit because of its similarity to the Holy Scriptures (Bagni 1968, 32-45). On the other hand, some other philosophers opposed by Bernard, e.g. William of Conches (ca. 1080-1154) considered poetry as an essential part of the philosophical enterprise (see e.g. *Glosae in Iuvenalem, passim*).

24 See Stock 1972; Westra 1986, 1-33.

25 Dahan 1980, 181-188. These discussions were also continued on the same lines during the Renaissance, see Mikkeli 1992, 59-79.

doctrina christiana (396-426).[26] Hugh proceeded through the entirety of philosophical doctrine and the methods of scriptural interpretation. He created an original division of the branches of knowledge in which the mechanical arts were first given the status of art.[27] Hugh was however more suspicious when it came to poetry:

> *Duo sunt genera scripturarum. primum genus est earum quae propriae artes appelantur. secundum genus est earum quae sunt appendica artium. artes sunt quae philosophiae supponuntur, id est, quae aliquam certam et determinatam partem philosophiae materiam habent, ut est grammatica, dialectica, et ceterae huiusmodi. appenditia artium sunt quae tantum ad philosophiam spectant, id est, quae in aliqua extra philosophiam materia versantur. aliquando tamen quaedam ab artibus discerpta sparsim et confuse attingunt, vel si simplex narratio est, viam ad philosophiam praeparant. huiusmodi sunt omnia poetarum carmina, ut sunt tragoediae, comoediae, satirae, heroica quoque et lyrica, et iambica, et didascalica quaedam, fabulae quoque et historiae, illorum etiam scripta quos nunc philosophos appellare solemus, qui et brevem materiam longis verborum ambagibus extendere consueverunt, et facilem sensum perplexis sermonibus obscurare. vel etiam diversa simul compilantes, quasi de multis coloribus et formis, unam picturam facere. nota quae tibi distinxi duo sunt, artes et appendicia artium.*

There are two kinds of writings. The first kind comprises what are properly called the arts; the second, those writings which are appendages of the arts. The arts are included in philosophy: they have, that is, some definite and established part of philosophy for their subject matter - as do grammar, dialectic, and others of this sort. The appendages of the arts, however, are only tangential to philosophy. What they treat is some extra-philosophical matter. Occasionally, it is true, they touch in a scattered and confused fashion upon some topics lifted out of the arts, or, if their narrative presentation is simple, they prepare the way for philosophy. Of this sort are all the songs of the poets - tragedies, comedies, satires, heroic verse and lyric, iambics, certain didactic poems, fables and histories, and also the writings of those fellows whom today we commonly call "philosophers" and who are always taking some small matter and dragging it out through long verbal detours, obscuring a simple meaning in confused discourses - who, lumping even dissimilar things together, make, as it were, a single "picture" from a multitude of "colors" and forms. Keep in mind the two things I have distinguished for you - the arts and the appendages of the arts. (Tr. Taylor.)[28]

Evidently the ambiguity and obscurity of poetry made it difficult for Hugh to accept it as a part of the scholarly canon. On the other hand, the same

---

26   Smalley 1952/1984, 84-106; Taylor 1961/1991, 7, 28-36; see also Sicard 1991.
27   Taylor 1961/1991, 1-19; Lemoine 1991, 20-24; Weisheipl 1965, 65-66; Dahan 1990, 9-10.
28   *Didasc.* III.iv, 54-55; translation Taylor 1961/1991, 87-88. Similar *topoi* about loquacious "philosophers" appear also elsewhere, e.g. in Daniel of Morlai (Stock 1972, 60-62).

ambiguity, obscurity and imaginary nature was characteristic of the Scriptures. Those medieval writers who for one reason or another considered poetry being valuable took this as a good reason or pretext to apply to poetry the same or at least analogous interpretative methods to those used on the Scriptures.[29] Whether the usual view on commentators of poetry pertaining to ethics was accepted, or only the view of Hugh about the inclination of poetry towards true philosophy, it meant that the philosophical or ethical elements of poetry had to be revealed. This revelation took place in its most simple form in the introductions, where the most complicated forms led to an interpretation of all the figurative elements of the text.

More positive about the value of poetry and its place among the *artes* or *scientiae* was the mid-twelfth-century Spanish scholar Dominicus Gundissalinus who, among other topics, scrutinised poetry and poetics as a part of human system of knowledge. His view was a mixture of the earlier Latin rhetorical tradition, and Aristotelian Arab philosophy which he utilized (and translated).[30] According to Dominicus, poetics was a part of the discursive disciplines *(sciencie eloquencie)*, which he placed outside philosophy proper *(sciencie sapiencie)*:

> *Poëtica est sciencia componendi carmina metrice... Genus huius artis est pars quod ipsa est pars ciuilis sciencie, que est pars eloquencie. non enim parum operatur in ciuilibus, quod delectat uel edificat in sciencia uel in moribus. Materia huius artis duo sunt: quia aut res gesta aut res ficta.*[31]

> Poetics is the science *(sciencia)* of composing songs in metre. ... The genre of this art *(ars)* is a part of civil sciences which is a part of eloquence [i.e. discursive science, TL]. In civil affairs, the effect of such things that delight or edify in sciences or behavior is not small. The matter of this art consist of two elements: either what took really place *(res gesta)* or is fictitious *(res ficta)*.

Dominicus defined poetry as a part of civil sciences which pertained to communicative or discursive arts (he seems to use the terms *sciencia* and *ars* almost as synonymous). These arts were essential in undertaking common or civil affairs. For him philosophy proper, or the science of wisdom, was identical with theoretical philosophy (physics, mathematics, theology or metaphysics) which treated the real understanding of being.[32] Dominicus

---

29 E.g. Bernard Silvester (see page 57-59); see also Stock 1972. Henri de Lubac emphasizes the differences between sacred and secular allegory and interprets them as two separate but interactive methods of reading (de Lubac 1959-64/1993 II, 182-183).

30 It seems evident that Dominicus did not know other works of Aristotle than those which already existed in Latin, i.e. the translations mostly made by Boethius (Weisheipl 1965, 69-72).

31 *De div. phil.*, 54.

32 *De div. phil.*, 11-17. Here Dominicus seems to follow Augustine's division into *sapientia* and *scientia* (see Gregory 1990, 11; and note 12 above).

divided practical philosophy into ethical, economic (or dispensative), and communicative branches of knowledge. The last heading did not follow the mainstream of ancient and medieval classifications. The communicative branch or arts laid the ground for other branches of practical philosophy. A similar interpretation of the significance of discursive arts *(eloquentia)* was also offered by John of Salisbury.[33] This interpretation seems to be a kind of synthesis of the Aristotelian division of Boethius and the Stoic version of Augustine (see note 12).

Dominicus divided discursive sciences *(sciencia disponendi conuersacionem)* into grammar *(sciencia litteralis)* and civil sciences *(sciencie civiles)*, the latter including poetics, rhetoric and the science of secular laws *(scientia legum secularium)*.[34] Logic was an intermediary discipline which was simultaneously a part of philosophy and an instrument for all disciplines.[35]

The terminology of Dominicus is vague: poetics is the art of composing poems but he also writes about the effects of its products, that is the effects of poetry, when he speaks about the significance of poetics as a part of the discursive sciences. Poetry, not poetics, is the force which delights and edifies in sciences or good morals. Dominicus later defines "poetical speeches", that is poetry, in discussing logic:

> *Proprium est poëtice sermonibus suis facere ymaginari aliquid pulchrum uel fedum, quod non est, ita, ut auditor credat et aliquando abhorreat uel appetat; quamuis enim certi sumus, quod non est ita in ueritate, tamen eriguntur animi nostri ad abhorrendum uel appetendum quod ymaginatur nobis. ymaginacio enim quandoque plus operatur in homine quam sciencia uel cogitacio; sepe enim sciencia uel cogitacio hominis contraria est eius ymaginacioni et tunc operatur homo secundum quod ymaginatur, non secundum quod scit uel cogitat... Iste ergo sunt species sillogismorum et arcium sillogisticarum et species locucionum, quibus utuntur homines ad uerificandum aliquid in rebus omnibus. Set hoc quinque hiis etiam nominibus appellari possunt: certificatiua, putatiua, erratiua, sufficiens, ymaginatiua.*[36]

> It is proper for poetical speeches to make one imagine something beautiful or ugly which does not exist. This is done so that the hearer

---

33 *Metalogicon* I.i, 6-8.
34 *De div. phil.* 16, 43-69, 81. A similar division is also attributed to Bernard Silvester *(Comm. in Mart.* 78-82).
35 *De div. phil.* 18, 69-83.
36 *De div. phil.* 74.
    This definition of "poetical speeches" may have influenced the views of Roger Bacon in the next century when he examined the "poetic argument" which he defined as pertaining to logic. However, Dominicus may have picked it up from Arab Aristotelians who probaly also influenced Bacon. The art of using efficient argument, that is, poetry, was for Bacon a part of moral philosophy just as in the traditional *accessus* formula. (In the works *Moralis philosophia* and *Opus tertium.*) John Buridan followed the path of Gundissalinus and Bacon when he defined poetry as "moral logic" in his commentary to Aristotle's *Ethica Nicomachea (Questiones in decem libros Ethicorum Aristotelis ad Nichomachum).* See Dahan 1980, 181-183. On Averroes and Avicenna and their influence in the Latin West see Black 1990; Dahiyat 1974; Hardison 1970; Minnis & Scott 1988/1993, 277-288.

might believe and be horrified or want something. Although we are sure that it does not exist in reality, yet our soul stretches itself towards the horrible or desirable thing imagined by us. Imagination is something that has more effects in the human than knowledge or cogitation. In fact, the knowledge or cogitation of man is often contrary to his imagination, and in such situations man acts according to what he has imagined, not according to what he knows or thinks .... Thus these [i.e. poetical speeches] are species of syllogisms, syllogistic arts, and locutions, which people use to verify something in the entirety of things. They can thus be called by these five names: demonstrative, putative, falsifying, sufficient and imaginative.

Poetics was thus a discursive art beside rhetoric and grammar. However, as a part of logic, or more precisely, as a part of logical argument, "poetical speeches" were an instrument for efficient (thus, persuasive) argument. Poetical speeches, in short, poetry, had an effect on the imagination and through the imagination was able to influence human behaviour. The opinion of Dominicus was not hostile to poetry as some modern scholars have argued,[37] neither did he place poetry exactly outside philosophy; indeed, poetry was a part of logic which was simultaneously an instrumental discipline and a part of philosophy. With the notions of Dominicus there were hardly any difficulties in placing the works of any individual poet as a part of philosophy.

William of Conches (ca. 1080/90-1154/55), a contemporary of Dominicus, did not precisely place poetry in the system of knowledge in commenting on the satires of Juvenal. Nevertheless, he defined satires as "undressing the vices";[38] that is, poems which include true arguments under the fictive surface.[39] However, further affirmation is given by an anonymous *accessus* which Bradford Wilson has included in his critical edition of William's Juvenal commentary. It follows the already traditional formula presented earlier in this chapter. To the question of which branch of philosophy Juvenal's satires belong to, the anonymous author answers:

> *Sunt qui querendum existiment et in hoc et in aliis auctoribus cui parti philosophiae subponantur. Magister vero Bernardus dicebat hoc non esse in actoribus querendum cum ipsi nec partes philosophie nec de philosophia tractant. Magister Wilelmus de Conchis dicit auctores omnes, quamvis nec partes sint philosophie nec de ipsa agant, philosophie suponi propter quam tractant, et omnes illi parti*

---

37 E.g. Paolo Bagni places Dominicus among the scholars opposing poetry and poetics with Hugh of St. Victor and Peter Abelard (1968, 40-42). This interpretation is false simplification because Dominicus accepts them as a part of disciplines. Even the place of Hugh of St. Victor in this "anti-poetical" side is problematic, because he admits certain functions for poetry, seeing it as tangential to philosophy. See also Klopsch 1980, 67-68.

38 *Glosae in Iuvenalem*, 110.

39 Et hoc quippe, quod ita de Polife <mo> legitur fabulosum est, non fabula; subestque veritas argumento. (*Glos. in Iuv.*, 101). William makes a distinction between fabulosa (fictitious) and *fabula* (untrue and improbable fictitious narrative). On the notion *fabula* and its veracity see Gompf 1973; Dronke 1974; Mehtonen 1991; *idem* 1992; *idem* 1996.

philosophie suponi, propter quam tractant. Utraque ergo lectio vera est; auctores suponuntur philosophie id est propter ethicam que pars est philosophie, tractant, ut scilicet moralem comparent instructionem, et actores non suponuntur philosophie, id est non sunt partes eius.

Some think that in his [i.e. Juvenal's] case and in that of the other authors *(auctores)* we must enquire to what part of philosophy they pertain. Master Bernard, however, used to say that this question should not be asked in the case of writers *(actores)*, since their works are not parts of philosophy, neither do they discuss philosophy. Master William of Conches, on the other hand, asserts that, even though they are not a part of philosophy, nor treat of philosophy itself, all authors *(auctores)* pertain to philosophy because of the subject-matter of which they treat, and all pertain to that part of philosophy of which their subject-matter treats. Each of these judgements, then, is true. Authors *(auctores)* do pertain to philosophy, that is, on account of the fact that they treat of ethics, which is a part of philosophy, in that they provide moral instruction; and writers *(actores)* do not pertain to philosophy, that is, they are not a part of philosophy. (Tr. Minnis & Scott.)[40]

The translation of A.J. Minnis and A.B. Scott follows the interpretation of Paul S. Miller based on the difference between *auctor* and *actor*, i.e. an authoritative author and a mere writer.[41] However, this explanation does not thoroughly clarify this obscure and elliptical passage. The text seems to make a distinction between three kinds of authors (or writers). First of all, there are authors whose pertinence to philosophy nobody doubts. Secondly, there are those whose authority is granted but who do not self-evidently pertain to philosophy even though they sometimes do treat philosophical subjects, and whose works do pertain to philosophy. Thirdly there seems to be a left-over category of writers whose works do not touch upon philosophy at all. Nevertheless, the twelfth-century commentators hardly considered this third group, and in practice all authors (and also all writers worthy of reading) were interpreted in some way or other as pertaining to philosophy without much attention to the counter-arguments of *magister Bernardus* and others like him.

William himself did consider Juvenal pertaining to philosophy, and did assert in his commentary that the poems of Juvenal included historical and natural facts as well as "poetical issues" which he defined a little later as fictitious or fabulous.[42] Thus poetry was understood primarily as an introduction to philosophy, and, especially to ethics. Its figurative and

---

40 *Accessus ab auctore incerto*, in William of Conches, *Glos.in Iuv*. 89-90; translation from Minnis & Scott 1988/1991, 135-136. I am following the ortography proposed by Minnis & Scott.

41 Minnis & Scott 1988/1991, 135-136 (also note 74). On the terms *auctor* and *actor* see Chenu 1957/1976, 353-354; Minnis 1984, 26, 157.

42 Sed hoc fabulosum est quia itaque poetarum est fingere, et de fabulis scribere. Dicens se fabulas nosse commendat se in poetica. *(Glos. in Iuv*. 99-100). On the threefold division into historical, natural and poetical issues: *ibid.* 96-99.

fictitious "surface" concealed "deeper truths" which had to be revealed in order that its function could be fulfilled. John of Salisbury (ca. 1115/20-1180), indeed, called poetry "the cradle of philosophy" which, while not forming an autonomous part of liberal arts, was included in other discursive arts, especially grammar and rhetoric.[43]

Poetry as moral science

Philosophy was defined as "the discipline of the disciplines and the art of the arts" which included all branches of knowledge.[44] In short, this art of arts was "correct understanding of that which is not visible but is, and as such, that which is and is visible"; that is comprehension of both incorporeal and corporeal reality.[45]

Philosophy – and all branches of knowledge – examined all being and provided the means to comprehend reality, and, of course, the right course of action. The reality examined was divided into two major spheres the first of which was unchanging superlunar reality, which belonged to the realm of *opus Dei*. The second sphere was the sublunar world which was in the realm of *opus naturae*. The sublunar world was on the other hand governed by unchanging divinely-ordered principles, *principia Naturae*, which, however, did not exclude human free choice (or will).[46]

Theoretical branches of knowledge examined the unchanging principles of being, that is the divine superlunar reality (theology) and the divinely-prescribed order of nature (physics and mathematics). The order of nature was often personified as *Natura*, which acted as a conceptual bridge between two spheres of reality.[47] In the common twelfth-century cosmology influenced by Neoplatonist conceptions, superlunar reality was understood as "the true reality", about which there was another source of knowledge besides divine relevation (i.e. the Scriptures) that is, perceptible nature. It was often called "the book of nature" which was interpreted as the writing of God.[48]

Science, *scientia*, was understood especially in the twelfth century as a study of the principles of nature, and on the other hand, as an interpretation of perceptible nature and the Scriptures intended to approach the invisible divine reality. The goal of science was not to produce new knowledge but to master the entirety of already existent knowledge, and to interpret this

---

43 *Metalogicon* I.xvii, xxii, 42-43, 52.
44 E.g. Isidore of Seville, *Etym.* II.24, ed. Marshall, 100-111; Hugh of St. Victor, *Didasc.*, II.i, 23-24; Dominicus Gundissalinus, *De div. phil.*, prol., 5, 11, 16-17. Brian Stock defines the medieval notion of science generally as "all things knowable" (1972, 3).
45 William of Conches, *Philosophia* I.I.4, 18-19. On the forms of knowledge and ideals of wisdom, see Gregory 1990, 10-69.
46 See e.g. Ralph of Longchamp, *In Anticlaudianum Alani commentum* I.i, I.lxx, 19-29, 63.
47 Gregory 1966, 27-65; Stock 1972, 227-273; Wetherbee 1972, 188-219; Sheridan 1980, 55.
48 Jackson 1969, 9-29; Gellrich 1985, 17-28, 34, 39 and *passim*; Pépin 1987, 251-252, 269-271; Gregory 1990, 10-69.

knowledge correctly.[49] Most often this lead scholarly pursuits to the available canon of authors, which was interpreted in the context of Christianity regardless of whether the authors were Christian or pagan.[50] In the case of ancient pagan poets this *interpretatio christiana* meant that, among others, the myths of ancient deities were interpreted as fictitious stories which had a deeper hidden sense comprehending their value for the medieval Christian reader.[51]

In standard ethical expositions, the interpretation of science as an already existing entirety together with Christian dogma led to a more or less unreflective normative moral philosophy. Thus, there was no real need to develop arguments to resolve what was good and what evil, but to give precepts *(praecepta)* and rules *(regulae)* to direct people to a correct and virtuous life. The primary problem of moral philosophy was the persuasive effectiveness of its teachings, and thus it was either explicitly (for instance Dominicus Gundissalinus) or implicitly associated with discursive arts concerned with persuasive effectiveness, that is rhetoric and poetics. Nor was more reflective moral philosophy concerned with the nature of good and evil which was known *a priori*. Thus the mainstream of reflection was directed to introspective speculation about the structure of the human mind and volition.[52] In some rare cases there was discussion of social issues which attempted to formulate more active moral speculation as a Parisian master Peter the Chanter (d. 1197) and his circle did.[53] Nevertheless, the basis of moral judgement remained untouched.

Poetry's persuasive effectiveness

The comprehensive view of poetry's persuasive effectiveness laid the basis for Christian interpretation of pagan poets, for instance Virgil, Horace, Juvenal and Ovid, as ethical authors persuading and directing their readers towards the true virtues. Both their fictitious and true stories provided examples of morally right or wrong decisions and their consequences. The persuasive effectiveness of poetry was an old conception. Plato would hardly have expelled the poets from his ideal state if he would not have believed that the works of poets had an exceptionally strong effect on the minds of people.[54] This conviction of the attractive power of poetical means such as tropes and fictitious stories is reiterated by Christian authors from Augustine to Thomas

---

49 Stock 1972, 273-283; *idem* 1978, 1-50; Weisheipl 1978, 461-482; Gregory 1990, 10-69.
50 E.g. Raban Maur, *De institutione clericorum* III.18, 225; Honorius Augustodunensis, *Speculum Ecclesiae* III (PL 172), 1056-1057.
51 E.g. Bernard Silvester, *Commentum super Eneidos libros*; see also examples above from the *accessus* literature, and Stock 1972.
52 Cf. Luscombe 1971; Lottin 1942/57-1960, *passim*; Baldwin 1970, 13-18, 80.
53 Baldwin 1970, xi-xiv, 13-16 and *passim*.
54 See also for Nussbaum (1993, 97-149) other ancient views.

Aquinas. The view of Dominicus Gundissalinus, which was influenced both by the Latin rhetorical tradition and Aristotelian Arab philosophers, of poetry as a species of argumentative logic becomes understandable in this context.

Poetry was not only interpreted as a source of moral knowledge. Twelfth-century poets not only wrote more or less didactic poetry, but moral philosophical works of the time really utilized poetry directly as an instrument of exemplification and argument. In logical terms poetical *exempla* were understood either explicitly or implicitly as incomplete inductions although they usually did not fulfil the conditions of logically valid argument.[55] On the other hand, the works and fragments of ancient authors were often compiled as moral *florilegia* in which poetry had a central role.[56] A third wide spread medieval fashion was to use poetry for openly moral purposes, composing poems *cum auctoritate*, that is, quoting a moral citation usually from an ancient author and writing a continuation which completed or explained the first.[57] The moral and exemplary role of poetry also becomes a conscious device used internally in satires, when they use authoritative quotations or generic forms of *exempla* for their own purposes. Distorted or false *exempla* and quotations, and the general moral function of poetry form a complex textual playground where ambiguous satires are constructed. I will return to this device in analysing the satirical poetry of the *Carmina Burana*.

It comes as no suprise that the Horatian doctrine of poetry as being of use by delighting was sown on favourable soil in the High Middle Ages, or that it was frequently repeated when the nature of poetry was under discussion.[58] Horace's definition identified poetry closely with the epideictic or demonstrative oratory similarly defined in classical rhetoric. Epideictic oratory did not have such an exact function in public life as other genres (i.e. forensic or legal and deliberative) but it was ethico-aesthetic, praising the beautiful and good and blaming their opposites.[59]

---

55 See Dahan 1980, 178, 182-183; Lehtinen 1993, 122-148, esp. 122-123; on similar views during the Renaissance see Mikkeli 1992, 59-66.

56 E.g. *Moralium dogma philosophorum* and *Distinctionum monasticorum et moralium*; Lehmann 1922, 3-28; Curtius 1948, 65-68.

57 Curtius 1948, 159-160; Witke 1970, 234; Schmidt 1974/1990. *Cum auctoritate*-structure resembles the *rhythmus / versus* variation in the *Carmina Burana*.

58 Anonymous, *Accessus*, 50; Bernard Silvester, *Comm. sup. Eneid.* prol. (tr. p. 4); William of Conches, *Glos. sup. Macr.*, 68; John of Salisbury, *Metalogicon* II.viii, 75; Ralph of Longchamp, *In Anticl. Al. comm.* I.xxviii, 39; Friis-Jensen 1988, 81-147.

Recently Glending Olsen has criticised the simplified interpretation of the medieval Horatian view. According to Olsen not only *prodesse* (benefit) but also *delectare* (amuse, delight) was seen as an important functions of poetry especially in medical therapeutic discussions (Olsen 1982, *passim*, esp. 19-38).

59 In classical rhetoric the different genres of oratory were defined according to their functional context. Deliberative oratory attempted to influence decisions concerning the future, and its audience was the governing body of society. Forensic or judicial oratory concerned the judgement of past deeds, and its audience was the court of justice. Epideictic (or demonstrative) oratory was concerned with the beautiful and good, and ugly and evil. Its audience was formed from the public gathered for the spectacle itself who evaluated the speech-act. This genre oscillated between aesthetic discourse which turned towards itself, and ethics. Epideictic oratory was clearly ideological discourse which defined and affirmed the ethical and aesthetic values of the society in question. It persuaded its public to behave

The twelfth-century learned interested in poetry not only contented themselves with the characterisation of poetry in general as "being useful by delighting", but examined the interpretative operations and linguistic means which made "being useful by delighting" possible. The interpretative operations were more or less parallel and analogous with all the allegorical methods of biblical exegesis. The *allegoresis* applied to poetry was, however, often limited solely to the moral-tropological sense and was not extended typologically to the "allegory of facts" *(allegoria in factis)* and to eschatological anagogic interpretation, which grew out of it, as was usual in the interpretation of the Scriptures.[60]

The notions applied in the analysis of the linguistic means proper to poetry were borrowed from rhetoric and grammar. This meant, the analysis of figurative representation, i.e. analysis of tropes (that is, the transference of meaning of single words) and figures (that is, wider expressions either transferring the meaning or otherwise breaking the conventional disposition).[61]

Moreover, the rhetorical concepts applying to one *genus* of argumentation, i.e. narration *(narratio)*, were picked up to clarify the representational nature and veracity of poetry. In classical rhetoric, exemplary stories *(paradeigmata, exempla)* were considered as one branch of persuasive argument. Three species of narration were distinguished: *historia*, that is, historically true story; *argumentum*, that is, probable or verisimilar story; and *fabula*, that is, purely imaginative or fictitious story.[62] For example Bernard Silvester, Ralph of Longchamp and John of Garland used the same distinction when they described the genres used in poetry.[63] The distinction leaves it unclear whether history existed in any other form than poetical. For instance, Otto of Freising (1114/5-1158) regarded his own world history which expanded from the Creation to his own life-time, as a story composed in the "mode of tragedy" even if his statement may have been meant to be metaphorical characterisation

---

morally properly and according the aesthetic principles. Nevertheless, it was clearly directed towards the speech itself and its aesthetics, and was identified rather with *delectare* than *movere* or *docere*. Hence its borderline with poetry was imprecise. E.g. Aristotle, *Rhetorica* 1358a 36 - 1358b 28; see also Lausberg 1960, 85-138; Kennedy 1980, 108-119; Vickers 1988/1990, 53-62.

60   E.g. Henri de Lubac emphasises the differences between sacred and secular allegories and interprets them as two separate but interactive methods of reading (de Lubac 1959-64/1993, II:2, 182-262). See also Chydenius 1960; Brinkmann 1980; Minnis & Scott 1988/1991, 65f. and *passim*; Strubel 1975, 342-347.

61   See Faral 1924; Murphy 1974/1981, 135f. I have borrowed the definitions of tropes and figures from Vickers 1988/1990, 315-316.

62   E.g. Bernard of Utrecht, *Comm. in Theod.* prol., p. 4; Bernard Silvester, *Comm. in Mart.* 2.971-985, p. 80-81; Ralph of Longchamp, *In Anticl. Al. comm.* I.xxxv, p. 44. See also Mehtonen 1992; *idem* 1996; Dronke 1974; *idem* 1975.

      The early version of this distinction appears in Aristotle who distinguished rhetorical examples *(paradeigmata, exempla)* of those which refer to past events, and those invented by oneself. The latter he divides into comparisons and fictitious myths *(Rhetorica* 1393a 28-1394a 15). The standard version was however transmitted to the Middle Ages by the pseudo-Ciceronian *Rhetorica ad Herennium* (I.viii.12-13) and Cicero's *De inventione* (I.xix.27).

63   Bernard Silvester, *Comm. in Mart.* 2.971-985, p. 80-81; Ralph of Longchamp, *In Anticl. Al. comm.* I.xxv, 44; about John of Garland see Mehtonen 1991, 131-133.

of human history.[64] This ambiguity is relevant in analysing the *Fortuna*-poems of the *Carmina Burana*.

In twelfth- and early thirteenth-century treatises the modes of poetical narration were not always considered as representing true, probable or fictitious states of affairs, but they were regarded as different levels of verisimilitude. A historical story was not necessarily referentially true but its literal meaning was identified with the probability of exemplificatory truthfulness.[65] It seems that many twelfth-century learned based the value of poetry on its deeper hidden meaning, and the persuasive effectiveness of poetical expression. Poetry was a morally efficient way for argument which guided the individual towards virtues (one has to remember that the domain of ethics was specifically the morals of an individual).

The distinctive features of poetry: metaphor and fictitiousness

Poetry was distinguished as specific genre of discourse but its boundaries with other genres of discourse remained vague. The distinctive criteria varied according to whether poetry was defined on the formal, semantic or veracity criteria. The formal criteria distinguished everything written in verse as poetry, the semantic criteria identified the distinctive quality as the use of metaphor while the veracity criteria emphasised the fabulous nature of poetry. The most problematic was the distinction based on linguistic facts when it was done in respect of the Scriptures. In this case the Christian learned needed a metaphysical argument which separated the human use of language from divine revelation.

Nevertheless, neither formal, semantic nor veracity features were separately characteristic of poetry alone. To mention an example, Thomas of Capua (d. 1239) enumerated prosaic, metrical and rhythmic forms as modes of letter-writing.[66] Further, the corporeal figures of language (i.e. tropes and figures) expressing incorporeal entities were considered as typical of the Scriptures. Fictitious stories were not used only in the sphere of poetry but pertained both to the means of rhetoric, and to philosophy.[67]

---

64 ... in modum tragediae texuisse... *(Chronica sive Historia de duabus civitatibus*, 4.) On the conception of the world history as tragedy, see Kelly 1993, 76-92; on Otto of Freising, *idem* 87-89.

65 Mehtonen 1991, 127f.; *idem* 1992; *idem* 1996; see also Morse 1991.

66 Dictaminum vero genera tria sunt, a veteribus definita: prosaicum scilicet, metricum et rhythmicum; prosaicum ut Cassiodori, metricum ut Virgilii, rhythmicum ut Primatis. *(Ars dictandis* 2, 13-14.) Correspondingly, according to several authors also poetry could be composed in metric or prosaic form (e.g. Ralph of Longchamp, *Anticl. Al. comm.* I.xxxv, 44).

67 On corporeal linguistical figures and incorporeal reality, see e.g. Augustine, *De doctr. christ.* I.ii.2-iv.4, 182-184; Gregory the Great, *Expositio in Canticis canticorum* I.2, 68-70; Hugh of St. Victor, *Didasc. V.iii, 96-97*; Ralph of Longchamp, *In Anticl. Al. comm.* I.iii, 24; Thomas Aquinas, *Summa theologiae* I.q.1.a.9; see also Chydenius 1960; Brinkmann 1980. On fictitious narratives in philosophical representation see e.g. Bernard Silvester, *Comm. in*

On the other hand, medieval scholars constantly spoke about poetry as a mode of expression distinctive from other categories of speech and written language. From various sources discussing about poetry and poetical language it is possible to abstract an implicitly accepted definition of poetry as a distinct discursive genre based on criteria for formal, semantic and veracity features. In the context of other genres of discourse these features were regarded as anomalies, but in the case of poetry they were the rule.

The idea of anomalous features typical of poetry in the other genres of discourse has been expounded by Thomas Aquinas (ca. 1225-1274) in a way that summarizes most of the views current already in the twelfth century. He attempts to solve whether Scriptures (in his vocabulary the theological and the highest branch of knowledge) should use metaphors which according to some are proper only for poetry (the lowest branch of knowledge). Characteristically both Scriptures and poetry used "similitudes" (*similitudines*) and "representations" (*representationes*) which seemed, according to views referred by Aquinas, rather to hide the truth beneath obscure and ambiguous expression than to present it clearly and unambiguously. However, the representation of incorporeal reality by means of corporeal similitudes arises from the human characteristic of proceeding from the perceptible to the conceptual. For this reason Scripture also uses metaphors, that is corporeal similitudes or likenesses signifying incorporeal entities.[68] In this kind of viewpoint the fundamental difference between poetry and Scripture is not based on distinctive internal characteristics but on the fact that the first is originally human and the second divine. Similarly, their semiotic systems are distinctive, since human text signifies only on the level of language (i.e. *allegoria in verbis*), while divine relevation includes the signification of "things" (i.e. *allegoria in factis*).

Thomas Aquinas extends this metaphysical difference to the functional basis of metaphors. Poetry uses metaphors to delight, while Scripture uses them for necessity and usefulness. To make this distinction, Aquinas cleverly exploited the traditional justification for the use of metaphor for delight, necessity, ornament and usefulness.[69] For him, the necessity grows out of representing incorporeal reality with the aid of tropes. Usefulness is based on two aspects: firstly, tropes (i.e. obscure and ambiguous expressions) help to hide the sacred secrets from unbelievers, and, secondly, they encourage scholars in pursuiting religious truths.[70]

Defining poetry *via* its metaphoric nature leads to interpretative need. Poetry in most of cases did not express its full meaning directly on the literal level. The "poetic speeches" had a hidden meaning – otherwise they had to

---

Mart. 70-92, 885-917, 998, pages 45-6, 78-9, 82; William of Conches, *Glosae super Platonem, passim*; also Jeauneau 1965, 20; Stock 1972, 11-62; Dronke 1974.
68 *Summa theologiae* I.q.1.a.9.
69 See e.g. Diomedes, *Ars grammatica*, 456-457.
70 *Summa theologiae* I.q.1.a.9. Saint Augustine explains the function of figurative and obscure passages in the Scriptures similarly *(De doctr. christ.* II.iv.7-8, IV.viii.22, 244-246, 458).

be regarded as mendacious. The problem of untruthfulness became especially acute when examining poetic narration, which often used the mode of *fabula*; that is the mode of imaginative or fictitious narrative which, by definition, could not in any case be taken as literally true.[71] Several twelfth-century scholars solved the problem of fictitious narratives (and, at the same time, of poetry) by explaining that the imaginary literal level concealed some deeper philosophical truths.[72] The method was analogous to the Stoic and Neoplatonist interpreters of Homer, Plato and other canonical writers.[73]

An interpretation seeking deeper truths was also characteristic of biblical exegesis in the High Middle Ages, which followed the fourfold allegorical interpretation. However, one can argue that it was rhetorical tradition that built the conceptual bridge which brought metaphor and allegorized *fabula* together, since in classical rhetoric metaphor was defined as a transference of the meaning of an individual word, while allegory was an "extended trope", that is a metaphorical narrative which had "another meaning".[74]

The figurative and fictitious nature of poetry (that is metaphor and *fabula*) indicated the need of interpretation, especially in the case of authoritative texts. Poetry was rather rarely regarded as being figurative if at all, because it expressed by corporeal similitudes something otherwise impossible to express, as the Scriptures were thought to do. The figurative nature of poetry was based on its entertaining and persuasive aspect, but because the goal of entertainment was to teach, the figurative (and/or fictitious) element had to be interpreted as attaining the didactic end.

In a commentary on Martianus Capella's *De nuptiis Mercurii et Philologiae* attributed to Bernard Silvester from the early twelfth century, this specifically figurative nature of poetry is taken as a challenge:

> *Genus doctrina figura est. Figura autem est oratio quam involucrum dicere solent. Hec autem bipertita est: partimur namque eam in allegoriam et integumentum. Est autem allegoria oratio sub historica narratione verum et ab exteriori diversum involvens intellectum, ut de lucta Iacob. Integumentum vero est oratio sub fabulosa narratione verum claudens intellectum, ut de Orpheo. Nam et ibi historia et hic fabula misterium habent occultum, quod alias discutiendum erit. Allegoria quidem divine pagine, integumentum vero philosophice competit.*

---

71   E.g. Ralph of Longchamp, *In Anticl. Al. comm.* I.xxxv, 44; cf. Curtius 1948, 223; Dronke 1974; Mehtonen 1991, 127-137; *idem* 1992; *idem* 1996.
72   Bernard Silvester, *Comm. sup. Eneidos*, prol. (tr.p. 5); *idem, Comm. in Mart.*, p. 45-46, 80-82, 133; William of Conches, *Glos. in Iuv.*, 96-108; *idem, Glos. sup. Macr.*, 68-69; Alan of Lille, *De planctu Naturae* VIII, 836-838; *Distinctionum monasticorum et moralium* I.xix, II, cxxxiv, 456-457, 470; see Dronke 1974, *passim*.
73   Coulter 1976, *passim*; Rollinson 1981, *passim*; Nussbaum 1993, 97-149.
74   Cf. Quintilian, *Inst. Or.* IX.ii.46; Diomedes, *Ars grammatica*, 456-462; Whitman 1987, 263-268.

Figure is a kind of instruction. Moreover a figure is a discourse which is normally called covered expression *(involucrum)*. It is subdivided into two types, *allegoria* and *integumentum*. Now an allegory is a discourse in the form of an historical narrative, enveloping an understanding true and different from external appearance, like the struggle of Jacob. But a integument is a discourse which encloses its true significance in the form of a fabulous narrative, as in Orpheus. Both history and fable contain a secret mystery which will be discussed elsewhere. In sum, allegory is suitable for Holy Scripture while integument is suitable for philosophical writing.[75]

These two terms, *involucrum* and *integumentum*, have a twofold role: first, they reproduce on the interpretative level the difference between otherwise disturbingly similar divine relevation and humanly created poetry. Secondly, they simultaneously present means for an apology for poetry. *Involucrum* is a general concept for texts which cover their "deeper" or "other" meaning under their surface, which may be literally true or not. Allegory proper to Holy Scripture (at least for those considered literally true which was not always the case) is the allegory of facts *(allegoria in factis)*. The literal surface is in itself a historically true description of factual events. The facts or "things" have themselves a meaning, being signs used by God.[76]

The notion of *integumentum* used by Bernard is often identified with the allegory of words *(allegoria in verbis)* which is proper to texts done by humans – including authoritative poetry – which have deeper meanings.[77] However, Bernard did not precisely distinguish the Scriptures from poetry, but Scripture and true historical narratives from fictitious or fabulous narratives. Thus historical events contained allegorical meanings of divine origin. The narrative could be told in the *Bible*, but true historical narratives could just as well be human (although correspondingly less reliable). On the other hand, Bernard nevertheless includes human historical narratives in poetry.[78] Thus it is possible to argue that historically true poetry could be allegorical, depending on the meanings of the events or facts narrated. Only poetry which was by nature fictitious used integuments to express philosophical truths.

According to Haijo J. Westra, Bernard applied always integuments when the literal meaning was obscure or otherwise not literally acceptable.[79] This view corresponds with the doctrine of St. Augustine on the indications of the

---

75 *Comm. in Mart.* 1.70f., p.45; I have used the translation by Stock (1972, 38-39) as my basis however altering some terms.
76 Auerbach 1959/1984, 49-54; Chydenius 1960; Gregory 1966, 27-65; *idem* 1990, 10-69: Jackson 1969, 9-29; Stock 1972, 40f.; Wetherbee 1972, *passim*; Brinkmann 1980, 3-51 and *passim*; Irvine 1987, 33-71.
77 Westra 1986, 23-27; see also Stock 1972; Wetherbee 1972; Brinkmann 1980.
78 *Comm. in Mart.* 2.971-985, 80-81. Dominicus Gundissalinus among others defined real and fictitious events as the subject matter of poetry *(De div. phil.* 54).
79 Westra 1986, 29.

need for allegorical interpretation in the Scriptures.[80]

Further, one can compare the interpretative strategy of Bernard on Martianus and Virgil for instance with the reading-rule for pagan poets given by a Carolingian scholar Raban Maur (776-856):

> *Poemata autem et libros gentilium si velimus propter florem eloquentiae legere, typus mulieris captivae tenendus est, quam Deuteronomium descripit: et dominum ita praecepisse commemorat, ut si Israhelites eam habere velit uxorem, calvitium ei faciat, ungues praesecet, pilos auferat et cum munda fuerit effecta, tunc transeat in victoris amplecus (Deuter. XXI.iif.). Haec si secundum literam intellegimus nonne ridicula sunt? Itaques et nos hoc facere solemus hocque facere debemus, quando poëtas gentiles legimus, quando in manus nostras libri veniunt sapientiae secularis, si quod in eis utile reperimus, ad nostrum dogma convertimus, si quid vero superfluum de idolis, de amore, de cura secularium rerum, haec radimus, his calvitium inducamus, haec in unguium more ferro acutissimo desecemus.*[81]

> If we want to read pagan poems and books according to the flowers of eloquence, we have to take them as Deuteronomy describes taking female prisoners of war. The Lord reminds us of this precept: if the Israelites wanted to take someone as their wife, one had to shave her head, pare her nails and pluck all her hair, and when she is cleaned, the winner may go and embrace her. Would not these precepts be ridiculous if we took them literally? Thus when we read pagan poets and when we receive books about secular wisdom, we have to convert them according our own dogma to make them useful for ourselves. We have to distinguish the truth from superfluities about idols, love and worrysome secular affairs. The unnecessities we rub off, pare and pluck bald as the nails are pared with a sharp blade.

The pagan poets and secular wisdom are useful reading if one proceeds according to "the flowers of eloquence" (that is "tropologically", or in transferred sense) and "converts them into our own dogma", that is into the Christian context. Laid down beneath the figures of Raban is a program of Christian allegorical reading. Even if Bernard uses less violent figures and metaphors, his interpretative strategy is the same when he removes the integuments of pagan poets and makes them pronounce Christian moral teachings.

Bernard Silvester adds a more formal definition to his interpretative definition of poetry in his commentary on Martianus:

---

80 *De doctr. christ.* III.i.1-ii.2, xxx.42-43. Also Hugh of St.Victor, *Didasc,* VI.x.
81 *De institutione clericorum* III.18, 225.
   The same opinion and example is repeated by several twelfth- and thirteenth-century authors, e.g. Honorius Augustodunensis, *Speculum Ecclesiae* III (PL 172), 1056-1057. See also Baldwin 1970, 78.

Poesis vero est scientia claudens in metro orationem gravem et illustrem. Oratio vero, quam sic claudit, <dividitur> secundum Tullium in fabulam, historiam, argumentum. Fabulam dicit nec veram nec verisimilem narrationem... Historia narratio rei gestae... Argumentum est res ficta, que tamen potuit fieri, ut comedie. Ad historiam satira, tragedia: sunt enim rerum gestarum narrationes. Historia illa, que satira est, tota in pugnandis viciis et extollendis virtutibus; tragedia quoque ad tolerandum laborum. ... Universaliter autem poema bonorum malorumque exempla proponit. Vnde poeseos est, nisi ea prave utamur, vicia erudicare et virtutes inserere.[82]

But poetry is a science which encloses grave and illustrious speech within metre. Speech enclosed this way is divided according to Cicero into fable *(fabula)*, history *(historia)* and argument *(argumentum)*. He calls fable narrative which is neither true nor verisimilar... History is narrative about famous deeds *(res gestae)*... Argument is fictive narrative *(res ficta)* which however could be comedy. Satire and tragedy pertain to history, that is, they are narratives about famous deeds. History which is satire concentrates on fighting against vices and emphasizing virtues, whereas tragedy teaches toleration of adversities. Generally speaking, a poem proposes examples of good and evil. Thus, 'to make poems', unless we use it improperly, means to eradicate vices and leads one to virtues.

Ultimately, poetry is not defined as poetry because of its fictitious nature – on the contrary, history, i.e. a true narrative, is also poetry for Bernard.[83] Poetry is poetry because of its exemplificatory nature, and its effectiveness is guaranteed by formal and semantic features. Poetry can be understood as an instance of epideictic oratory, for which it is proper to praise the good and beautiful (and blame their opposites) in a speech composed in metre, and use meaning hidden beneath tropes and figures, and fictitious narratives.

Bernard's definition corresponds with the common usage of poetry as

---

82   *Comm. in Mart.* 2.971-985, 80-81.
    Cf. the almost identical definition given by Ralph of Longchamp, *In Anticl. Al. comm.* I.xxxv, 44. It appears also in a twelfth-century treatise *Ysagoge in theologiam*; see Kelly 1993, 92; Mehtonen 1996.
    Isidore of Seville has a corresponding view about fictitious narratives in a passage where he discusses poets (... in argumentis fabularum ad veritatis imaginem fictis; *Etym.* VIII.vii.5, ed. Lindsay 1911/1987).

83   The dichotomy between fictitious and truthful narratives was polarized by the notions *historia - fabula*. However, *historia* was included among the forms of poetic narration regardless of whether it was literally true or not. This is clearly visible e.g. in the definitions of an anonymous author from the turn of eleventh and twelfth centuries. Referring to Horace, he described a poet *(poeta)* as inventor *(fictor)* or shaper *(formator)* (Anon., *Accessus ad auctores*, 50-51; Bernard of Utrecht repeats the same definition in *Comm. in Theod.*, 59, as does Conrad of Hirsau in *Dial. sup. auct.*, 75-76 in slightly altered form). On the other hand, bishop Otto of Freising described his world history as tragedy in his dedication to Emperor Frederick Barbarossa. Thus, he also seems to think that historiography pertains to poetry, or at least that tragedy can be seen as a metaphor for world history *(Chronica*, 4; see also Kelly 1993, 87-89). However, among others Isidore of Seville did earlier differentiate historical narratives from poetry *(Etym.* VII.vii.10-11, ed. Lindsay). About *historia* as a form of narration, see Mehtonen 1996.

exemplary material in twelfth- and thirteenth-century *florilegia* and *distintiones* collections and other moral-philosophical works offering moral precepts and examples.[84]

The notion of satire: a paradigmatic case for ethical poetics

The first part of the *Carmina Burana* is dominated by moral-satirical poetry. The generic definition is relevant from the point of view of modern interpretation, especially as satire is often considered the most "social" of the classical poetic genres.[85] Indeed, satire was an especially popular and important genre during the Middle Ages. Moreover, it fitted well within the definitions of Christian ethical poetics. As a matter of fact, satire was often defined in the same terms as poetry in general – in a certain sense, satire formed the paradigmatic case of Christian ethical poetics. On the other hand, the definitions of satire included aspects which diverged from the general definition we have constructed above. Satire was a sub-case which obviously pertained to moral discourse but which in the semantic sense was usually thought to be "open to understanding", i.e. according to commentators it did not require such interpretative efforts as poetry usually did. The moral sense of a satire was most often considered as easily achievable. Further, on the level of form and content satire included indications of the authority. Thus its special standing was affirmed both by its paradigmatic nature and by indications of its special position.

From the point of view of historical interpretation satire is however far from a simple and unequivocal object. From the perspective of a modern interpreter it may often be rather obscure what and who are satirized. Even if the object of satire, e.g. the Roman curia, is explicit, it remains uncertain how fundamental the critique was meant to be, and whether it included elements which question the whole ecclesiastical hierarchy and Christian value-system.[86] On the other hand, satire undoubtedly functioned as a means to describe and criticise the contemporary society - its historical connections are obvious, and often they are expressed quite explicitly. Its historical importance has been remarked by modern scholarship. Indeed, with erotic poetry, it has been the most widely-studied among the medieval Latin secular genres and, as distinct from the scholarship of love-poetry, the studies of

---

84 See e.g. *Distinctionum monasticorum et moralium* and *Moralium dogma philosophorum*. Also Lehmann 1922, *passim*; Curtius 1948, 64-68; Delhaye 1949/1988, 59-81; *idem* 1958/1988, 83-134; Le Goff 1985, 99-102; Lehtinen 1993, 126-127.

85 Witke 1970, 2-3.

86 Some scholars have argued from different perspectives that satirical poetry fundamentally questions the ecclesiastical hierarchy or Christian dogma, see e.g. Le Goff 1957/1985, 35-40; Jackson 1960, 237; Morris 1972, 112-133; Mann 1980, 63-80. However, the interpretation of medieval Latin satire as reformative, and not as an offence against the Christian church and its values seems to be more plausible, see Yunck 1963; Witke 1970; Schüppert 1972; and part III in this work.

satire are most often clearly directed to historical and social questions.[87] Furthermore, the generic definitions of satire have been discussed more than other Latin secular genres.[88] In fact, this comes as no suprise because the historical interest and problems are obvious, and, there is plenty of material for generic satire studies.

In the following, I will examine the generic definitions of satire in the first plan in relation to general definitions of poetry, and, in the second, in relation to medieval Latin satires. What kind of textual space is constructable from the diverse definitions of satire, and what kind of indications does it offer for the analysis and interpretation of medieval Latin satire?

The notion of satire in the High Middle Ages can be examined on several levels: firstly, satire was often defined by formal criteria; secondly, it could be defined by its content and function, and thirdly, by semantic crtiteria. Generic definitions were made in rather miscellaneous contexts, medieval Latin authors did not recognize or use any coherent generic theory following the principles of form and content.[89] This does not mean that medieval authors did not notice the various poetic genres and their differences, or that the poets themselves would not have been conscious of them. Medieval generic theory was heterogeneous and fragmentary, leaning on generic terms picked up rather haphazardly from authors of antiquity whose original poetical references were often unknown. On the other hand, the generic system of poetry was only partly connected with explicitly stated generic theory, and the greater part of poetry was completely independent of it. As a consequence, the medieval generic theory was a hybrid theory which aimed both at being faithful to models of antiquity, and at adopting material foreign to it (including the *Bible*) into its structure.[90]

However, when medieval poetry and generic theory are examined, misunderstandings of antiquity's generic theory are not crucial, albeit that the terms borrowed from antiquity were used regardless of their original meaning. Further, it is not important that theory did not describe its contemporary poetry, but that the contemporary medieval poetry was created and understood in a complicated textual network which was composed of the poetry of ancient authorities, commentaries dealing with them, generic theory borrowed from antiquity, different medieval adaptations (e.g. prescriptive poetics)[91], the corpus of Christian texts, medieval interpretations of the texts of antiquity,

---

87 E.g. Yunck 1963; Elredge 1970; Schüppert 1972; Schmidt 1974/1990; Pepin 1988.
88 E.g. Kindermann 1978; *idem* 1989; Paul S. Miller 1982 (unpublished, see Minnis & Scott 1988/1991, 116-117 n. 14 and 15). More recently, conceptions of tragedy in the Middle Ages has been thoroughly examined by Henry Ansgar Kelly (1993).
89 Kindermann 1989, 303-313.
90 E.g. The Venerable Bede analysed the different genres appearing in the *Bible (De arte metrica et de schematibus et tropis* I.xxv.1-25, p. 139-141); also Bernard of Utrecht, *Comm. in Theod.* 181-83, p. 62.
91 On the basis of ancient poetical tradition in the Middle Ages a new kind of prescriptive poetics whose purpose was to offer instructions in Latin verse appeared. See Faral 1924; Murphy 1974/1981, 145, 162-193; Mehtonen 1992; *idem* 1996.

etc. The borrowed generic theory forms a constituent in the intertextual network of medieval poetry. Thus the incompatibility of generic theory with the medieval poetry itself does not make it irrelevant when considering the poetry itself.

In the medieval generic theory the central qualifiers were, on the one hand, truthfulness and on the other, general moral function. Formal generic criteria remained secondary, although not completely insignificant. One could structure texts by formal means, emphasize the significance of their contents, and stress the authoritative status of a particular text.[92]

On the model of the poetry of Horace, Juvenal and Persius, satire was considered to be poetry composed in hexameter (or in its variations).[93] In the *Carmina Burana* the metre occurs in the *versi* finishing the groups. The hexameter was apparently associated with the authoritative nature of texts independently of whether the *versi* were direct quotations from authors or not (actually, they were most often combinations of authoritative texts and new verses). However, metric authority alone was insufficient: among the playful rhythmic or prosaic parodies and satires, the *versi* are normally solemn and safely didactic. As a counter-weight to "goliardic" play, the moral message is affirmed with multiple authority; that is, with direct authoritative quotations, metrical authority, and, finally, with a normative message and interpretative unambiguity.

Medieval writers also associated rhythmic, so-called "goliardic" or "vagant" metre, with satire, even if it commonly occurred in other genres too (as did hexameter).[94] This metre, or more correctly metrical system based on the syllabic stress, was a new form originating from Late Antiquity and the Early Middle Ages, and was especially popular in the Latin poetry of the High Middle Ages.[95] In the *Carmina Burana* the goliardic metre dominates and is

92 E.g. the alternation of *rhythmi* and *versi* in the *Carmina Burana*. Matthew of Vendôme (d. before 1175) defined *versus* as follows: Versus est metrica oratio succincte et clausatim progrediens venusto verborum matrimonio et flosculis sententiarum picturata, quae nihil diminutum, nihil in se continet otiosum. *(Ars versificatoria* I.1, p. 110-111.)

93 Kindermann 1978, 12-18.

94 Kindermann 1978, 18-21; see also Rigg 1977a, 65-109.

95 The distinction between metric and the new rhythmic metre was made quite early. For example, Bede (673-735) wrote: Videtur autem rithmus metris esse consimilis, quae est uerborum modulata compositio, non metrica ratione, sed numero syllabarum ad iudicium aurium examinata, ut sunt carmina uulgarium poetarum. Et quidem rithmus per se sine metro esse potest, metrum uero sine rithmo esse non potest. Quod liquidius ita definitur: metrum est ratio cum modulatione, rithmus modulatio sine ratione. Plerumque tamen casu quodam inuenies etiam rationem in rithmo, non artifici moderatione seruata, sed sono et ipsa modulatione ducente, quem uulgares poetae necesse est rustice, docti faciunt docte. *(De arte metrica et de schematibus et tropis* I.xxiv.10-19, p. 138-139). Thomas of Capua differentiates between three forms of (letter) writing, i.e. prose, metric and rhythmic form in the early 13th century *(Ars dictandi* 2, p. 13-14). See also Beare 1954, 254-291; Jackson 1960, 216-220.

   In the terms of modern poetics the distinction is the same as between the durational (cf. metric) and dynamic (cf. rhythmic) metre-system (Viikari 1990, 61). Mikhail Bakhtin argues that the medieval (originally vernacular) rhythmic accentuating system in the Latin poetry is an example of "polyglossia", i.e. synchronicity of various discourses and levels of meaning because it conflates the authoritative Latin language and vernacular metric system (Bakhtin

characteristic of both satires and erotic poetry and drinking songs.

Thirdly some medieval writers drew a distinction between satire written in metre (whether 'metrical' or 'rhythmic') and that written in prose which they called *invectio*.[96] Fourthly, a mixed 'Menippean' form, or in medieval terms *prosimetrum*, that is, a mixture of prose and metre, was also considered a proper form for satire. This definition led to a slight anomaly in that since the three first formal criteria stated not so much the characteristics of satire but the forms used in satiric poetry and the satire was in the end distinguished by criteria related to content and function, the *prosimetrum* was a purely formal way to define a work as a satire, i.e. all works composed in *prosimetrum* were considered satires.[97]

The medieval commentators could define as satirists writers using *prosimetrum* such as Seneca, Martianus Capella, St. Jerome and Boethius, whether their texts fulfilled the criteria of content and function or not.[98] This conception is also repeated in the *Carmina Burana* in a slightly obscure scholarly poem *Quocumque more motu volvuntur tempora* (CB 65) treating time, mutability, and erotic love. In its latter part "the choir of scholars" sings the praise of Venus:

> *Hec memor corde serva, / quod te mea Minerva / nunc prudens, nunc proterva / multiformis hactenus declarat harmonia: / prosa, versu, satira psallens et rhythmachia / te per orbem intonat scolaris symphonia.*[99]

Adore this memory (of love) in your heart of which my now prudent, now impudent, multiform Minerva declares to you as follows in harmony: the symphony of scholars sings all over the world with prose, verse, satire, and rhythmic songs for you.

Udo Kindermann interprets this strophe as presenting a formal fourfold division into prose, metrical poetry, satire or *prosimetrum*, and rhythmic poetry. The choir of scholars praises Venus and the memory of love with different forms, satire among them. Thus the term seems to be understood purely in formal terms without any reference to its contents.[100]

1940/1994, 75f., 431). Bede's remark about the connection between rhythmic metre and vernacular poetry affirms this hypothesis. The metric system would function as a kind of musical key which tunes certain substantial and generic expectations.

96 ... satira enim metrice sed invectio prosaice scripta est reprehensio. (*Accessus ab auctore incerto*, p. 90). See also Kindermann 1978, 23-25.

97 Kindermann 1978, 22-24; about the Menippean satire see Riikonen 1987.

98 An anonymous commentator from the twelfth century (Stock 1972, 90, n. 46) specified the genre of *Philosophiae consolatio*, and compared it to the work of Martianus Capella: ... hos libros per satiram edidit imitatus uidelicet Martianum Felicem Capellam, qui prius libris de nuptiis Philologiae et Mercurii eadem specie poematis conscripserat *(Saeculi noni auctoris in Boetii Consolat. Philos. Comm.* I, p. 4).

99 CB 65.10ᵃ; CB I.2, 27-28.

100 Kindermann 1978, 22. However, it is possible that the satirical "praise" can be understood as ironical satire which only seemingly praised vices while actually attacking them (see e.g. Bernard of Utrecht, *Comm. in Theod.* 104-105, p. 62).

An influential synopsis of ancient generic theory was presented by Isidore of Seville in the eighth book of his *Etymologiae* dealing with religion, philosophy and poetry. He quoted some ancient Latin authors about the religious origins of poetry and then proceeded to a description of the generic system. As a subgenre of comic poetry, he presented the "new comedy", represented by satirical writers as Horace, Persius and Juvenal. Comic poetry treated "light matters", and the "new comedy", i.e. satire, was described as revealing vices by painting them openly and truthfully. At the same time, abundance and profusion was proper in satire as simultaneous treatment of the great variety of its subject-matter.[101]

The definition of satires given by Isidore is simultaneosly similar and dissimilar to the later medieval conceptions. It is partly dissimilar because it defines satire as a comic genre, although the risible effects of satire were also thought as its characteristics later in the Middle Ages.[102] Satire and comedy were however later most often understood as separate genres.[103] The rest of Isidore's definition more or less follows the lines which became a common-place in the Middle Ages: satire reveals and reprehends vices, it exposes them and, on the other hand, treats matters "in profusion" or exaggerates them.

Isidore defines satire as comic poetry dealing with private affairs – thus, it naturally falls into the sphere of ethics. However, Isidore himself does not here mention anything about the relation between poetry and philosophy. By his own definition, comedy would belong to ethics but tragedy to politics because it treats of public matters.[104] On the other hand, the variety of subject matter characteristic of poetry according to Isidore could mean that satire reaches beyond the private sphere. In practice medieval satire did not respect the borderline between private and public, or individual and general matters, and it dealt with topics pertaining to both ethics and politics. Thus among the topics of satire one can find private vices, and moreover, vices occurring in regal courts, the Roman curia and among the ecclasiastical estate in general, and satires could handle problems of jurisdiction, the selling of ecclesiastical offices, etc.[105] It is evident that satiric poetry was not composed having in

---

101 *Etym.* VIII.vii, ed. Lindsay 1911/1987; Isidore writes about satire in other passages also: DE LEGE SATVRA. Satura vero lex est quae de pluribus simul rebus eloquitur, dicta a copia rerum et quasi a saturitate; unde et saturas scribere est poemata varia condere, ut Horatii, Iuvenalis et Persii. (Isidorus, *Etym.* V.xvi, ed. Lindsay 1911/1987.) See also Kelly (1993) on the influence of the Isidorean definition of tragedy.
102 Kindermann 1978, 83-113.
103 Bernard of Utrecht, *Comm. in Theod.* 85-124, p. 61-63; Bernard Silvester, *Comm. in Mart.* 2.971-985, p. 80-81.
104 Sed comici privatorum praedicant acta; tragici vero res publicas et regum historias. *(Etym.* VIII.vii.6-7.)
   E.g. Bernard of Utrecht shared this view: ... est enim comicum, quo privatorum facta per personas representatur, ...; est tragicum, quo publicae res est et potentum scelera depinguntur, ... Est satiricum quod communiter vicia reprehendit... *(Comm. in Theod.* 85-107, p. 61-62.) According to Henry Ansgar Kelly the identification of comedy with private affairs and tragedy with public ones originates from Horace and was transmitted to the Middle Ages by Isidore, Diomedes and others (1993, 6, 46, 62-65 and *passim*).
105 Lehmann 1922-23/1963, 25-93; Raby 1934, 45-54, 89-102, 204-214; Yunck 1963, *passim*;

mind the distinction between ethics and politics, which were more or less fused with each other.

I have above already quoted the division of poetry by Bernard Silvester into three genres according to their level of veracity. *Fabula* was an untrue fictitious narrative, *argumentum* was verisimilar and probable narrative, and *historia* was a narrative of real deeds. The generic terms of antiquity, i.e. comedy, tragedy, and satire Bernard interpreted as the modes of true and verisimilar poetry; that is, modes of *historia* and *argumentum*.[106]

The generic theory of Bernard Silvester has two levels, the first one being the tripartition based on the level of veracity, and the second is based on content and function which is also composed of three parts. Comedy is the genre characteristically using *argumentum*, verisimilar narrative. Bernard does not complete this definition with further characterisations, but his division implies conceptions common in the High Middle Ages. Several authors thought that it was indeed the fictitious narratives *(fabulae)* that were next to metaphors the essential feature bringing pleasure and enjoyment.[107] Thus Bernard apparently meant by comedy verisimilar and probable poems bringing pleasure and ending happily.[108] *Historia* was however divided into two kinds of narratives, that is, tragedy and satire. Tragedy was most commonly in twelfth-century terms a poem (or just a writing, *scriptum*) beginning in prosperity and ending in adversity, taught one to bear adversity. It seems that this conception had something in common with the cathartic theory in the *Poetics* of Aristotle, and, with the view of Boethius about adversity as morally edifying.[109] When he turns to satire, Bernard defines it simply as the reprehension of vices and praise of virtues.

Witke 1970, 200-266; Schüppert 1972, *passim*; Pepin 1988, *passim*.

106 *Comm. in Mart.* 2.971-985, p. 80-81 (see above quotation on page 60); also Ralph of Longchamp, *In Anticl. Al. comm.* I.xxxv, p. 44.
  Bernard of Utrecht presented the same description originating from ancient rhetorical treatises (see note 63): Fabula igitur est quod neque gestum est nec geri potuit, dicta a fando quod in dictis tantum, non in factis constet. ... et aut delectationis fingitur causa ut quae vulgo dicuntur, aut causa instruendi mores ut quas auctores referunt et sub quibus plerumque veritas occulitur. Historia autem est res gesta sed a memoria hominum remota, tracta *apo to ystorin* id est videre: solos enim fieri rem videntes olim scribere licebat. ... Argumentum vero est quodammodo res ficta, quae tamen fieri potest, ut in comediis... *(Comm. in Theod.* 127-140, p. 63).

107 See Olsen 1982.

108 In his his commentary on the *Aeneid* Bernard divides writers into three groups; that is, those who write to teach as satirists, those who write to give pleasure as writers of comic plays, and those who write for both reasons as historians. In the same passage Bernard quotes Horace *(AP* 333-334) and explains that Virgil's *Aeneid* gives pleasure on the basis of verbal ornaments, figures and adventures described. It is useful because it gives an example of pursuit of virtues and of avoidance of vices *(Comm. sup. Eneidis*, prol., p. 4).

109 The *Poetics* of Aristotle was unknown in Western Christendom before the mid-thirteenth century, and even after its first translations (1278) it remained relatively unknown before the Renaissance (Dahan 1980, 171-173; Kelly 1993, 111-125; Lehtinen 1994). On the moral theory of Boethius see *Philosophiae consolatio* (esp. II.pr.viii, p. 224; see part II n. 136 in this study); also Chadwick 1981/1990. Indeed Boethius makes *Fortuna* ask if tragedies are anything else than representation of her deeds *(Phil. cons.* II. pr.ii, p. 182; Kelly 1993, 32-35, 69).

The connection between satire and philosophy is repeated by several medieval authors. Bernard Silvester calls personified satire *(Satira)* a friend of philosophers, whose name is according to him traced from salt *(sal)* because it cures vices as one cures wounds with smarting salt. Bernard also emphasizes the exuberance of satire which he connects with opulence *(opulentia)*: satire warns of the pursuit of material and secular riches.[110] At the same time, Hugh of Saint Victor placed satire among the "appendage arts" *(appenditia artium)* leading to philosophy when he enumerated the different genres of poetry.[111]

Thus, satire was considered as being copious in its contents, abundant or exaggerating, reprehending human vices and directed people towards virtue. The definitions based on content and function regarded it clearly as a part of moral poetry, which corresponded perhaps most unambiguously to the classical rhetorical definition of epideictic oratory.[112] One may argue that satire constituted the core of poetical moral discourse. Satire was also unambiguously useful by delighting through ridicule *(ridentibus)*. "The common people" may have understood it only as amusing, but "the learned" understood the didactic level and serious truths concealed under its risible surface.[113]

According to medieval authors, "nakedness" and "openness" were proper to satire. Isidore asserted that satires exposed sinful manners.[114] Bernard of Utrecht connected the ridiculous nakedness of satyrs and the revelation of vices through ridicule in satires.[115] According to some authors the exposure of vices turned into the openness of satires, although ironic satire especially was understood according to allegorical thinking as hiding truths beneath the literal surface.[116] However, the openness of satire to understanding won more ground among the writers of the High Middle Ages. For example, Conrad of Hirsau connected the nakedness of satyrs with the unconcealed expression of satirical poetry.[117] On the other hand, Bernard Silvester's interpretation of satire as a sub-branch of history leads to the identification of historically and literally true narrative and satire.[118]

Satire's simple and literal openness to understanding did evidently not mean that satirical poetry was considered to devoid of figurative means. Rather, it seems that an emphasis on direct exposure meant directness of moral content. Satire could be ironic, it may have used *integumenta*, and it might demand a learned reader before its didactic message could be understood (although in the High Middle Ages all *readers* were by definition learned[119]), but its

---

110 *Comm. in Mart.* 4.206-216, 238-243, p. 90-91.
111 *Didasc.* III.iv, p. 54-55.
112 See above note 59: also Kelly 1993, 123-124.
113 To modify the definition of *fabula* by Bernard of Utrecht freely *(Comm. in Theod.* 127-140, p. 63). See note 106 above.
114 *Etym.* VIII.vii.7, ed. Lindsay 1911/1987.
115 *Comm. in Theod.* 99-101, p. 62.
116 *Ibid.* See also notes 8 and 9.
117 *Dial. sup. auct.* 1460-1483, p. 118-119; Minnis & Scott 1988/1991, 60-61.
118 *Comm. in Mart.* 2.971-985, p. 80-81. See Minnis & Scott 1988/1991, 116-118.
119 Grundmann 1958, 1-65.

moral message was not concealed in ambiguous and obscure expression so that one would have to harness the allegorical interpretative apparatus to clarify it.

An anonymous author who complemented the commentary on Juvenal by William of Conches wrote:

> *Quid sit satira et unde sit dicta videamus. Satira igitur est reprehensio metrice composita, et distat inter satiram et invectionem, satira enim metrice sed invectio prosaice scripta est reprehensio. Palinodia vero est reprehensionis recantacio ut si aliquem prius reprehendas, postea eum laudas; pertinet tamen ad reprehensionem. Satira secundum quosdam dicitur a satiris diis nemorum eo quod in proprietatibus omnibus pares conveniant. Satiri enim nudi sunt et dicaces; saltando incedunt. Immitantur gestus hominum; caprinos habent pedem. ...*
>
> *Satirorum ergo proprietates habet satira: illi nudi et hec nuda, sunt enim quidam <qui> reprehensiones suas velant, ut Lucanus de pinguedine Neronis ait... Satira vera nude et aperte reprehendit. Dicaces sunt satiri. Satira nihil tacet et nulli parcit; illi saltando incedunt, hec modo, unde statim alium tangit; hec quemadmodum ille gestus hominum imitatur, quam turpiter enim agunt homines, tam turpiter hec reprehendit. Caper vero fedidum est animal, unde satira propter viciorum fecorem similis est satiris caprinos pedes habentibus.*

Let us consider the nature of satire and the origin of its name. Satire is reprehension *(reprehensio)* composed in metre, and there is a difference between satire and invective *(invectio)*, for satire is reprehension written in metre, while invective is reprehension written in prose. Palinode is a recantation of reprehension, as if you were first of all to reprehend someone, and then to praise him, but it pertains to reprehension. According to some, satire is so called from the satyrs, who were woodland gods, because the two are perfectly matched in all their characteristics. For satyrs are naked and have an unbridled tongue, advance with a leaping motion, imitate human movements, and have goats' feet. ...

Satire, then, has the characteristic of satyrs. They are naked and it is naked. For there are some writers who cover up *(velant)* their reprehension, as when Lucan, speaking of Nero's obesity... True satire consists of naked and open reprehension. Satyrs have an unbridled tongue; satire passes over no person in silence, and spares no one. Satyrs advance with a leaping motion, while satire [touches on one person] one moment and immediately jumps from there to deal with another. Both imitate the movements *(gestus)* of human beings. For satire in its base reprehension exactly matches the base lives of men. The goat is a smelly animal, and so satire, by reason of the stench of vices, is like goat-footed satyrs. (Tr. Minnis & Scott.)[120]

---

120 *Accessus ab auctore incerto*, p. 90; translation by Minnis & Scott 1988/1991, 136-137.

William of Conches briefly states in his proper commentary on Juvenal that "satire is called a lamp which strips and reveals vices".[121]

Satire, then, reprehended directly and openly, and its exposure was compared with nakedness of satyrs. This analogy constituted a theory about the semantic nature of satires. Contrary to the common definition of poetry as moral discourse, one did not have to dig for the ethical truths beneath the surface of satire.

Contradictions between different definitions of satire do not cease. On the one hand, there were satires whose moral meaning was open immediately at the literal level, and on the other hand, satires which demanded more interpretative work, e.g. satires which may have seemingly praised vices. The *Carmina Burana* shows that a third type of satire might also have existed, that is, satire which for one reason or another veiled its true target with *integumenta* but did not hide its moral indignation. These texts resemble the description given by the anonymous commentator on Lucan.[122] All three types were however such that the ordinary cleric did not have to strain his interpretation to understand their moral message.

Poetry and the sublunar world

Even if in the High Middle Ages nobody gave an overall definition of poetry, we can construct a fairly reliable and commonly-accepted definition from commentary literature and general treatises on sacred and secular learning. Moreover, we can argue that this definition was implicitly applied by clerical scholars, and that it was widespread among all who had an elementary clerical education.[123]

In this context secular Latin poetry pertained to practical philosophy; more specifically it was a part of ethics, a human discourse on the sublunar world, most often on human action there, whose mode was normative exemplification (i.e. it gave *praecepta* and *exempla*), and its aim was moral persuasion by praise of virtues and vituperation of vices. The secular poetry was distinguished from other ethical genres, or other discursive genres in general, by its use of metre, rhyme, metaphoric language, and by its more or less fictitious character. Each of these features could be found in other discursive genres too, but one can argue that the underlying (if not explicitly stated) *differentia specifica* of poetry was an ensemble of formal and semantic

---

121 Satira dicitur lucerna quia nudat et aperte vicia. (In another manuscript it is explained: Lucernam vocat satiram quia quo modo lucerna abscondita manifestat, ita viciorum occulta denudat), *(Glos. in Iuv. in Satiram primam*, p. 110.)
122 E.g. CB 41; CB I.1, 65-76.
123 Judson Boyce Allen writes: ... no medieval poet could have learned his Latin without having submitted his reading to a school accessus, nor could he have read at all widely without having encountered more or less marginal commentary (1982, xiv).
  See also Glauche 1970; Vance 1987, 3-13 and *passim*; McGregor 1978; Häring 1982, 173-200.

features. Its specific mode of veracity was essential: poetry was not in itself untrue, but its truth was found in its moral meaning, not necessarily in its literal or referential sense.

Medieval scholars emphasized the importance of the correct use of poetry. One had to excavate the deeper ethical truth which corresponded to "our dogma" beneath the surface of the fictitious narratives of pagan authors. Poetry did not necessarily carry out its function without interpretation. Secular poetry did not utilize tropes, figures and fictitious narratives to represent the non-corporeal reality as the Scriptures did but to delight the reader or hearer. Above all, poetry proposed examples *(exempla)* which had evident moral implications as satires. That meant that they were either "open to understanding" *(aperta)*, i.e. they were comprehensible without complicated interpretative effort, or their moral meaning was concealed in figurative expression *(integumenta)* which demanded interpretation to uncover their ethical meaning. The demand for allegorical interpretation was based on obscurity of moral implications, not on their figurative elements.

We should notice, that tropes, figures, fictitiousness or evident allegorical nature (i.e. allegory which had no sense on the literal level alone) did not demand allegorical interpretation as such, because their moral sense *(sensus* or *sententia)* was immediately understandable. The allegorical interpretation ought not be applied unless the text failed to reveal its moral sense directly. It is this conception that is behind William of Conches' view of satire as directly (morally) understandable or "open" texts.

Part II

■ *Fortuna* and the sublunar world

Fortuna becomes popular

Originally the Roman goddess *Fortuna* was a goddess of fertility. Transferred to the Middle Ages she was often thought to control wordly success, destiny and luck in the sublunar world. Her popularity arose from her appearance in the works of Ovid and Horace and in the allegorical and scholarly poem *De nuptiis Mercurii et Philologiae* (ca. 410-29) by Martianus Capella. However, Boethius' *Philosophiae consolatio* (524), in which the goddess had a central role as a personification of the change of wordly luck and fortune in human action, was the most important influence.[1]

During the twelfth century the pictorial and literal representations of *Fortuna* where becoming ever more common. At the same time her iconography was changing. Earlier the goddess has been represented standing with cornucopia on a wheel or globe but now she herself was rotating the wheel, on whose rim four men, usually kings, were rolled from success to defeat and vice versa.[2] Many writers were simultaneously discussing *Fortuna* as a personification of earthly luck, following Boethius by using her as the name of randomness in human action. The goddess was also popular in contemporary poetry. For example, Alan of Lille gave her an important role in his allegorical poem on human perfection *Anticlaudianus* (ca. 1181/84). *Fortuna* was represented as a central force in the sublunar world. Despite the fact that she was subject to personified *Natura*, *Fortuna* threw the ideal order of nature into disorder with her randomness.[3] In the *Carmina Burana Fortuna* appears both as a literary and as pictorial figure. The miniature representing *Fortuna* is on the first folio of the manuscript, where it has been shifted from its original place after the group of *Fortuna* poems (CB 14-18).[4]

The popularity of *Fortuna* in the High Middle Ages may be traced back to the literary tradition. Boethius was one of the most popular authors – so much, that the twelfth century has been called *aetas Boetiana*.[5] For Boethius

---

1   Chadwick 1981/1990, 242-253; Cioffari 1935, 67-70; Courcelle 1967, *passim*; Doren 1924, 71-144; Kajanto 1960, 27; Patch 1927, *passim*; Pickering 1966, 112-121; *idem* 1967, 18-34, 98-153; Kitzinger 1973, 362-363.
2   Courcelle 1967, 145-158; Pickering 1966, 132-145; Murray 1978/1990, 98-102; however, Hahnloser and Kitzinger have argued that iconography changed from mechanical and active to more abstract and passive types at the turn of the twelfth and thirteenth centuries (Kitzinger 1973, 364-366; see also Steer 1982, 184-186).
3   *Anticlaudianus*, VII and VIII books.
4   Schumann 1930/1961, 5*-6*, 31*-39*, 42*.
5   Chenu 1957/1976, 142-158; cf. also Courcelle 1967, *passim*.

Fortuna is not at all an ill-defined allegorical personification; he used her to adapt the *Physics* of Aristotle as a concept for the fortuitious aspect of causality and intentional human action.[6] Furthermore, the position given *Fortuna* by other authors of antiquity as a representation of the change of wordly fortune made her one of the most important figures borrowed from the pagan Pantheon.[7] As such, *Fortuna* had an essential role in discussing the relations between divine providence, the divinely determined order of nature, human free will and the fickleness of the terrestrial world.

In the Middle Ages *Fortuna* personified a group of different and partly contradictory aspects from the bringer of luck and prosperity (and their remover), chance and inevitable fate.[8] As a force regulating wordly success she seemed to be simultaneously in conflict with Christian divine providence and divinely-ordered natural determination.[9] Despite (or perhaps because of) her contradictory features she was extremely popular in literary and pictorial representations from the twelfth century.

Why did *Fortuna* become such a popular figure in the twelfth century? The general and easily acceptable answer is that *Fortuna* became popular just as other figures in the classical Pantheon from Jove to Venus did. Moreover, one can argue that the new emergence of discussions of concepts and representations of causality, determinism and randomness were a consequence of the growth of the speculation in both moral philosophy and natural events.

Alexander Murray does not accept this as an adequate explanation because with the emergence of representations of *Fortuna* her iconography changed. From a passive personification of randomness she turned to an active force rotating the wheel of fortune. Active *Fortuna* seemed to act purposefully when she brought some to the pinnacle of success and threw others down to adversity and misfortune. According to Murray, *Fortuna* did not become popular only as a byproduct of the growth of scholarly activities, but had a special function as a conceptualisation of the new social mobility which emerged at the same time. Murray thus explains the popularity of *Fortuna* and her wheel as a reflection of the economic, social and cultural transition in the High Middle Ages. The effects of the expansion and a new monetary economy in advanced areas of Western Europe were clearly visible especially in the clerical world. New bureaucratic, impersonal and monetary relations first started to penetrate the clerical social order governed by personal and reciprocal lordship. At the same time Latin literature on *Fortuna* and her pictoral representations became widespread and their nature altered.

---

6 Boethius, *Phil. cons.* V.pr.1, p. 384-388; Aristotle, *Physica* 195b31-197a35; *idem*, *Metaphysica* 1025a14-20; Chadwick 1981/1990, 244.
7 Patch 1927, *passim*.
8 Patch 1927, *passim*.
9 Cioffari 1935, 71-116; Courcelle 1967, 109.
   St. Augustine denies *Fortuna* as a senseless concept, although he too thinks that it can be used in ordinary language as a name in the human perspective seemingly fortuitous events (cf. *De libero arbitrio* III.ii.5, p. 388-390; *De civitate Dei* I.viii, IV.xvii, xxxiii, V.i, viii-x, p. 212, 582-584, 634, 644, 668-688).

Alexander Murray argues that from the twelfth century on the globe with *Fortuna* on it was changed to the wheel of *Fortuna* which was now rotated by the goddess herself. On the rim of wheel appeared human figures turning around with it. The change was a reflection of the new social situation, increasingly common social mobility being strange phenomenon for which contemporaries had no explanatory concepts.[10]

Alexander Murray's thesis is persuasive even if his own documentation is not thorough and not grounded on systematic research. Neither does he present much detailed analysis of medieval literature. Despite the weaknesses in documentation Murray's interpretation seems to be plausible in its main lines while not exhausting the contemporary literal and pictorial representations of *Fortuna*. It is quite possible that the popularity of the goddess was related to the social tumult especially strong among the clerical order, but the role of *Fortuna* was at least as essential as a means of conceptualizing human action in the sublunar world. As a matter of fact, some contemporary authors used *Fortuna* when they characterised historical processes which did not seem to be guided in all their details by divine providence but seemed to be more chaotic and random.[11]

I wish to analyse the *Fortuna* poems in the *Carmina Burana* in their contemporary intellectual context. First I outline various themes relating to *Fortuna* and their historical and intellectual sources and then proceed to the *Fortuna* poems in the *Carmina Burana*. What did the medievals talk about when they talked about *Fortuna*? Seemingly quite general and almost trivial poems in the *Carmina Burana* appear in quite a different light when their intertextual elements in and outside the collection are traced. Seemingly imprecise and stereotypical complaints about the fickleness of luck are related to essential contemporary discussions on the terms of human action, social change and nature of the sublunar world. These are simultaneously linked to the rupture between the monastic and clerical ways of thinking.

---

10   Murray 1978/1990, 96-100. The change in *Fortuna* iconography is documented by Pickering (1966, 132-145) and Courcelle (1967, 157-158; cf. also plates no:s 65-86). See also Kitzinger (1973) and Steer (1982). On *Fortuna* standing on the wheel or globe see also Robinson 1946, 212.

11   For example Otto of Freising, *Gesta Frederici*; Pickering 1967, 12-13, 35, 88 & *passim; idem*, 1976, 69-118; Steer 1982, 188; Henry Ansgar Kelly discusses about the concept of *Fortuna* of Otto of Freising in his *Gesta Fredericii*. According to him *Fortuna* is presented here more like a genius or a guardian angel of Frederick Barbarossa (i.e. *Fortuna cesarea*) but, on the other hand, Otto's definition of the sublunar history is very close to definitions of *Fortuna* as a personification of randomness and wordly fickleness.

Providence, free will, chance and earthly luck

The medieval characteristics of *Fortuna*

In the last section of the *Architrenius* (ca. 1180s), a general, partly autobiographical and partly allegorical poetical work, composed by John of Hauvilla, there is a brief description of *Fortuna* sharing prosperity and adversity in the sublunar world: she is simultaneously *sors*, that is, lot or "fate", *Tyche*, *Rhamnus*, *Nemesis*, *Casus* (chance) who makes bishops, and *Fortuna* giving offices. The catalogue given by John connects the Fates and the philosophical concept of chance personified by *Fortuna*. Furthermore, it seems to list all essential medieval connotations inherited from Graeco-Roman mythology, poetry and philosophy.[12]

In Roman poetry, the characteristics of Greek deities and personifications ruling over randomness and destiny *(Heimarmene, Moira, Tyche)* were identified with *Fortuna*, originally a goddess of fertility, and as a consequence, she was not clearly separated from the concept of *Fatum*, fate or destiny. Iiro Kajanto has differentiated three separate meanings of *fatum* in Roman literature – prophecy or divination, *fatum-moira* or the agent of death and destruction, and *fatum-heimarmene*, which was mediated by Stoic philosophy and meant the predetermined causality *(causa aeterna rerum)*.[13] However, *Fortuna* was especially identified with *Tyche*, the goddess of destiny, who regulated wordly success, and was simultaneously a personification of luck or randomness independent of human decision. In principle, *Fortuna-Tyche* and *Fortuna-Heimarmene* excluded each other and thus were opposite concepts. The first conceptualized indeterminate events while the latter was expressly a notion of determined causality or, in other words, fatality. In practice these opposite notions were often confused with each other in literature.[14]

---

12 Quod Fortuna favit nuptiis. Respicit et blandis epulas percurrit ocellis / Et vultus adhibet animi cum melle favorem / Sors inopum vindex, regum Tuchis ultra tumores, / Ramnis opum terror, Nemesis suspecat tirannis, / Casus agens mitras, tribuens Fortuna curules. / O data vel raro vel nulli fercula, solis, / Degustanda viris! o felix mensa, Catoni, / Forsitan et nostro vix evo nota! beatis, / Immo beativis, indulge sumptibus. absit / Meta dum clausura dapes, connubia Virtus / Sanctiat et dempto convivia fine perhennet. *(Architrenius* IX.25.452-462, ed. Schmidt 1974, p. 283; *idem,* ed. Wetherbee 1994, p. 250-252.)

13 The *Moirai* were *Parcae* in Latin (Kajanto 1960, 5-6, 9-11, 25-29).

14 Kajanto 1960, 6, 25-29.
    Tyche and *Heimarmene* both had philosophical connotations: while the latter represented determined causality, which left no place for free will and choice, *Tyche* was a personification of undetermined fortuitousness. For example, Aristotle made a distinction between inevitable causality and fortuitousness. According to Vincenzo Cioffari, he also made a distinction between necessary, probable and unusual, and, on the other hand, purposed and non-purposed events. *Tyche* was a cause of those events which were unusual and connected with meaningful human action. *Automaton* however was a cause for randomness in nature, that is a cause for indeterminated unusual events. (Cf. Aristotle, the 5. and 6. chapters in the second book of *Physica*; also *Metaphysica* 1032a12). Cioffari relates this fortuitousness thus: "That is: hazard *(automaton)* is a privation of Nature, and Fortune *(Tyche)* is a privation of techne (of Mind) ... Now as Mind and Nature are surely

---

The figure of *Fortuna* and all the epithets associated with her were transmitted to the Middle Ages through Roman poets, particularly by Horace and Ovid. Nevertheless, the impact of Boethius was decisive when he decided to give *Fortuna* a central role in his *Philosophiae consolatio*. On the general level, *Fortuna* was depicted by Boethius as a personification of the unreliability of the sublunar world and the fickleness of luck. Boethius's work was indeed read as a kind of *contemptus mundi*.[15] Nevertheless, *Fortuna* and her randomness was a problematic notion in the context of Christian beliefs. For example, Saint Augustine left no room for causality independent of divine providence, neither was there any randomness out of its reach.[16]

Boethius also reduced in his *Philosophiae consolatio* the general causality of Nature to providence and to the world order created by God. However, he differentiated the "fate" *(fatum)* which he assimilated with inevitable causality and which was, by definition, dependent on divine providence. Human free will was logically independent of fate. However, while it was also subject to omniscient providence, Boethius argued that predestination did not follow from the divine foresight.[17]

In the High Middle Ages, the views of the learned were divided between St. Augustine and Boethius.[18] Augustine left no space for chance – or for *Fortuna* – and free will *(libera voluntas, liberum arbitrium)* became first of all a necessary condition for the possibility of morals.[19] In the view of

---

efficient causes, a privation of them is a lack of causality. In fact this is the very reason why Aristotle *(Phys.* II.iv.193a3) places Fortune among the efficient causes." (Cioffari 1935, cit. 31, otherwise 13-44; on the confusion between the concepts of Fortune and Fate 45-70; cf. also Cioffari 1940, 1-2; Cioffari uses the notion 'Fortune' as synonymous with Aristotle's *tyche.*

15 Pickering 1966, 112-145; *idem* 1967, 98-153; Courcelle 1967, *passim*; Bultot 1969, 823-824.
16 *De civitate Dei* V.viii-xi, p. 668-691; *De libero arbitrio, passim*, p. 190-529; cf. also Cioffari 1935, 76-81.
17 Boethius, *Phil. cons.* the fifth book, especially V.pr.iii, pr.iv, p. 394-402, 404-412; Chadwick 1981/1990, 242-247; see also Courcelle 1967, 203-221; Kretzmann 1985, 23-50; Craig 1988, 79-98; Knuuttila 1993, 45-62.
    The IV and V book of *Phil. cons.* are quite explicit in stating this. However, Boethius seems to be more on indeterministic lines in his commentary on Aristotle's *De interpretatione* (especially on its chapter 9) where he discusses of future contingents and the conceptions of possibility, actualizing agency and free will. Here he presents change as a sort of outcome of free will operating on real potentiality *(Comm. in Arist. Peri Hermeneias* I, 103-126; ibid. II, 185-250; see Kretzmann 1985, 28-36 and *passim*; also Chadwick 1981/1990, 157-163; Craig 1988; Knuuttila 1993).
    In the Middle Ages the relation between providence, foresight, predestination and free will formed a central logical problem which was discussed especially from the late 13th century onwards. In the twefth century and early thirteenth century the relation between providence and foresight was still more or less undefined. For example the anomymous *Moralium dogma philosphorum* treats *providentia* as simple foresight (I.A.1, p. 9-10), and Ralph of Longchamp identifies providence and preordination with each other (I.lxx, p. 63). On the medieval theological tradition see Pelikan 1978, 80-98, 271-277; on philosophical speculation about free will, detremination and contingency see Korolec 1982/1990; Courtenay 1984b; Craig 1988; Knuuttila 1993; see also Lottin 192-57/1960.
18 Pickering 1967, 18-23 (see cit. in note 22); *idem* 1976.
19 *De lib. arb.* III.ii.5 & *passim*, p. 388-390; also *ibid.* I.xvi.34, II.i.1, xvii.45-xx.54, III.ii.4-iv.11, p. 262, 264, 358-379, 388-404.; *De civ. Dei* I.viii, IV.xvii, xxxiii, V.i, viii-x, p. 212, 582-584, 634, 644, 668-688; Cioffari 1935, 76-81.

Boethius, *Fortuna* and change araising from intentional human action had much more central status even if in the frame of *Philosophiae consolatio* they were not seen genuinely indeterminated and free of providential order.[20]

The difference between Augustine and Boethius (of *Philosophiae consolatio*) is not necessarily in their ideas about divine omnipotence, foreknowledge and indetermination although they do analyse these concepts from a different point of view and with different emphasis. Essential to the medieval discussions is rather the fact that they offer radically different views and conceptual tools. Augustine underlines the divine plan and his work is permeated by his deep mistrust of the possibility of chance. Hence he excludes *Fortuna* and chance as meaningful concepts and accepts them only as names in ordinary speech for unexpected and unusual events (as in Cicero). Free will has two functions in his system: firstly, it is a precondition for the existence of morals, and secondly, it allows Augustine to explain the existence of evil. Human agents willing and choosing freely either good or bad do not however produce proper contingency in the course of history.[21]

Contrary to Augustine, Boethius underlines *Fortuna* as a name randomness which seemingly arise from human action while she manifests the unreliable nature of the sublunar world. Thus she becomes a mediating instance which according to Frederick P. Pickering gave motivation for writing human dynastic history.[22] She is a providential agent subjected to the order of nature

---

20   In the fourth book of *Philosophiae consolatio* Boethius discusses "the causes of hidden things", *providentia, praedestinatio* and free will (IV. pr.vi, p. 356). He distinguishes *providentia* and *fatum* followingly: Nam providentia est ipsa illa divina ratio in summo omnium principe constituta quae cuncta disponit; fatum vero inhaerens rebus mobilibus dispositio per quam providentia suis quaeque nectit ordinibus. Providentia namque cuncta pariter quamvis diversa quamvis infinita complectitur; fatum vero singula digerit in motum locis formis ac temporibus distributa, ut haec temporalis ordinis explicatio in divinae mentis adunata prospectum providentia sit, eadem vero adunatio digesta atque explicata temporibus fatum vocetur. Quae licet diversa sint, alterum tamen pendet ex altero. Ordo namque fatalis ex providentiae simplicitate procedit (IV. pr.iv, p. 358). Later in the same chapter he states bluntly that: Haec actus etiam fortunasque hominum indissolubili causarum conexione constringit, quae cum ab immobilis providentiae proficiscatur exordiis, ipsas quoque immutabiles esse necesse est. Ita enim res optime reguntur, si manens in divina mente simplicitas indeclinabilem causarum ordinem promat. Hic vero ordo res mutabiles et alioquin temere fluituras propria incommutabilitate coerceat (IV. pr.vi, p. 362).

    See also *Cons. Phil.* V.pr.i, p. 386-388 (see further p. 79-80); also Pickering 1967, 18-36, 88, 98-153; *idem* 1976, *passim*.

21   Craig 1988, 59-78; Kirwan 1989/1991, 82-128; Knuuttila 1993, 45-62.

    For Augustine, history was ultimately directed by divine providence which strecthed as a typological narrative between the Creation and the second coming of Christ. Human aspirations are not really significant when the course of events are understood as the writing of God, prefigurations and its actualisation. The models of possible events had already been stated in the relevation of the Old and New Testaments (Auerbach 1959/1984, 49-76; Chydenius 1960, 16-24; Frye 1981/1983, *passim*; Guenée 1980, 29-33; cf. also Lehtonen 1990, 193-195).

22   Pickering writes: Den gedanklichen Apparat zu dieser Art Geschichte bietet nicht Augustinus sondern Boethius. Damit meine ich natürlich nicht, daß bei Augustinus in der *Civitas Dei* nichts Verwendbares zu finden gewesen wäre, sondern daß man sich nach Boethius richtete, wo man alles fand, was man brauchte. Dort in *De consolatione Philosophiae* findet der Autor das dieser Gattung zugeordnete Begriffssystem und die relevante Instanz-Hierarchie, sozusagen die Spielregeln oder, wie man besser sagen wird, die Proprietäten der Gattung. ... Hier hatte unter anderen Instanzen *Fortuna* ihren Platz, ihre in einer Instanzen-Ordo

and also points up the vanity of pursuit of earthly prosperity through her unreliability. Randomness personified by *Fortuna* is itself a part of providential plan but, in a certain sense, she becomes simultaneously an emblem for the sublunar world and human history. Stable only in her instability she deceives all who put their hopes in her. The whole *Philosophiae consolatio* hinges on the difference between *Fortuna* and *Philosophia*: the first represents the wordly success and wealth which are wiped away in a moment, while the latter offers durable contemplative values.[23]

Behind the association of chance and *Fortuna* was already the fact that the word *'fortuna'* was associated both conceptually and etymologically to the word *'fortuitus'* ('random', 'haphazard'). This defition appears for example in Isidore of Seville.[24]. The personified Lady Philosophy and the *persona* discuss about this randomness in the work of Boethius:

> *"Quod igitur," inquam, "nihilne est quod vel casus vel fortuitum iure appellari queat? An est aliquid, tametsi vulgus lateat, cui vocabula ista conveniant?" "Aristoteles meus id," inquit [Philosophia], "in Physicis et brevi et veri propinqua ratione definivit." "Quonam," inquam "modo?" "Quotiens," ait, "aliquid cuiuspiam rei gratia geritur aliudque quibusdam de causis quam quod intendebatur obtingit, casus vocatur, ut si quis colendi agri causa fodiens humum defossi auri pondus inveniat. Hoc igitur fortuito quidem creditur accidisse, verum non de nihilo est; nam proprias causas habet quarum inprovisus inopinatusque concursus casum videtur operatus. Nam nisi cultor agri humum foderet, nisi eo loci pecuniam suam depositor obruisset, aurum non esset inventum. Haec sunt igitur fortuiti causa compendii, quod ex obviis sibi et confluentibus causis, non ex gerentis intentione provenit. Neque enim vel qui aurum obruit vel qui agrum exercuit ut ea pecunia reperiretur intendit; sed uti dixi, quo ille obruit hunc fodisse convenit atque concurrit. Licet igitur definire casum esse inopinatum ex confluentibus causis in his quae ob aliquid geruntur eventum; concurrere vero atque confluere causas facit ordo ille inevitabili conexione procedens, qui de providentia a fonte descendens cuncta suis locis temporibusque disponit.*

> "Why then," I said, "is there nothing which can rightly be called chance or fortuitousness? Or is there something, although it is hidden from common men, to which these names belong?"
> "My Aristotle," she said, "defined it in his *Physics* in an argument brief and close to the truth."
> "How?" I asked.
> "Whenever," she said, "something is done for the sake of some given

---

genauestens definierte Rolle (1967, 18).
  See Boethius, *Phil. cons.* the fifth book (on free will and divine foresight V.pr.ii, pr.iii. pr.v, p. 166-170; Kretzmann 1985, 23-50; Knuuttila 1993, 45-62. *Phil. cons.* I.pr.vi, p. 166-170; Pickering 1967, 88 & *passim; idem* 1976.

23 Eg. *Phil. cons.* II.pr.1, p. 176; Chadwick 1981/1990, 223-253; see also Kretzmann 1985; Craig 1988; Knuuttila 1993.

24 *Etym.* VIII.11.94, ed. Lindsay 1911/1987

end, and another thing occurs, for some reason or other, different from what was intended, it is called chance *(casus)*: as, for example, if a man digging in the ground in order to till his field were to find he had dug up a quantity of gold. Now this is indeed believed to have happened by chance, but does not come from nothing; for it has its proper causes, and their unforeseen and unexpected coming together appears to have produced a chance event. For if the man tilling his field were not digging the ground, and if the man who put it there had not hidden his money in that particular spot, the gold would not have been found. These are therefore the causes of that fortuitous profit, which is produced by causes meeting one another and coming together, not by the intention of the doer of the action. For neither he who hid the gold, nor he who worked the field, intended that money to be found, but as I said, where the one buried it the other happens and chances to have dug. We may therefore define chance as the unexpected event of concurring causes among things done for some purpose. Now causes are made to concur and flow together by that order which, proceeding with inevitable connexion, and coming down from its source in providence, disposes all things in their proper places and times." (Tr. S.J. Tester)[25]

The randomness associated with *Fortuna* according to Boethius is not only events without known causes (as for example Cicero and Augustine argue), but the unusual crossing of two independent intentional lines of action.[26] Boethius quotes the example given by Aristotle in his *Metaphysics* of a peasant who finds a treasure while tilling his field.[27] This event is intelligible in the context of general natural causality but in the context of meaningful human action it lacks the final cause, the goal of action (neither does it have a natural final cause which it should have according the Aristotelian view). The treasure has a meaning and value in the context of human action. Similarly, the tilling of peasant has a goal (and meaning) which, however, is not the search for a treasure. The lack of intention makes the event a chance event, in other words it belongs in the sphere of *Fortuna*.

Boethius seems to have argued for indeterministic stand in his commentary to Aristotle's *De interpretatione* (see note 27) but in his *Philosophiae*

---

25 *Phil. cons.* V.pr.1, p. 386-389.
    Boethius is referring to Aristotle's analysis of chance *(tyche)*, spontaneous events *(automaton)* and intentional action in the 4th, 5th and 6th chapters of the second book of *Physica* (195b 31-198a 13). Cf. Knuuttila 1992, 202; also *idem* 1993, 45-62; Cioffari 1935, 13-21, 82-90; Kretzmann 1985, 23-50.

26 Boethius, *Phil. cons.* V.i, p. 384-388; Cioffari 1935, 82-84.
    Boethius criticises its notion of chance in his commentary on Cicero's *Topica* and argues for the Aristotelian interpretation (Chadwick 1981/1990, 119).

27 The example about a peasant finding a treasure is from the 30. chapter of the fifth book in Aristotle's *Metaphysica* (1025a14-35). However Boethius refers otherwise to *Physics* II.4-6, where Aristotle is discuss the notion of accidence (195b31-198a13). See also Kretzmann 1985.
    When defining *casus* by using the same example in his commentary to Aristotle's *De interpretatione* Boethius however takes an indeterministic stand *(Boet. comm. in Arist. Peri herm.* II p. 193-198 and *passim*, also I p. 112) which is quite contrary to what he later argued in *Philosophiae consolatio* (e.g. also IV. pr.iv, see cit. in note 20).

consolatio he had changed his mind as the quoted passage above clearly demonstrates (see also note 20). However, he seems to accept even in the latter work that in the phenomenal world it is reasonable to speak of *casus* and *Fortuna* as names for unexpected and unintended events and thus, inspite of his deterministic stand in it he actually offered conceptual tools to treat *Fortuna* almost as an independent force in this world (of course the emphasis was on *Fortuna*'s independence of human intentions). Thus the majority of the clerical learned who spoke explicitly about *Fortuna* seem to have picked up their concepts from Boethius and not from Augustine or others similarly minded. Some of them, like Thierry of Chartres in 1130's, emphasized the role of *Fortuna* as randomness connected with human action or, as they sometimes stressed, prosperity in the sublunar world which ought to distinguished from the rather obscurely defined (pure) chance. Thierry wrote in his commentary on Cicero's *De inventione*:

> *Differt autem casus a fortuna, quod casus est eventus alicuius damni quod solet homini accidere, fortuna vero est condicio cuiusque, id est status vitae quem quisque adipiscitur vel ex arbitrio vel ex casu temporis vel ex hominum institutione.*[28]

> But chance differs from *fortuna* since chance is an occurence of something harmful which usually happens to men. But *fortuna* is someone's condition, that is, standing in life, which he has achieved either because of his choice, temporal coincidence or human institutions.

Thierry explains the choice as a solution through someone's own will (to acquire temporal good). As an example of temporal coincidence he gives a defeat or victory in war which may lead one to sink into poverty or rise in dignity. Institutional *Fortuna* occurs for example when someone happens to be born into a noble family since it is not caused by nature but institutions created by men.[29] It is not quite clear if Thierry had in his mind Boethius's definition above but he seems to follow the same line of thought. He widens the Boethian definition in the sense that in the secular world one can prosper because of one's own choice or because of temporal coincidence – which, in principle, may be understood according to the concurrent intentional lines of action as Boethius defined them. What is especially interesting is that Thierry also includes human institutions in his definition, that is, collective human forces. He seems to be giving an overall definition which comprises those causes influencing the human regime in the sublunar world, and as such a

---

28   Thierry of Chartres, *Com. s. de inv.* 59-61, p. 136; see also 75f., p. 133; 91f., p. 241; 86f., p. 259; 33f., p. 286; Fredborg 1988, 36-37.
29   Ex arbitrio, veluti si quis sponte se faciat pauperem, ut aliquod temporale bonum acquirat; ex casu temporis, veluti si quis oppressus bello cadat in paupertatem vel factus victor in aliquam dignitatem elevetur; ex institutione, veluti si quis servus a parentibus nascatur, non hoc naturae est, sed humanae institutionis, non ad naturam pertinet. *Ibid.* 62-67, p. 136.

certain theory of human (historical) action.

The influence of Boethius was pervasive and even more explicit than in the writings of Thierry, whose definition became available to others. The Boethian background is visible for example in such authors as Bernard Silvester (first half of the twelfth century) and at the beginning of thirteenth-century in Ralph of Longchamp. In commenting on Martianus Capella, Bernard Silvester explained the difference between providence and fate:

> *Fatumque nostrum. Hic tangitur illa que in Boetio est sententia, quod scilicet quecumque subiacent fato et providentie, sed non quecumque subsunt providentie et fato. Ea enim que superlunarem tenent regionem, ut pote spiritus et stelle, providentie subiecta sunt; temporali vero permutationi non subiuciuntur cum potius sub eorum ministerio et effectu tempora disponantur...*[30]

> And about our fate. Here Boethius's notion that everyone is disposed to fate and providence but is not yet subjugated to providence and fate is touched upon. Those who stay in the superlunar region, as the spirits and stars may do, are subjected to providence. But the temporal mutations are not so much beneath their yoke than rather imposed under their service and effects of time...

Bernard, relying on Boethius, included fate *(fatum)* under providence. Fate can be understood as synonymous with a causal chain following the principles of nature. Similarly Martianus Capella drew a distinction between providence and fate. Futhermore, calling fate a servant of providence originates with him - to be exact, Martianus spoke about the Fates *(Clotho, Lakhesis* and *Atropos)* who acted as the scribes of Jove and entered his providential orders (which were different from fatal determination) in their books.[31]

In the early thirteenth-century Ralph of Longchamp explained the divine providence, fate and free will:

> *Quid sit Divina providentia, quid fatum, quid liberum arbitrium, quid casus?*
> *Hic iterum considerabat Ratio:* quid cogat fatum etc. *(Anticl. I.504). Ad hic nota quod aliud est divina providentia, aliud fatum, aliud libertas, aliud casus.*
> *Divina providentia est Dei preaordinatio qua Deus ab aeterno omnia providit et praeordinavit. Ab hac nascitur fatum. Fatum enim est temporalis rerum series quae nascitur ab aeterna praeordinatione. Libertas est humana ratio quae operatur mendiante voluntate. Casus est, ut superius diximus, inopinatus rei eventus ex causis confluentibus.*
> *Penes providentiam est necessitas absoluta, penes fatum est*

---

30 *Comm. in Mart.* 4.568f., p. 243. Bernard's presentatiom seems to be based on the distinction made by Boethius in the IV book of *Phil. cons.* (IV.pr.vi, p. 358); see note 20 above.
31 Cioffari 1935, 67-68.

necessitas determinata, penes libertatem est facilitas, penes casum nec
facilitas nec necessitas. Et ita libertas est inter casum et fatum.[32]

What could Divine Providence, fate, and free will be?

This was considered by the Reason again and again, *what fate determines etc. (Anticl.* I.504). Here one has to note that divine providence, fate, freedom and chance are all different things.

Divine providence is God's preordination by which God foresees *(providit,* also: provides, takes care) and preordains everything from his eternity. From this is born fate. Fate is then a series of temporal things which is born from eternal preordination. Freedom is human reason which operates through the will. Chance is, as we said above, unexpected event from confluent causes.

In the realm of providence is the absolute necessity, in the realm of fate is the determined necessity, in the realm of freedom is the aptitude, in the realm of chance is neither aptitude nor necessity. And so freedom is between chance and fate.

Ralph, like Bernard, clearly follows Boethius: everything is ordained by providence but it does not involve itself actively in the course of events in the sublunar world which is a consequence of fatal necessary determination, i.e. causality.[33] Randomness or chance is some unexpected exception from ordinary regularity and is connected with human action. Free will, then, is placed by Ralph between necessity and randomness which are both aspects of the sublunar world.[34] One should notice that Ralph was hardly treating fate simply as a logical notion even if he spoke of it as a determined necessity. Events depending on fate are those which are indubitably possible to anticipate as human mortality, the alternation of seasons and day and night. Randomness and events not possible to anticipate approach each other – for example Bernard Silvester even seems to think that all natural event not regularly recurrent belong to the sphere of randomness (or at least *Fortuna*).[35] Nevertheless, unexpectedly concurrent intentional lines of actions belonged properly to the sphere of *Fortuna*. According to Ralph, in the sublunar world reason was able to decide freely whether to seize the occasions offered by

---

32 *In Anticl. Al. comm.* I.lxx, p. 63.
33 The notion can be reduced to an analysis of divine foresight by Boethius: because God is outside time he is able to see all events in a diachronic continuum synchronously with one glance. He has left the human will free, but because of his extratemporal faculty of vision he sees in advance all decisions, all causes and consequences. The world is regulated by natural causality, but after its original imposition divine providence does not involve itself actively in the course of events nor thus on individual human destiny on earth. *(Phil. cons.* V.pr.vi, p. 422-435.) See also notes 20 and 30 above.
34 Ralph's cosmology is essentially the same as Hugh of Saint Victor's, in which it is argued that the characteristics of the superlunar providential sphere were immutability and stability or constancy. The divinely-created nature defined by Hugh can be identified with Ralph's determinant causality, i.e. Fate (cf. the Stoic *heimarmene*). Hugh defines mutability and instability as properties of the sublunar world. Mutability is a consequence of determined necessity (annual seasons, mortality, etc.) and instability of fortuitousness (i.e. unpredictability). See Hugh of Saint Victor, *Didascalicon.*
35 *Comm. in Mart.* 8.600-615, p. 193.

chance or not. The content of the choice was primarily moral – one may achieve prosperity (or not) by free decision but eventually the choice had an effect on destiny in the eternal life.

In the High Middle Ages the concept of *Fortuna* was not limited only as notion of randomness but also meant good luck and worldly success and prosperity quite as in classical antiquity.[36] If worldly success and prosperity has been connected with chance before, this tendency became now even more stronger with the Christian faith, which emphazised contempt for this world. Worldly success and prosperity were indeed those elements which were to be avoided by a good Christian taking care of the salvation of his soul. At least one should not actively pursue them. In antiquity the Aristotelian and the Epicurean philosophical traditions regarded good luck as one of the conditions of the good life (and the good life, at least partly depended on chance).[37] The Christian (and among philosophies of antiquity, the Stoic) tradition opposed this view – earthly success and prosperity had nothing to do with real good life and they were identified even more closely with randomness. Chance and propitiousness were an inevitable pair and as such, because of their unstable and unreliable nature; one more proof of the contemptible nature of all earthly goods. Boethius made of chance and bad luck an educative factor: the disgrace of *Fortuna* directed one away from appreciation of material world to stable and immutable virtuous values.[38]

An exceptional, more Augustinian view in *Speculum Ecclesiae*, attributed to Honorius Augustodunensis and presumably dating from early twelfth century, describes *Fortuna* as follows:

> *Scribunt itaque philosophi quod mulier rota innexa jugiter circumferatur; cuius caput nunc in alta erigatur, nunc in ima demergatur. Rota haec quae volvitur est gloria huius mundi quae jugiter circumfertur. Mulier rotae innexa est fortuna gloriae intexta. Hujus caput aliquando sursum, aliquando fertur deorsum, quia plerique multocies potentia et divitiis exaltantur, saepe egestate et miseriis exalliantur. Dicunt etiam quod quidam apud inferos damnatus per radios rotae sit divaricatus; quae rota sine intermissione ab alto montis in ima vallis feratur et iterum alta repetens denuo relabatur.*
>
> *Ferunt iterum quod quidam ibi saxum in altum montis evolvat, ac pondus saxi volventem de vertice montis praecipitem pellat, rursumque*

---

36 An anonymous author explained the "goods" of *Fortuna* (*De bonis Fortunae*) in an ethical work composed during the twelfth century: Fortune autem bona sunt ista: opulentia, prelatio, gloria. (*Moralium dogma philosophorum* I.B.1, p. 22.)

For example, Aristotle (in *Rhetorica*) said that he means by the notion *tyche (Fortuna)* noble birth, wealth, power and their opposites, ie. to generalise good and bad luck *(Rhet.* 1389a1-2). Similarly, Boethius interpreted *Fortuna* as a possessor of material good things (*Phil. cons.* II.pr.ii, pr.v, p. 180-182, 198-206); see also St. Augustine, *De lib. arb.* I.xv, p. 254; Thierry of Chartres, *Com. s. de inv.* 135.59 (see notes 28 and 29).

See also Patch 1927, 63-65, 80; Cioffari 1935, *passim*; *idem* 1940; Kajanto 1960, *passim*.

37 Cioffari 1935, 24-32; *idem* 1940, 1-2; see for example Aristotle, *Rhetorica* 1360b19-30, 1368b24-37, 1389a1; *idem, Ethica Nicomachea* 1099a31-1099b8, 1112a32.

38 *Phil. cons.* II.pr.viii, p. 222-224.

miser saxum in altum revolvat. Tradunt iterum quod cujusdam jecur ibi vultur exedat...[39]

> Thus philosophers write that a woman attached to the wheel rotates on it forever. Now one's head rises to the height, now it sinks to bottom. This revolving wheel is the glory of this world which is rotated forever. The woman attached to the wheel is *Fortuna* intertwined into glory. Her head rises a while, and sinks a while, because most are first exalted to power and wealth and then hurled down to poverty and misery. Philosophers say also that one among the damned in the hell has spread the wheel with his rays and that the wheel rolls from the top of mountain down to valley floor without intermission and then rises again and repeatedly falls.
>
> Again and again the one rises on the wheel up to the mountain-top and then by the weight of the wheel is again hurled down from it. And then again the axle revolves one from misery to eminence. Those whose liver is gnawed by this vulture are to be deceived...

Honorius addresses his description as advice and a warning to those who want to beware of the wheel of *Fortuna* – and also to those who are gnawed by earthly lusts in the manner of a vulture and who cannot resist the temptation to throw themselves into the game of *Fortuna*.[40] However, Honorius deviates from the conventional representations of the High Middle Ages in that his *Fortuna* neither rotates the wheel nor stands on it, but is tied to the wheel and rotated with those rotated on the rim. Honorius clearly gives a monastic, almost Augustinian, interpretation of *Fortuna* which seems to ward off more secular clerical interpretations. As distinct from other descriptions such as Boethius or Alan of Lille, *Fortuna* is represented as a prisoner of her own wheel. She does not seem to have any independent power of herself but rather is also subordinated to the change of luck. As such, her power is an illusion. Probably Honorius would have agreed with Augustine that *Fortuna* can be used in ordinary speech as a name for unexpected events with unknown causes but it would be absurd to assume that such an independent agent as *Fortuna* could exist, or that any such fortuitiousness is needed to explain the universal order, as Augustine claimed in *De civitate Dei*.[41]

---

39   *Speculum Ecclesiae* III, PL 172, col. 1057.

40   Haec quia sapiens ratio composuit, debet scire vestris dilectio quid velint. Is qui in rotae vertigine de monte in ima praecipitatur, est is qui de altitudine potestatis vel divitiarum in profundum baratri praeceps rotatur. Qui autem saxum in montem evolvit, quod ipsum mox revolvit, est is qui eum magna difficultate dignitotes vel quaelibet cupita assequitur et per eadem ab ima inferni dimergitur. Cujus vero jexor vultur vescitur et tenuo reviviscere fertur, est is de cujus corde luxuria pascitur; et expleta concupiscentia, iterum foeda libido renascitur. In jecore enim est concupiscentia; vultur vero amat mortuorum cadavera. (*Speculum Ecclesiae* III, PL 172, col. 1057-1058).

    Honorius seems to allude to Sisyfos and Tityos who both appear originally in the IX song of *Odyseia* but are probaly familiar to Honorius *via* Ovid's *Metamorphoses* (IV.457, 460; X.43-44). I am indebted for this to Antti Ruotsala who pointed me the similarities between *Odysseia* and this passage.

41   *De civ. Dei* I.viii, IV.xvii, xxxiii, V.i, viii-x.

In the texts of the twelfth and thirteenth centuries *Fortuna* was not defined only in respect of divine providence. Her relation to nature became more and more essential – most often in relation to personified *Natura* which did not mean so much earthly reality perceived by the senses as the regularity and order governing natural processes.[42] It is from this idea that Bernard Silvester seems to derive the extreme notion of subjecting all seemingly irregular events to *Fortuna*:

> *Fortuna est temporalium eventus mutabilis; fortunarum autem dicitur pluraliter quia diversa genera sunt. Earum enim que temporaliter proveniunt, quedam proveniunt ex natura tantum, ut cum aqua in glaciem vertitur, quedam ex nobis tantum, ut cum auctorem nature aliqua culpa offendamus; quedam ex natura et nobis, ut cum baculum frangis. A natura enim aptitudo frangendi, a nobis vero actus. Rursus eorum que ex nobis sive solis, sive ex nobis et natura proveniunt, quedam consilio, quedam casu contingunt. Consilium quidem est alicuius faciendi vel non faciendi deliberatio. Casus vero inopinatus rei eventus, productus ex causis propter aliud inceptis, ut contingat aliquem in agro aurum deponere, ne inveniatur, et alium ibidem fodere, non ut aurum inveniat, sed ut agrum excolat. Tunc, si aurum inveniat, casus erit. Populum itaque fortunarum dicit homines casui se committentes nichilque consilio disponentes.*[43]

> *Fortuna* is a mutable event in time, but we speak of the properties of *Fortuna* (*fortunarum*) in the plural because there are diverse genres of them. There are those which come into existence temporally, those which come into existence wholly from nature, as water changing to ice, those which depend totally on us, as when we offend the author of nature with some sin. Some originate from us and from nature as a snapped stick. From nature comes the aptitude to snap, from us the act. Those again which come into being from us alone, or from us and nature happen either by consideration or by chance. Consideration (*consilium*) means that something is done or not done deliberately. But chance is an unexpected event caused by deeds done for some other purpose, as when someone hides gold in a field so it could not be found, and another digs it up, not to find the gold but to till the field. Then, if one finds gold, it is by chance. People call those men fortunate who prosper by chance and do not do things by deliberation.

In this passage, Bernard is faithful to Martianus Capella, whom he comments on. Martianus differentiated between *Fortuna* and the Fates *(Clotho, Lakhesis, Atropos)* acting as the scribes of Jove and, furthermore, between her and inevitable determined natural processes *(Heimarmene)*, leaving in the power of *Fortuna* the allotment of earthly success and prosperity as well as a part

---

42 On the notion of nature see Gregory 1966, 27-65; Delhaye 1966, 272-278; Sulowski 1966, 320-327; Wetherbee 1972, *passim*; Stock 1972, *passim*; Courtenay 1984a, 1-26.
43 *Comm. in Mart.* 8.600-615, p. 193.

of determined causality.[44] The significance of *Fortuna* as a force affecting the sublunar world was even further emphasized. It is significant that Bernard contrasted deliberate action particularly and its results with success caused by chance. These were not only separated because of the existence or lack of intention but also the results since a prudent and wise man pursues the purity of soul and its salvation, and is not interested in worldly success.[45] The definition of *Fortuna* as a label for all irregular mutability even in nature and not only an aspect of human intentional action is suprising, evidently underlining the connection of *Fortuna* with the mutable and unreliable essence of the terrestrial world.

The shared view of Martianus and Bernard is repeated by Alan of Lille (1116/7-1202/3), whose broad poetical work *Anticlaudianus* treats *Fortuna* certainly as a traditionally unreliable figure revolving men on earth from prosperity to adversity and back, but simultaneously as a servant of *Natura*, i.e. the universal order. Furthermore, one of the daughters of *Fortuna* is the indistutably positive force *Nobilitas*.[46] Thus for Alan, three aspects of *Fortuna* are combined: the changability of worldly success, the irregularity of natural events in the world, and a condition of good life.[47]

As a consequence of the supremacy of *Fortuna* and her two daughters, namely *Casus* (Chance) and *Sors* (Lot), and of the displacement of *Nobilitas*,[48] the natural order is disturbed and the sublunar world is degenerated by these forces representing randomness and disorder. The ideal order is replaced by a world turned upside down.[49] The effect of this is general misery. Alan's

---

44 Cioffari 1935, 67-69.
45 See also the anonymous *Moralium dogma philosophorum* I.B.1, p. 22.
46 *Anticl.* VII.397-400, VIII.63-64, p. 168-171, 174.

   Alan describes *Fortuna*'s ambiguous figure and her residence as followings: Hic est Fortune sua mansio, si tamen usquam / Res manet instabilis, residet uaga, mobilis heret, / Cuius tota quies lapsus, constancia motus, / Voluere, stare, situs discurrere, scandere casus, / Cui modus et racio racionis egere, fidesque / Non seruare fidem, pietas pietate carere. / Hec est inconstans, incerta, uolubilis, anceps, / Errans, instabilis, uaga, que, dum stare putatur, / Occidit et falso mentitur gaudia risu. / Aspera blandiciis, in lumine nubila, pauper / Et diues, mansueta, ferox, predulcis, amara, / Ridendo plorans, stando uaga, ceca uidendo, / In leuitate manens, in lapsu firma, fidelis / In falso, leuis in uero stabilisque mouendo, / Hoc firmum seruans quod numquam firma, fidele / Hoc solum retinens quod nesciat esse fidelis, / Hoc solo uerax quod semper falsa probetur, / Hoc solo stabilis quod semper mobilis erret, / Ambiguo uultu seducit forma uidentem. / Nam capitis pars anterior uestita capillis / Luxuriat, dum caluiciem pars altera luget. / Alter lasciuit oculus, dum profluit alter / In lacrimas; hic languet hebes dum fulgurat ille. *(Anticl.* VIII.13-35, p. 173-174.)

47 *Anticl.* VII-VIII. James J. Sheridan writes in his translation of Alan's *The Plaint of Nature*: "Nature is the principle of order in the sublunary world and when he speaks of Nature he has the world of the four elements in mind. ... Only the things in the sublunary world are subject to change, decay and death." (Sheridan 1980, 95.) According to Simo Knuuttila both Plato (in his *Timaeus*) and Aristotle (in the *Physics*) regarded change as an element without which there could not be such an ordered universe as ours. (Knuuttila 1993, 35.)

48 Post alias sua dona libens et leta dedisset / Filia Fortune, Casus cognata propinqui / Nobilitas, si quid proprium cecisset in eius / Sortem, quod posset Nature lege tueri. / Sed quia nulla potest, nisi que Fortuna ministrat, / Nil sine consilio Fortune perficit, immo / Matris adire locum disponit filia, gressum / Aggreditur superatque uie dispendia gressu. *(Anticl.* VII.397-404, p. 168-169).

49 *Anticl.* VII.405-480, p. 169-171.

description culminates in a battle between *Natura* and *Fortuna* in which the first wins. The order of nature is restored, *Fortuna* is returned to her original position subject to *Natura*, and the balance of the three daughters of *Fortuna* is re-established.[50] *Ratio*, reason as well as moderation, regular and proportionate relation between things, level out the extravagance of *Fortuna*.[51] The restoration of the ideal order also makes possible the creation of a new ideal man, for according to Alan exactly the same elements affect nature (macrocosm) as the human mind (microcosm).[52]

Alan of Lille's work was commented on quite soon after its composition. The commentators summed it up as a description of four artificers *(artifices)* which were *Deus, Natura, Fortuna* and *Culpa* (or *Vitium*). In some manuscripts of *Anticlaudianus* an anonymous summary appears, which is also included in the modern edition by R. Bossuat:

> *Quia in hoc opere agitur de quatuor artificibus, Deo, Natura, Fortuna et Vicio, primi autem dicitur artificis, id est Dei, quatuor sunt opera: opus in mente, opus in materia, opus in forma et opus in gubernatione; Nature uero [duo]; unum in pura natura consideratum, ab omni corruptione alienum, quale opus Nature fuit ante Ade peccatum, aliud uero uaria corruptione uiciatum, quale fuit post peccatum Ade; Fortune eciam duo: unum prosperitatis, alterum adversitatis; unum uero Vicii, scilicet deprauacionis. Liber iste in quo de hiis agitur non inconsequenter nouem distinctionibus completur: primo autem agitur in hoc opere tam de operibus Nature quam operibus Dei, quia per ea que facta sunt inuisibilia conspiciuntur Dei; secundo autem de opere diuino; tertio de opere Fortune; quarto de opere Vicii.[53]*

This work treats of four artificers God, Nature, Fortuna and Vice. The deeds of the first artificer, that is God, are four kinds: deed in mind, deed in matter, deed in form and deed in governing. But deeds of Nature are of two kinds some concern pure nature, which are alien to all corruption and which Nature did before the Fall of Adam, but the other deeds of Nature are corrupted by various vices - such are the deeds of Nature after the fall of Adam. The deeds of Fortuna are of two kinds: some lead to prosperity, the others to adversity. The deeds of Vice are of only one kind, that is depraved. This book which treats these facts completes them consistently with the following distinctions: firstly, the deeds of Nature are more discussed in this book than the deeds of God because by these (visibles) God's invisibles are perceived; secondly, it treats divine deeds; thirdly, it treats the deeds of Fortuna; fourthly, it treats the deeds of Vices.

---

50 *Anticl.* VIII.70-105, p. 175-176.
51 *Anticl.* VIII.140-146, p. 176-177.
52 This summary is based on books VII-IX of *Anticlaudianus*. On the analogy between nature and mind, see *Anticl.* VII.1-116, p. 157-160; on misery as a consequence of the reign of *Fortuna*, the victory of *Natura* and the birth of a New Man, see *Anticl.* VIII.171-369, IX, p. 177-198.
53 *Appendice in Anticl.*, p. 199.

The principal theme of the *Anticlaudianus* is to represent a reversion to the prelapsarian ideal state where a yet uncorrupted order of nature prevailed. The section describing the reign of *Fortuna* then, in principle, represents the postlapsarian state of the sublunar world. Further, the passage is reminiscent of Boethian view of the constitution of the world. In a commentary on Boethius' *Philosophiae consolatio* an anonymous author states that every work is either the work of God, the work of nature, or the work of an artificer *(artifex)* imitating nature.[54] Alan's commentator has completed his theory with *Fortuna* and vices – the first can be seen as a Boethian extension, and the latter seems to point to the theodicy of St. Augustine in which evil is interpreted as a consequence of human free will and sinful deeds.

The same anonymous commentator explains under which branch of philosophy Alan's work belongs to and how one should read it:

> *Ex hiis liquet que sit materia huius auctoris in hoc opere. Est tamen materia duplex, una historialis, alia mistica, quod satis diligenti liquet lectori, et quia circa materiam uersatur intentio, per materiam intentionis comparatur noticia. Liber uero nulli parti uel speciei philosophie tenetur obnoxius, nunc ethicam tangens, nunc phisicam delibans, nunc in mathematice subtilitatem ascendens, nunc theologie profundum agrediens.[55]*

> On this basis it is clear what the author's matter *(materia)* in this work is. Indeed, the matter is double: on the one hand, it is historical, on the other, it is mystical, which is perceived by a sufficiently diligent reader. From the matter, we turn to intention, and compare the intended message with the matter. The book does not belong to any part of philosophy alone, but it now touches upon ethics, now it savours physics, now it ascends among the subtilities of mathematics, and now it agreeds with the depths of theology.

Alan's poem deals with all branches of knowledge (or philosophy), and is simultaneously readable literally (or historically) and mystically, i.e. the "surface" of the poem contains a narrative true in itself, and, on the other hand, beneath it there is hidden a deeper meaning.[56] Although, Alan's work

---

54 Omne enim opus aut est opus Dei aut opus naturae aut artificis imitantis naturam. *(Saeculi noni auctoris in Boetii Consolationem Philosophiae commentarius* III.7-8, p. 157; now ascribed to the twelfth century, see Stock 1972, 90-92, also note 46, p. 90).

55 *Appendice in Anticl,*, p. 201.

56 Another commentator on Alan, namely Ralph of Longchamp, argues that the work touches upon all branches of philosophy. He sees its usefulness in adding a self-knowledge. Ralph gives no opinion as to whether the work should be understood literally or mystically (or allegorically): Utilitas sive finalis causa est illud coeleste proverbium "nothis elittos" id est "cognoscere teipsum". Est enim maximum et perutile suae originis habere cognitionem. Hanc enim utilitatem consequitur lector in hoc opere ut sciat, quis ex Deo habeat, quid ex natura contrahat, quid a fortuna recipiat, in quo ei vitium detrahat.

Nulli parti philosophiae specialiter liber iste tenetur obnoxius, immo per omnes philosophiae partes evagatur: quandoque enim ethicam tangit tractando de moribus et morum informationibus; nunc naturam sive physicam agendo de naturalibus; nunc mathematicam subtilitatem attingit; nunc theologiae subtilitatem ascendit; unde patet quod omnes partes

is obviously an allegory, that is to say, the commentator has probably meant by his claim of twofold meaning that the allegorical meaning is conspicious and understandable as such. At the same time, the more learned reader was able to find under the conspicious and understandable allegory a hidden mystical sense, i.e. Alan's poem was a double allegory.[57]

When read in parallel with Bernard Silvester and Otto of Freising the historical sense can be understood as a representation of the "mutability of events" *(mutabilitas eventuum)* in the sublunar world. The reign of *Fortuna*, the world turned upside down and the corrupted order of nature signify all the sublunar world awaiting the second coming of Christ.[58]

By early thirteenth-century Ralph of Longchamp (ca. 1150-1220) wrote a thorough commentary on first four books of Alan's *Anticlaudianus*.[59] He repeats the interpretation given in the anonymous writer's summary but treats the action of the four artificers from a different point of view:

> *Materia huius libri sunt quattuor artifices et quattuor artificium opera. Est enim artifex Deus, artifex natura, artifex fortuna, artifex culpa.*
>
> *Deus autem specialiter dicitur artifex eorum, quae facit de nihilo, ut sunt spiritus et animae; unde Deus dicitur proprie creare et eius operatio dicitur creatio.*
>
> *Natura autem proprie dicitur artifex eorum, quae sunt ex praeiacente materia, quia natura est potentia naturaliter rebus sive causis inferioribus insita, similia ex similibus procreans, ut hominem de homine, bovem de bove. Unde dicitur procreare, quasi procul creare, id est aliunde creare, scilicet ex praeiacente materia.*
>
> *Fortuna sive casus, quia pro eodem hic accipitur, est artifex eorum, quae casualiter fiunt vel eveniunt, ut si rusticus fodiens agrum inveniat thesaurum. Est autem fortuna sive casus inopinatus rei eventus ex causis confluentibus, uti patet in praemisso exemplo. Inventio enim thesauri est inopinatus rei eventus. Causae confluentes sunt ea, quae ad hoc concurrunt, ut accessus rustici ad thesaurum, terrae fossio et similia. Huius artificis opera sunt libertas, servitus, divitiae, adversitas, prosperitas.*
>
> *Artifex culpa malus artifex est, cuius opera sunt diversa vitiorum genera.*[60]

---

philosophie gustat et deliberat. *(In Anticl. Al. comm.* I.i, p. 20.)

57 Cf. Ochsenbein 1975; Meier 1977.

58 Alan of Lille also composed another remarkable allegorical poetical work *De planctu Naturae* (1160/65) which is a complaint put in the mouth of *Natura* about the state of this world where language and sexuality are analogically perverted. In the world different *idolatriae* (for example *Bacchilatria* and *Nummilatria*) are flourishing. When Alan speaks of the order of nature, he is ultimately speaking of moral order. See also Wetherbee 1972; Sheridan 1980, 1-66.

59 The commentary discusses Alan's work's prologue, books I-III and the beginning of the fourth book. It is dedicated to the bishop of Narbonne, and it was probably composed around 1212/14. The commentary may be linked with the ecclesiastical power-struggle against the heretical Cathars in Languedoc (Sulowski 1972, I-XXXIV).

60 *In Anticl. Al. comm.* I.i, p. 19-20.

The matter of these books is four artificers and their works. The artificers are God, nature, *Fortuna* and sin.

God is especially said to be an artificer of those which are made of nothing, as the spirits and souls. For this reason God is said to create in the proper sense and his work is called creation.

Nature, then, is said properly to be an artificer of those which are made from pre-existent matter because nature is a power which naturally combines lower things or causes and procreates similar from similars, as human from human or bovine from bovine. For this reason it is said to procreate *(procreare)*, to create proximately *(procul creare)*, that is, to create from something else as it creates from pre-existent matter.

Fortuna or chance (because here these two are the same) is the artificer of those who come into being or happen randomly as when a rustic tilling his field finds a treasure. So *Fortuna* or chance is an unexpected event which is a consequence of confluent causes as one can see from the preceding example. The discovery of treasure is an unexpected event. The confluent causes are those, which concur with each other here, such as the access of rustic to treasure, tilling of land and similar things. The works of this artificer are freedom, slavery, wealth, adversity and prosperity.

Sin is the artificer of evil, and its works are diverse genres of vices.

For Ralph of Longchamp, unlike the anonymous summarizer, it was important to draw a distinction between God's creation from nothing *(creare)* and procreation or generation in nature *(procreare)*. Furthermore, he does not seem to be interested in differentiating the works of nature before and after the fall of Adam.

Ralph also gives a more profound account of *Fortuna*, defining her with the help of the traditional example of a peasant finding a treasure. Likewise, his definition differs from Bernard Silvester's and lists for *Fortuna* only acts which result from meaningful to human action such as freedom, slavery, wealth, adversity and prosperity - not irregular changes in nature. Later on he reverts to *Fortuna*:

> *Fortuna proprie dicitur status vitae quem quis adipiscitur vel ex arbitrio vel ex casu temporis vel ex hominum institutione. ... Sub fortuna enim comprehenditur libertas, servitus, nobilitas, ignobilitas, paupertas, divitiae, bonos filios vel non bonos habere. ... Qualitas etiam mortis apprehenditur sub fortuna. ... Ideo in versibus superioribus dicitur, quod: Fortuna vultus praetendit dubios, vel hoc ideo dicitur, quod fortuna mutabilis est et dubia; vel propter imaginem ipsius Fortunae, quae erat Romae ex una parte calva et oculosa, ex altera parte capillata at caeca.*[61]

> *Fortuna* is properly called a position *(status)* in life, which is achieved either by will, by temporal chance or by human institutions. ... Under *Fortuna* is comprehended freedom, slavery, nobility, ignobility,

---

61   *In Anticl. Al. comm.* V.lxiii, p. 166.

poverty, wealth and having either good or bad sons. ... The quality of death is apprehended under *Fortuna*. ... That is why following verses say that *Fortuna* presents her dubious face; or it is said that *Fortuna* is mutable and doubtful; or according to the image of *Fortuna* herself which was in Rome, it is said that one side of her head was bald and seeing, and other was hairy and blind.

Ralph is quite clear in his statement that *Fortuna* is central in deciding the human position in the mundane life. He distinguishes between *Fortuna* and chance, which is quite contrary to his earlier definition:

> *Differat autem casus a fortuna, quia casus est inopinatus rei eventus ex causis confluentibus, fortuna vero proprie dicitur conditio corporis cuiusque, id est status vitae, ut iam diximus, quem quis adipiscitur vel ex arbitrio vel ex casu temporis vel ex hominum institutione.*[62]

> But chance is different from *Fortuna* because chance is an unexpected event occurring through confluent causes. But someone's corporal condition is called *Fortuna* proper, that is, position or state in life, and as we already said, it is achieved either by will, by temporal chance or by human institutions.

Here Ralph seems to have borrowed his definition from Thierry of Chartres. *Fortuna* becomes an almost intentional force influencing human position and earthly success alone. Position is achieved either by individual pursuit (will), by "social" causes (human institutions) or by temporal chance. *Fortuna* is still connected with chance despite the fact that they are not equivalents – together they cover the field of events not directly caused by either divine providence or natural order. From the Christian point of view the difference between *Fortuna* and chance is however irrelevant because both were aspects of wordly matters in any case. Free will operated between the necessity and *Fortuna*: its function was to make the moral choice of whether to pursue earthly success, i.e. join in the game of *Fortuna*, or to seek a place in heaven in the afterlife. The pursuit of worldly success was by definition irrational because people were ultimately unable to decide their success: the nature of human action in the world being ironic, that is, its results never met the goals of the agent – and were often the contrary.[63] A narrative about the sublunar world, i.e. history, was either a satire or tragedy which taught one to beware of worldly achievement, and urged taking care of the soul's salvation. As Ralph of Longchamp asserted – under *Fortuna* one apprehends the quality of death, that is, the ephemeral nature of flesh and spiritual steadiness.[64] Nevertheless, *Fortuna*'s field was now broader than mere randomness,

---

62 *In Anticl. Al. comm.* V.lxiii, p. 166.
63 In this respect Thierry of Chartres seems to offer a radical theory which offers some possibility of intentionally pursuiting earthly prosperity (even if, for him too, worldly prosperity is ultimately vanity). See above p. 81-82 and notes 28 and 29.
64 *In Anticl. Al. comm.* V.lxiii, p. 166.

including all human action for mundane purposes – sublunar history, whether it was a consequence of chance, individual human intentions or collective decisions, i.e. human institutions, was in the realm of *Fortuna*.

Fortuna, the *Carmina Burana* and the sublunar world

Fortuna in the *Carmina Burana*

On the first folio of the manuscript of the *Carmina Burana* is a miniature which represents the wheel of fortune and four human figures on its rim. Inside the rim is the goddess *Fortuna* herself, face turned to the spectator with four opened book scrolls. Each human figure has a caption: on the left by the side of the upward moving figure is written *regnabo*, I shall govern; on the top by the side of the crowned figure, *regno*, I am governing; on the right downward moving figure with the falling crown, *regnavi*, I have governed; and, by the side of the figure beneath the wheel, *sum sine regno*, I have nothing to govern.[65] The figures can be interpreted as four kings whirled around by *Fortuna*.

In a commentary on Martianus Capella, written in the early twelfth century, there is a corresponding verbal description:

> *Notandum est fortunam quatuor status habere: superius, inferius, ascensum, et descensum. Ideoque eam rotam et figurant scriptores et pingunt pictores. Est enim in rota quoque superius, inferius, ascensus, descensus. Ei autem rote solent quatuor viri ascribi, quorum qui superius tenet, rosis et violis stipatus dicit: "Glorior elatus." Secundus autem, a capite deorsum deiectus pedibus superpositis, dicit: "Descendo minorificatus." Tercius autem deorsum depressus: "Infimus axe teror." Quartus autem a capite sursum erecto brachiis alta petentibus: "Rursus ad alta feror." Superius itaque in has rota prosperitas, inferius adversitas; motus de adversitate in prosperitatem <ascensus>; descensus deiectio de prosperitate in adversitatem. Hos ergo quatuor status hic notat philosophus. Tractum enim dicit ascensum qui ad alta trahit. Set quia et descensus - cum ad ima trahat - tractus poterat intellegi, subiungitur; <eminentis> scilicet sursum ferentis.*[66]

One should note that *Fortuna* has four states: superior, inferior, ascending and descending. Thus is her wheel depicted by writers and painted by illustrators. Similarly, the wheel has four positions: superior, inferior, ascending and descending. On this wheel four men should be depicted. On the top is the one decorated with roses and violets and

---

65   CB facs. fol. 1; CB I.1. 18a, 37. The captions of the figures are probably an addition made at the turn of 13th and 14th centuries (Schumann 1930/1961, 55*; Bischoff 1970a, 19-25). See the picture on page 95 and the cover of this book.
66   Bernard Silvester, *Comm. in Mart.* 8.772-787, p. 198-199.

he says: "I am elevated to glory". The second one, heading down with feet in the air says: "And I am descending humiliated". The third one, inferior, depressed says: "I am ground on the bottom". But the fourth one, heading upwards with arms in the air, says: "I am being brought back to the top". The superior position of the wheel means prosperity, the inferior position adversity; the ascending position means movement from adversity to prosperity and descending means the fall from prosperity to adversity. The philosopher notes these four states. He calls pulling the ascending position which pulls upwards, but because the descending position - the one which pulls towards the bottom - can also be understood as pulling, the top and ascending positions are connected to descending and bottom positions.

This description, attributed to Bernard Silvester, is not identical with the miniature in the *Carmina Burana* but it gives us an interpretation of its meanings and relates it to contemporary learned discourse.

The basic idea in the miniature and Bernard Silvester's description is the mutability of earthly luck. Bernard does not specify the position of *Fortuna* herself in various representations, saying only that the wheel of *Fortuna* has four positions, i.e. superior, inferior, ascending and descending. The miniature in the *Carmina Burana* is not much clearer: a crowned feminine figure in the center of the wheel obviously represents *Fortuna*. However, she is not actively rotating the wheel but she sits in the frontal position holding open book scrolls in her hands. The figures on the top and descending position have much the same epithets as *Fortuna*: both their crowns and robes are similar. On the contrary, the bottom figure and the ascending one are depicted without crown and robe, clothed only in a white tunic.

Medieval *Fortuna* represented the mutability of the sublunar world and fickleness of worldly prosperity and she can be understood as an overall integument *(integumentum)* representing the nature of the sublunar world generally.[67] On the other hand, *Fortuna* was connected distinctively with the moral character of human decisions to the extent that the choices based on *liberum arbitrium* (free will or choice) were made in a gap left between divine providence and uncontrollable capricious terrestrial chance, i.e. *Fortuna*. As such, *Fortuna* is an essential element in all discourse concerning the sublunar world and human action there. If the *Carmina Burana* can be defined as the poetry of the ancients, as moral discourse concerning terrestrial affairs, then the group of *Fortuna* poems can be interpreted as a one of its key groups.

The *Fortuna* poems in the *Carmina Burana* form the sixth group in the manuscript. *Fortuna* is an explicit subject in *rhythmi O varium Fortune lubricum* (CB 14), *Fortune plango vulnera* (CB 16), *O Fortuna, velut luna* (CB 17) and in *versus Fortuna levis* (CB 18). *Celum non animum* (CB 15)

---

67 For example in the work of Bernard Silvester quoted above the *integumenta* are, like *Fortuna*, most often individual allegorical figures or metaphors for which Bernard gives a figurative sense (Westra 1986, 23-33, cf. ibid. *index of integumenta*, 269-279, on *Fortuna*: 272).

Fortuna *and her*
wheel from the
Carmina Burana.
Figure is taken from
Schmeller 1847, p. 1.
In colours as in the
manuscript clm.
4660, see the cover
of this book.

is an exception dealing with mutability and the virtue of *constantia*.[68] The goddess *Fortuna* and her epithets also appear elsewhere in the collection. When the corruption of the clergy, especially simony, selling and buying ecclesiastical office, is vituperated, the fickleness of *Fortuna* is also mentioned.[69] In a love-poem discussing of youth (and its transient nature) *Fortuna* appears as a supplier of the lover's attractions, handsomeness and good behaviour.[70] And, of course, when gambling is discussed, *Decius*, a personification of the dice, carries "the shield of *Fortuna*" and is "the messenger of *Fortuna*".[71] In other gambling poems in which *Decius* or *sors* (i.e. lot) appears, *Fortuna* can be assumed to be a power behind the scenes.[72] The old classical epithet of the goddess *Fortuna*, cornucopia, shows itself separately in the last *rhytmus* of the manuscript just before the two religious plays – the poem is a complaint over degradation of the times *(Zeitklage)* and corruption in manners.[73] A structural allusion, in identical rhythmic metre, links CB 17 *(O Fortuna velut luna)* to CB 24 *(Iste mundus furibundus)*, which deals with the unreliability and transitory nature of "this world", i.e. "the way of all flesh" *(lex carnalis)*.[74]

All in all, the *Carmina Burana*'s *Fortuna* is a capricious, fickle and fraudulent force which for a moment takes one into her favour just to deny everything arbitrarily at the next moment. This unreliability is even more obvious with the praise of virtue of *constantia*, persistent activity in pursuit of undeviating steadiness in CB 15. However, *Fortuna*'s call to join her game and the pursuit of her favours is represented as almost irresistible. Christian views are to be found in the fundamental interpretation of the sublunar world and in some allusions; for example, in the first stanza of CB 14 when the overwhelming power of *Fortuna* is described in words close to those of Samuel (I. Sam. 2:6-8): *de stercore / pauperem erigens*. The same allusion appears also in CB 11 when the subject is personified Money *(Nummus)*.[75]

---

68 In the *Fortuna* group CB 16 and 17 are known only from *Carmina Burana*. The others appear partly or entirely in other mansucripts. (CB I.1, 31-37; Walsh 1976, 140; Parlett 1986/1988, 204-205.)

69 In diebus iuventutis / timent annos senectutis, / ne fortuna destitutis / desit eis splendor cutis. (CB 8.6.1-4; CB I.1, 11.)

70 Cum Fortuna voluit me vivere beatum, / forma, bonis moribus fecit bene gratum / et in altis sedibus sedere laureatum. (CB 93a.1; CB I.2, 121.)

71 Terminum nullum teneat nostra contio, / bibat funditus confisa Decio. / nam ferre scimus eum / Fortune clipeum. (CB 195.1^c; CB I.3, 31.)
     Qui perdit pallium, / scit esse Decium / Fortune nuntium / sibi non prospere, / dum ludit temere / gratis volens bibere. (CB 195.2^a; CB I.3, 32.)

72 *Sors*, a lottery ticket, (human) lot or destiny, was an epithet directly connected with *Fortuna* both in *Carmina Burana* (CB 14.2.12 and 4.14, CB 17.2.1 and 3.1, CB 18.IV) and outside it (Patch 1927, 80-81). *Decius*, a dice or the "god" of the game, is connected with *Fortuna* indirectly through gambling, and within its range, as a surrender to the mercy of chance (for example CB 17 discusses gambling).

73 CB 226.3.3; CB I.3, 85; about the cornucopiae and *Fortuna*: Patch 1927, 120-121.

74 CB I.1, 35-36, 44; Hilka & Schumann 1930/1961, 28-29, 37-38; Parlett 1986/1988, 205-207.

75 Erigit ad plenum de stercore Nummus egenum. (CB 11.9; CB I.1, 15.)
     Dominus mortificat et vivificat, deducit ad inferos et reducit. Dominus pauperem facit et ditat; humiliat et sublevat. *Suscitat de pulvere egenum, et de stercore pauperem*, ut sedeat cum principibus et solium gloriae teneat. (I. Sam. 2:6-8.)

The power of God omnipotent is equated in these poems with the power of *Fortuna* and *Nummus* on the earth if as divine providence were powerless in the sublunar world. Evidently the *Fortuna* poems and miniature are connected with the widespread *contemptus mundi* literature, although their tonality is more moderate and affirmative towards this world than stricter monastic texts.[76]

Chance and history

The first poem among the *Fortuna* poems of *Carmina Burana O varium Fortune lubricum* (CB 14) treats *Fortuna* as an historical force and the victims of her fickleness are the past heroes, cities and nations:

> *1. O varium / Fortune lubricum, / dans dubium / tribunal iudicum, / non modicum / paras huic premium, / quem colere / tua vult gratia / et petere / rote sublimia, / dans dubia / tamen, prepostere / de stercore / pauperem erigens, / de rhetore / consulem eligens.*
> *2. Edificat / Fortuna, diruit; / nunc abdicat, / quos prius coluit; / quos noluit, / iterum vendicat / hec opera / sibi contraria, / dans munera / nimis labilia; / mobilia / sunt Sortis federa, / que debiles / ditans nobilitat / et nobiles / premens debilitat.*
> *4. Subsidio / Fortune labilis / cur prelio / Troia tunc nobilis, / nunc flebilis / ruit incendio? / quis sanguinis / Romani gratiam, / quis nominis / Greci facundiam, / quis gloriam / fregit Carthaginis? / Sors lubrica, / que dedit, abstulit; / hec unica / que fovit, perculit.*
> *3. Quid Dario / regnasse profuit? / Pompeïo / quid Roma tribuit? / succubuit / uterque gladio. / eligere / media tutius / quam petere / rote sublimius / et gravius / a summo ruere: / fit gravior / lapsus a prosperis / et durior / ab ipsis asperis.*[77]

1. O Fortuna's various and slippery court of justice, you give dubious and undue prizes even for he who wants to cultivate your grace and obtain the heights of your wheel. But you give only dubious gifts and preposterously raise up the poor out of the dust and choose a rhetor as consul.
2. Fortuna builds up and destroys. Now she abandons those she nurtured before. To those whom she does not accept, she offers misfortunes and gives extremily labile presents. The promises of

---

76 Cf. Bultot 1969, 815-827.
77 CB I.1, 31-32.
   I have restored the order of stanzas as it was in the manuscript (i.e. I have changed the order of the third and fourth stanzas), but, however, I have retained the numbers of the modern edition. The version edited by Hilka and Schumann is a collage of several different sources. It also includes one extra stanza (see the next note).
   Nevertheless, I shall analyse the version from the manuscript of the *Carmina Burana* because my aim is not to present an inquiry as to the "correct" versions (or those believed to be correct) but, specifically, a scrutiny of the text of the *Carmina Burana* which was compiled around 1225/30. The poem is anonymous and according to Hilka and Schumann it is composed sometime around the turn of the twelfth and thirteenth centuries (1930/1961, 25).

Chance *(Sors)* are mobile - the worthless are ennobled with riches, the nobles are put down and subdued.
4. What was the use of the subsidies of labile *Fortuna* in the battle when noble Troy was miserably ruined by fire? Who drowned in blood the grace of the Romans? Who made the name of Greek oratory disappear? Who broke down the glory of Carthage? Slippery Chance *(Sors)* took away all it had given and rejected everyone it had favoured.
3. What was the profit of Darius from his reign? What were the tributes of Rome for Pompeius? Both of them succumbed to the sword. It is better to choose lasting protection than obtain the heights of the wheel and then be dashed down: it is always more grave to fall from prosperity back to asperities.

The poem gives a conventional description of *Fortuna*. However, *Fortuna* is exceptionally compared to a court of justice *(tribunal iudicium)* whose sentences are random and arbitrary. She raises up the poor out of the dust and chooses a mere rhetor as consul; she builds up and destroys; she rewards the worthless *(debiles)* and punishes the noble *(nobiles)*. She did not save Troy from flames nor Rome from a bloodbath. All the potentates of history were destroyed by her – who indeed could seriously put his faith in such an untrustworthy force?[78]

The mode of CB 14 is an *exemplum*: it represents a cautionary tale about the true nature of *Fortuna* without any reflection on the relation between *Fortuna* and divine providence or *Fortuna* and the randomness in the sublunar world. While it typically uses more or less explicit allusions to classical pagan literature, Christian authors and the *Bible*, it also employs thematic complexes which act as its interior triggers of intertextual exemplary chains.

Various and slippery *Fortuna (varium Fortune lubricum)* is an allusion to the fifth poem in the first book of Boethius' *Philosophiae consolatio*, in which the first person narrator speaks to the Creator of the universe and complains that God takes care of the proper order of everything else but the sublunar lot of an individual human - what else one could think when one's fortune is slippery and the innocent endure pains and evil ones prosper and get unjust rewards? Virtue is hidden in darkness and virtuous and just men are calumniated.[79] The whole of the first book of Boethius's work is a complaint

---

78 The modern editors of the *Carmina Burana* have added the fifth stanza, which originates from a manuscript from Bodleian library by Oxford (CB I.1, X, 31-32). The stanza praises glory as the sweetest of the gifts of *Fortuna*, if it would only last. But it disappears as fast as a flower-meadow withers following the annual seasons. While otherwise remaining on the general level (although it speaks directly to *Fortuna*), the fifth stanza adds a *persona* who refuses to present an inappropriate song (perhaps praising the glorious gifts of *Fortuna*?) and warns about her "slippery presents" by quoting the words of the first stanza:

   Nil gratius / Fortune gratia, / nil dulcius / est inter dulcia / quam gloria, / si staret longius. / sed labitur / ut olus marcidum / et sequitur / agrum nunc floridum, / quem aridum / cras cernes. igitur / improprium / non edo canticum: / o varium / Fortune lubricum. (CB I.1, 31-32.)

79 Nam cur tantas lubrica versat / Fortuna vices ? Premit insontes / Debita sceleri noxia poena, / At perversi resident celso / Mores solio sanctaque calcant / Iniusta vice colla nocentes. / Latet obscuris condita virtus / Clara tenebris iustusque tulit / Crimen iniqui. *(Phil. cons.*

against the injustice of human earthly destiny. The *persona* demands from Lady Philosophy an explanation of the injustice of the world. If God is good and omnipotent why does he allow the good to suffer and the evil prosper? Why does a force regulating the order of nature so perfectly seem to leave humans to the mercy of *Fortuna*?

Fortuna in CB 14 is not only identified with the arbitrary and cruel *Fortuna* governing the sublunar world in the first parts of Boethius' work but the description in the first stanza with its comparisons with court of justice also provides an image of imbalance of justice and injustice, virtue and vice on earth where evil does not seem to get its just punishment. The last four verses of the first stanza strengthen the representation of *Fortuna* with an emphatic description of her power which is in itself a combination of a biblical source and an allusion to Juvenal: *de stercore / pauperem erigens, / de rhetore / consulem eligens.*[80]

Fortuna's power to raise up the poor out of the dust is compared to God omnipotent in the first book of Samuel where God gives and takes away human life and maintains the world:

> *Dominus mortificat et vivificat, deducit ad inferos et reducit. Dominus pauperem facit et ditat; humiliat et sublevat. Suscitat de pulvere egenum et de stercore elevat pauperem, ut sedeat cum principibus et solium gloriae teneat. Domini enim sunt cardines terrae, et posuit super eos orbem.*

> The Lord killeth, and maketh alive: he bringeth down to the grave, and bringeth up. The lord maketh poor, and maketh rich: he bringeth low, and lifteth up. *He raiseth up the poor out of the dust, and lifteth up the beggar from the dunghill,* to set them among princes, and to make them inherit the throne of glory: for the pillars of the earth are the Lord's, and he hath set the world upon them. (I quote the Authorized version of the English Bible thoughout)[81]

Both in Samuel and in Boethius God is responsible for maintaining the universe and order but in the poem's sublunar world of human action *Fortuna* has taken the place of divine providence who used to take care of everything and everyone. It is this view which CB 14 shares with the *persona* in the beginning of *Philosophiae consolatio*. *Fortuna* not only seems to be arbitrary and despotic but is easily interpreted as a perverted force contrary to providence. Through the figure of *Fortuna* the perpetually changing sublunar world is contrasted to the eternally stable world beyond. The inverted state of things is underlain by a quotation from the textual authority, i.e. the *Bible*,

---

I.vers.28-36, p. 160.)

80   CB 14.1.13-16 (CB I.1, 31).

81   I. Sam. 2:6-8.
      The verse does not allude to Samuel alone, but among others to a hymn for Maria presented by Luke: Deposuit potentes de sede et exaltavit humiles. Esurientes implevit bonis, et divites dimisit inanes. (Lk. 1.52-53.)

in an unholy nexus of *Fortuna* and *Nummus* (Money).[82]

A mere rhetor is made a consul in the seventh satire of Juvenal (ca. 60-100 AD.) which complains of the uselessness of learning when one fights for worldly prosperity and success:

> *Si Fortuna volet, fies de rhetore consul; / si volet haec eadem, fiet de consule rhetor.*

> If Fortune so choose, you will become a Consul from being a rhetor; if again she so wills, you will become a rhetor from being a Consul. (Tr. by Ramsay)[83]

Success is brought by *Fortuna*, not by one's own ability and merits. The theme of *Fortuna* sharing her favours was naturally very popular as such. But from the viewpoint of learned clerics the allusion to Juvenal added to this general theme the essential specification that among other things, great learning did not guarantee good fortune. This was an ambivalent, although understandable, statement when compared to the social reality of the time in that twelfth and thirteenth century clerics were benefitting from the new social mobility but, at the same time, the competition was fiercer than before and the alternation of success and adversity was more acute (especially compared to closed monastic life).

In the final chapter of *Architrenius* of John of Hauvilla, a counterpart to the *Fortuna* of CB 14 appears, i.e. "chance makes bishops and *Fortuna* shares offices": *casus agens mitras, tribuens Fortuna curules.*[84] This parallels *Nummus* (Money) presented a little bit earlier in the *Carmina Burana* (CB 11). He is, like *Fortuna*, a seemingly omnipotent force in the sublunar world: *In terra summus rex est hoc tempore Nummus.*[85] Kings and popes are in its power, it governs monasteries and ecclesiastical councils, it fights wars and causes quarrels. Slightly different versions of the same poem are known from several sources. Some of them include a verse missing from the manuscript of the *Carmina Burana* but which is added to its modern edition: *Erigit ad plenum de stercore Nummus egenum.*[86] Money and *Fortuna* are identified with each other with the intermediation of the book of Samuel and both seem to be equated with God. They are both apparently independent forces

---

82 I will analyse such ironic intertextuality more closely in the context of the *Carmina Burana*'s money satires and especially the gospel parody in part III.

83 Juv., *Sat.* VII, 197-198. The strophes were also quoted by John of Salisbury in his *Policraticus* (I.3.viii, p. 192; I.5.iv, p. 293).

84 *Architrenius* IX.25.452-462, ed. Schmidt 1974, p. 284; *idem*, ed. Wetherbee 1994, p. 250.

85 CB I.1, 15-29.

86 CB 11.9 (CB I.1, 15, 22).
    The same allusion appears twice later: first, in a long satire *Propter Sion non tacebo* (CB 41) on the vice of the Roman curia, in verses 25.4-6: intrat saccus ere plenus, / pauper autem et egenus / tollitur a ianuis. (CB I.1, 67). Secondly, it appears in *Heu voce flebili cogor enarrare* (CB 50) which is a complaint on the loss of the Holy Land - verses 2.3-4 run as follows: quo respexit Dominus mundum sorde pleno / erigens de pulvere, pauperem a ceno. (CB I.1, 99.)

influencing the terrestrial lot of man, who have in their power not only the success of individuals but generally all events connected with human action in the sublunar world.

The second stanza of CB 14 continues the description of power and *Fortuna*'s ways of action: she builds up and destroys, she abandons her recent favourite and punishes him with adversities. *Fortuna* and *Sors*, one's lot or "destiny", are the one and same. The third stanza in the manuscript (the fourth in Hilka and Schumann) moves from general characteristics to examples *(exempla)* such as what was the fate of Troy, Rome, Greece, and Carthage?

In the poem, history provides as examples the histories of antiquity taken from various sources, functioning as moral picture-book. Moral and historical examples, *exempla*, not only strengthen the central theme of the poem but simultaneously enlarge its basic statement. *Fortuna* not only tried individuals but also communities, nations and kingdoms. The whims of *Fortuna* were a principal element in sublunar human history.[87]

On the other hand, the examination of the caprices of *Fortuna* taught trust in the true God as well as patience, serenity of mind and its correct control as Otto of Freising (1114/5-1158) wrote in a dedication to emperor Frederick Barbarossa in his world history *Chronica sive Historia de duabus civitatibus*:

> *Honesta ergo erit et utilis excellentiae vestrae historiarum cognitio, qua et virorum fortium gesta Deique regna mutantis et cui voluerit dantis rerumque mutationem patientis virtutem ac potentiam considerando sub eius metu semper degatis ac prospere procedendo per multa temporum curricula regnetis.*[88]

> Knowing history, which represents both the deeds of brave men and God and mutations of kingdoms, is an honest and useful pursuit for Your Excellence. In the mutation of things, it gives you the virtue of patience and power of consideration whose measure will help you always to live and prosper and proceed reigning through the course of different times.

In Otto's prologue, the historical course of events and *Fortuna*'s mutability and instability are implicitly related. Otto announces that he is guiding his reader through the change of times and ambivalent states and, further, to their various and unusual origins.[89] Change, characteristic of the temporal world,

---

87 Cf. the description of the caprices of *Fortuna* by Alan of Lille: Summa rote dum Cressus habet, tenet infima Codrus; / Julius ascendit, descendit Magnus et infra / Silla iacet; surgit Marius, sed cardine uerso / Silla redit, Marius premitur; sic cuncta uicissim / Turbo rapit uariatque uices Fortuna uolutans. *(Anticl.* VIII.58-62, p. 174.) The examples of Alan are the same that were associated with tragedies as exemplificatory stories of human history leading from prosperity to adversity and being as such representation on the whims of *Fortuna* (Kelly 1993, 76-92, also 27, 32-34, 49, 55, 69f., 101).

88 *Chronica*, in the dedication to Frederick Barbarossa, p. 4.

89 Sepe multumque volvendo mecum de rerum temporalium motu ancipitique statu, vario ac inordinato proventu, sicut eis inherendum a sapiente minime considero, sic ab eis transeundum ac migrandum intuitu rationis invenio. *(Chronica* I. prol., 10.)
   Cf. "Birth" or "Coming into existence" *(proventus).* Birth is temporal and creation

is analogical with the conventional epithets for *Fortuna* (naturally, when *Fortuna* is a personification of change and mutability). However, Otto explicitly follows the tradition of Saint Augustine and his *De civitate Dei*:

> *Sapientis enim est officium non more volubilis rotae rotari, sed in virtutum constantia ad quadrati corporis modum firmari. Proinde quia temporum mutabilitas stare non potest, ab ea migrare, ut dixi, sapientem ad stantem et permanentem eternitatis civitatem debere quis sani capitis negabit? Haec est civitas Dei Hierusalem caelestis, ad quam suspirant in peregrinatione positi filii Dei confusione temporalium tamquam Babylonica captivitate gravati. Cum enim duae sint civitates, una temporalis, alia eterna, una mundialis, alia caelestis, una diaboli, alia Christi, Babyloniam hanc, Hierusalem illam esse katholici prodire scriptores.*[90]

> The task of wise man is not to rotate like a whirling wheel but to be firm with constant virtues in the mode of the quadrate corpus. Who with a sane head would deny that temporal changes will not last, and that one must wisely avoid them, as I said, for the everlasting eternal City? This is the heavenly City of Jerusalem to which the sons of God, languished in terrestrial peregrination and oppressed by temporal confusion and the captivity of Babylon, aspire. Because there are two cities, one temporal, other eternal, one mundane, the other celestial, one belonging to the devil, the other to Christ - the catholic writers call this Babylon, that Jerusalem.

The distinction between the temporal world and the heavenly world beyond has implications for discussion of divine providence and free will since according to Boethius providence was beyond time and therefore was able to know everything in advance without binding human free will to preordination or predestination.[91] St. Augustine did not differentiate between providence and predestination as did Boethius.[92] Otto stays faithful to Augustine, and does not name *Fortuna* directly, but a medieval reader might well interpret his description of the temporal world in Boethian terms especially when the world history was seen as tragedy of the mutable events and turning from prosperity to adversity just like the wheel of *Fortuna*.[93]

The two last stanzas present *Fortuna* as a personification of destruction and transitoriness. The examples in the second last stanza (the fourth in Hilka and Schumann) are not only familiar from pagan authors but also recall to mind a description of the destiny of the realms of antiquity and the vain worship of pagan deities in the *De civitate Dei* of St. Augustine. In Augustine there is of course a polarity between uncertain earthly history and the certainty

---

extratemporal.

90 *Chronica* I. prol., p. 10. See also Steer 1982, 188.
91 Boethius, *Phil. cons.* IV & V; ks. Chadwick 1981/1990, 221-247.
92 *Phil. cons.* IV.pr.iv, p. 356-372; Chadwick 1981/1990, 241-242, 250.
93 Kelly 1993, 78-92.

of God's world beyond. Troy in CB 14 especially brings to mind the example of Augustine in which the refugees from Troy find no protection in pagan temples and meet their unhappy end at the hands of conquerors – and the contary example of Christian refugees in churches in year 410 who were left untouched by Alaric's Goths.[94] The parallel with Otto of Freising and through him, with Augustine, strengthen the Augustinian interpretation.

The last stanza in the manuscript version (the third according to Hilka and Schumann) presents a group of examples of individual destinies. They seem to relate the poem to the concept of tragedy. In the Latin translation of Eusebius by Rufinus, and later in the works of Remigius of Auxerre (at the turn of 10th c.) and in several twelfth-century texts tragedies were defined as "poems that bewail the miseries of men, whether based on 'examples of dead men', or 'battles of dead men'".[95] Furthermore, tragedy was thought to deal with public affairs and often crimes of the great men and it was thought to proceed from prosperity to adversity – and to represent the whims of *Fortuna*.[96] Darius and Pompeius are such great men whose figures may be a recollection from the *Elegia de diversitate Fortunae et Philosophiae consolatione*, a work composed after the model of Boethius by an Italian, Henry of Settimelle, around the turn of the twelfth and thirteenth centuries,[97] although they both may also originate from some *florilegium* or heroic poem of deeds in antiquity.[98] In both cases they point to the nexus of *Fortuna*, tragedy and history.

Stability or mutability

Otto of Freising advised following the path of a wise man and cherishing the virtue of *constantia* in the midst of temporal change and having recourse to the eternal heavenly world beyond. *Celum non animum* (CB 15) is indeed a eulogy of the same virtue of constancy described by Otto. One of its versions in another manuscript is titled *De stabilitate:*[99]

> *1. Celum, non animum / mutat stabilitas, / firmans id optimum, / quod mentis firmitas / vovet - cum animi / tamen iudicio; / nam si turpissimi*

---

94 *De civ. Dei* I.iv, p. 202-204.

95 Kelly 1993, 55-57, 68-110, cit. 72-73.

96 Boethius formulates this very clearly although it appeared already earlier e.g. in Apuleius (Kelly 1993, 25, 33, 54, 68). Later in was often repeated in the High Middle Ages *(ibidem,* 74-75, 78-92, 99, 102). Boethius makes *Fortuna* ask rhetorically: Quid tragoediarum clamor aliud deflet nisi indiscreto ictu fortunam felicia regna vertentem? *(Phil. cons.* II. pr.ii, p. 182.)

97 Mater Pompeio, deinde noverca fui / Verba sic Dario, post verbera; Mello Cyro, / Fellea post, nutrix ingeniosa dedi. *(Elegia* II, 68-70, PL 204, col. 851.)
   Quid Darium referam? Quid Cyrum? quidve Neronem? (ibid. III.153, 859).

98 Bernt for example presumes that this is possible in his commentary on the German translation of the *Carmina Burana* (Bernt 1975, 459-460).

99 CB I.1, 34.

/ voti consilio / vis scelus imprimi / facto nefario, / debet hec perimi / facta promissio.

2. Non erat stabilis / gradus qui cecidit, / pes eius labilis / domus, que occidit. / hinc tu considera, / quid agi censeas, / dum res est libera; / sic sta, ne iaceas; / prius delibera, / quod factum subeas, / ne die postera / sero peniteas.

3. Facti dimidium / habet, qui ceperit, / ceptum negotium / si non omiserit, / non tantum deditus / circa principia, / nedum sollicitus / pro finis gloria; / nam rerum exitus / librat industria, / subit introitus / preceps incuria.

4. Coronat militem / finis, non prelium; / dat hoc ancipitem / metam, is bravium; / iste quod tribuit, / dictat stabilitas; / istud quod metuit, / inducit levitas; / nam palmam annuit / mentis integritas, / quam dari respuit / vaga mobilitas.

5. Mutat cum Proteo / figuram levitas, / assumit ideo / formas incognitas; / vultum constantia / conservans intimum, / alpha principia / et o novissimum / flectens fit media, / dans finem optimum, / mutans in varia / celum, non animum.[100]

1. Stability *(sic!)* changes heavens, not soul, and strengthens the optimum that is promised by firmness of mind because it is with one's soul that one goes to judgement. If the impudent break their holy promises knowingly, in the end they are doomed to destruction.
2. The steps of a fallen one were not stable, neither was the foundation of a ruined house solid. You should consider all this carefully when you are freely choosing your actions; so stand up, do not crouch. First, consider what you are going to do, and do not repent too late the next day.
3. What is begun is half-finished if one does not cut business short. If your work does not get stuck at the beginning you do not have to worry about the glory at the end because the business is brought into a well-balanced end by industriousness - but being capsized by carelessness leads downwards.
4. The soldier is crowned by the result, not by the battle; the award is given with a double measure. The one rewarded is he who spreads stability; he who had a reason to fear was leading to levity. The palm was earned by integrity of mind, which the vagant mobility cast off.
5. So levity changes its figure with Proteus, and therefore it adapted unknown forms. Constance keeps its familiar face: alpha stays at the beginning and omega at the end; between them the middle bends and gives the best end by changing in variety heavens, not soul.

The poem begins with a quotation from Horace[101] and then alludes to the last judgement. The moral sense quite obvious seems to be that by practising the virtue of *constantia* one is rewarded in the life hereafter but it also helps in one's terrestrial undertakings. It seems to emphasize finalistic ethics when, at the end of the fourth stanza, the conclusion of an action is proposed as a

---

100 CB I.1, 33-34. The attribution and dating are obscure.
101 ...caelum, non animum, mutant, qui trans mare currunt... (Hor. *Epist.* I.11.27) Cf. also Schmidt 1974/1990.

measure of its evaluation. Despite the Christian motivation, the intertextual structure is remarkably classical: with the exception of a couple of biblical allusions, the subtexts are authors of antiquity from Horace to Boethius. The virtues of the poem seem to oscillate between a rather simplified Christian reward-ethic and an almost bourgeois purposefulness in the terrestrial undertakings. Its ethics are faraway of from the Stoic strength of mind and the aristocratic views.[102] Even the teachings of Boethius in his *Philosophiae consolatio* are different - rewards of virtuous life are not earthly achievements but peace and strength of mind.

The second stanza clearly connects the poem intertextually with Boethius. The two first verses *Non erat stabilis / gradus, qui cecidit* [103] are a modification of the last verse of the opening poem of *Philosophiae consolatio*: *qui cecidit, stabili non erat ille gradu.*[104] The first-person narrator of Boethius' work complains of his miserable destiny: the one favoured by *Fortuna* has now fallen into misfortunes. The *Carmina Burana*'s poem proceeds from groping steps to a house standing on a yielding footing which alludes to the parable of Jesus about the wise man who built his house on solid rock and the fool who built on sand.[105] The following verses *(hinc tu considera, / quid agi censeas)* recalls the definition of forethought *(consilio)* given by Bernard Silvester.[106]

The third stanza returns to Horatian allusions: *Facti dimidium / habet, qui ceperit*[107] repeats the words from a moralising epistle to young Lollius Maximus in which Horace reads Homer as a kind of *exempla*-collection.[108] After various examples representing virtuous purposefulness, the epistle concludes by emphasizing the purity of body and soul and the end of the text becomes a bundle of various moral maxims.[109] The verse modified in the *Carmina Burana* is the following: *dimidium facti qui coepit habet; sapere aude; incipe* – "Well begun is half done, dare to be wise; begin!"[110] Teaching of this type may of course be quoted without knowing its origin, but when it is joined with other Horatian allusions and quotations at the beginning and

---

102 Cf. e.g. a poem of Bertrand de Born which presents warfare as purpose in itself (Bloch 1939-40/1983, 409f.); see also Murray 1978/1990, 350f.
103 CB 15.2.1-2 (CB I.1, 33).
104 *Phil. cons.* I.vs.i.22, p. 132.
　　The intertextual chain can be continued from Boethius to Ovid who speaks about the "ambiguous steps" of *Fortuna* in *Tristia* (V.viii.15-18) - the strophe is quoted in CB 18 (CB I.1, 36); see further page 115-116.
105 Et omnis qui audit verba mea haec, et non facit ea, similis erit viro stulto qui aedificavit domum suam super arenam: Et descendit pluvia, et venerunt flumina, et flaverunt venti et irruerunt in domum illam, et cecidit, et fuit ruina illius magna. (Matt. 7:26-27.)
　　Qui autem audit et non facit, similis est homini aedificanti domum suam super terram sine fundamento; in quam illisus est fluvius, et continuo cecidit, et facta est ruina domus illius magna. (Lk. 6:49.)
106 CB 15.2.5-6 (CB I.1, 33); Bernard Silvester, *Comm. in Mart.* 8.600-615, p. 193.
107 CB 15.3.1-2 (CB I.1, 33).
108 Hor. *Epist.* I.ii.1-31.
109 *Epist.* I.ii.55-71.
110 *Epist.* I.ii.40-41.

the end of the poem it seems not merely accidental but consciously and systematically Horatian.

The fifth stanza again uses Horatian and further Ovidian echoes. Proteus appears in both their works as a personification of frivolity and mutability.[111] The stanza concludes in a couplet: *mutans in varia / celum non animum.*[112] Both explicit surface and implicit intertextual webs connect the text with moral-philosophical currents from Stoics *via* the Roman poets to Boethius, but it is at least partly contradictory with its authors, Stoic and aristocratic virtues being changed to simplified Christian "reward-ethics".

The Christian tonality therefore makes the text slightly ambivalent, the first stanza warning of the last judgement (however, without menacing pathos), the second alluding to Christ's parable - and naturally to all its medieval implications, the rock being Jesus, Christian faith, and the Church. The house built upon sand means leaning on this world. The last stanza then urges keeping oneself stable from the beginning to the end with an allusion from the last chapter of the *Apocalypse* of the Apostle John, i.e. a description of the New Jerusalem. God is both alpha and omega, the Beginning and the End. Thus CB 15 also closes up with an Horatian allusion, promising a stable soul and the best possible end.[113]

The allusion to the *Apocalypse* of the Apostle John brings a Christian world-historical tension to a text which began with Stoic strength of mind, but contradicted it immediately with simplified reward-ethics and then emphasized almost bourgeois earthly purposefulness. The poem, seemingly thoroughly oriented to selfish salvation and success in this world, suddenly finds itself between the antagonism of earthly and heavenly Cities, Babylon and Jerusalem, as do the world-histories from St. Augustine to Otto of Freising. The probable author of the poem, a learned cleric who knew his pagan and Christian authors, has turned the whole classical apparatus to conform to the Christian teachings with skillful sophistication – and, on the surface, with very light and neutral *topoi*. He did not have to recourse to the violent cutting of the nails and plucking out the hair as Raban Maur and Honorius Augustodunensis recommended.[114]

In the theological cosmology of the High Middle Ages, the division into stable and changing, immutable and mutable was essential; the first being the properties of divine providence and the superlunar world. Regular change, i.e. the intermediate form between the immutable and the mutable (and the mediator between two spheres of beingness), was in the power of *Natura* (Hugo of St. Victor, Alan of Lille) or the Fates *(fata, Parcae*; Boethius, Bernard Silvester) both preordained by God. Even if the reckless and irregular

---

111 ... quo teneam voltus mutantem Proteo nodo? (Hor. *Epist.* I.i.90).
     Utque leves Proteus modo se tenuabit in undas. (Ovidius, *Ars am.* I.761.)
112 CB 15.5.11-12 (CB I.1, 33).
113 ... alpha principia / et o novissimum / flectens fit media. (CB 15.5.7-9, CB I.1, 33).
114 See above part I, p. 59, also note 81.

change, the transitoriness of all material things, and randomness were ultimately in the power of God, they were all proper to the perceptible sublunar world where fatal chance, *Fortuna*, was the personification of all mutability and transitoriness.

While CB 15 stayed at the general and exemplificatory moral level, the next poem in the *Carmina Burana* is in a certain sense its complementary opposite. Now *Fortuna* is depicted in a private complaint. It is "historical", that is, particular and bound to an individual *persona* (however, it is true that this *persona* does not acquire personal traits and, as such, remains general). According to the threefold partition of Bernard Silvester *(historia, argumentum, fabula)*, the poem would probably belong to history, although it does not refer to any broader story of historical events but is representing the nature of events in the world. In Bernard's terms, all history is either tragedy or satire, the first teaching one to bear adversities, and the latter one combating vices and promoting virtues.[115] According to this definition CB 14, with its descriptions of the destruction of civilisations and great men of history, was a tragic poem, and CB 16 perhaps a satire being apparently a treatment of private affairs. This generic definition is confirmed by the common medieval notion of tragedy as a poetical genre treating generalities such as kingdoms and the "crimes of princes" while satire examined private vices.[116]

Fortune plango vulnera (CB 16) runs as follows:

> *1. Fortune plango vulnera / stillantibus ocellis, / quod sua michi munera / subtrahit rebellis. / verum est, quod legitur / fronte capillata, / sed plerumque sequitur / Occasio calvata.*
> *2. In Fortune solio / sederam elatus, / prosperitas vario / flore coronatus; / quicquid enim florui / felix et beatus, / nunc a summo corrui / gloria privatus.*
> *3. Fortune rota volvitur: / descendo minoratus; / alter in altum tollitur; / nimis exaltatus / rex sedet in vertice - / caveat ruinam! / nam sub axe legimus / Hecubam reginam.*[117]

1. I am complaining to Fortuna of my wounds with weeping eyes because rebelliously she took back her favours from me. It is true what we read about the long forelock which is usually followed by a bald occasion.
2. I sat elevated on the throne of Fortuna and was crowned by various

---

115 *Comm. in Mart.* 2.971-985, p. 80-81.
116 See Isidore of Seville, *Etym.* VIII.vii.5-7, ed. Lindsay 1911/1987; Bernard of Utrecht, *Comm. in Theod.* 85-107, p. 81-82. Origins of this view can be traced to Horace (AP 89-98; see Kelly 1993, 5-6; its transmittance to medieval authors, see *ibidem*, 10, 36-40, 46, 62-65, 105). This view is quite contrary to the view that virtuous persons may be treated in tragedies also current in the High Middle Ages. Even Christ's passion was described as a tragedy but this conception was more unusual definition in the twelfth and early thirteenth century even if it originated from Boethius' *Contra Eutychen* (V.85-86, p. 106; see Kelly 1993, 24, 32-33, 52, 74-75).
117 CB I.1, 34-35. The attribution and dating are obscure.

riches and flowers. So I flourished, happy and blessed - now, I have fallen down from the top and my glory has been wrenched from me. 3. Fortuna's wheel goes round and round; from up I am going down. Another is rising up, exalted to the heights. The king is sitting on the top - beware your ruin! for beneath we read about Queen Hecuba.

In the classical generic terms, the poem is an elegy (Lat. *planctus*), a personal complaint about the fickleness of earthly destiny, with to a subtext common to all texts on terrestrial fickleness, i.e. alluding to the *Philosophiae consolatio*. The connection with the first book of the *Philosophiae consolatio* is particularly evident as the first-person narrator complains of his miserable destiny and Lady Philosophy answers him, arguing that terrestrial adversities are only good for a human. The characteristic trait of the nature of *Fortuna* is mutability and, things being so, it is absurd to blame *Fortuna* for acting in a way which is proper for her. The narrator's complaint about the change of *Fortuna*'s attitude is wrong because *Fortuna* is stable in her mutability:

> Tu fortunam putas erga te esse mutatam, erras. Hi semper eius mores sunt ista natura. Servavit circa te propriam potius in ipsa sui mutabilitate constantiam. Talis erat cum blandiebatur, cum tibi falsae incelebris felicitas alluderet. Deprehendisti caeci numinis ambiguos vultus.

> You imagine that *Fortuna*'s attitude to you has changed; you are wrong. Such was always her way, such is her nature. Instead, all she has done in your case is remain constant to her own inconstancy; she was just the same when she was smiling, when she deluded you with the allurements of her false happiness. You have merely discovered the changing face of that blind power: she who still conceals herself from others has completely revealed herself to you. (Tr. S.J. Tester).[118]

The general subtext by Boethius is replenished by a cluster of allusions to classical and medieval sources which all complete the poem's explicit content. They do not however build up such a sophisticated Christian interpretation on the ground laid by pagan allusions as in CB 15.

In the opening stanza the *persona* complains the wounds made by perfidious *Fortuna* in words originating from Cicero, Lucan, Ovid and Juvenal.[119] The stanza concludes with an enigmatic affirmation: *verum est, quod legitur / fronte capillata, / sed plerumque sequitur / Occasio calvata.*[120]

"Forelock" and "bald occasion" originate from the *disticha Catonis* which were very popular in the Middle Ages. There *Fortuna* is described having a hairy forehead and a bald back of the head.[121] This description found favour

---

118 Boethius, *Phil. cons.* II.pr.1, p. 176.
119 Vulnus Fortunae (Cic. *Acad. I.1*,; Lucan 8.72); ... sic ego continuo Fortunae vulneror ictu. (Ovid, *Ex Ponto* II.7.41, p. 352.)
    ... gibbus et acre malum semper stillantis ocelli. (Juvenal, *Sat.* VI.109.)
120 CB 16.1.5-8 (CB I.1, 34).
121 Fronte capillata, post est Occasio calvat. Cit. Parlett 1986/1988, 205; see also Patch 1927,

with medieval authors, and, among others, Alan of Lille, his commentator Ralph of Longchamp and the imitator of Boethius, Henry of Settimello, all present its variations.[122] The "long forelock" meant, according to David M. Robinson, *kairos*, the right or opportune monent.[123] However, it is continued by *occasio calvata* meaning, in addition to "a bald occasion", death. *Fortuna*, mutability and mortality are formed into a chain as a series of textual associations - being suborded by *Fortuna* one learns the quality of death, as Ralph of Longchamp wrote.[124]

The second stanza tells of the favours of *Fortuna*. Once again the complaint structure brings to mind the *Philosophiae consolatio*, specially its opening poem where the narrator remembers *Fortuna*'s favours. The first verse CB 16 alludes to the "tearful eyes" in Boethius' text (Boethius: *flentes oculos*; CB: *stillantibus ocellis*). On the level of literal content the CB poem's "I" alludes from beginning to end to an analogous getting and losing the favours of *Fortuna*. The last verses of Boethius's poem are also the source of the "unstable steps" in the second stanza of CB 15.[125]

The description of the wheel of *Fortuna* in the second and third stanzas refers to several literal and visual representations which I have alluded to above. The *persona* who sits flowered on the top is similar to the figure adorned with roses and violets and who boasts on the heights of the wheel depicted by Bernard Silvester.[126] The representation of *Fortuna*'s wheel concludes with an *exemplum*: *nam sub axe legimus / Hecubam reginam.*[127]

116-117; Robinson 1946, 213.

122 Ambiguo uultu seducit forma uidentem. / Nam capitis pars anterior uestita capillis / Luxuriat, dum caluiciem pars altera luget. (Alan of Lille, *Anticl.* VIII.31-33, p. 173-174.)
    Fortuna vultus praetendit dubios, vel hoc ideo dicitur, quod fortuna mutabilis est et dubia; vel propter imaginem ipsius Fortunae, quae erat Romae ex una parte calva et oculosa, ex altera parte capillata et caeca. (Ralph of Longchamp, *In Anticl. Al. comm.* V.lxiii, p. 166.)
    Fronte capillata, sed in retro rasa caput. (Henry of Settimello, *Elegia de diversitate Fortunae et Philosophiae consolatione* II.202, PL 204, col. 855.)

123 Robinson 1946, 213.

124 *In Anticl. Al. comm.* V.lxiii, p. 160.

125 Carmina qui quondam studio florente peregi, / Flebilis heu maestos cogor inire modos. / Ecce mihi lacerae dictant scribenda camenae / Et veris elegi fletibus ora rigant. / Has saltem nullus potuit pervincere terror, / Ne nostrum comites prosequerentur iter. / Gloria felicis, olim viridisque iuventae / Solantur maesti nunc mea fata senis. / Venit enim properata inopina senectus / Et dolor aetatem iussit inesse suam. / Intempestivi funduntur vertice cani / Et tremit effeto corpore laxa cutis. / Mors hominum felix quae se nec dulcibus annis / Inserit et maestis saepe vocata venit. / Eheu quam surda miseros avertitur aure / *Et flentes oculos claudere saeve negat. / Dum levibus male fida bonis fortuna faveret, / Paene caput tristis merserat hora meum. / Nunc quia fallacem mutavit nubila vultum, / Protrahit ingratas impia vita moras. / Quid me felicem totiens iactastis amici? / Qui cecidit, stabili non erat ille gradu.* (Boethius, *Phil. cons.* I.vs.i, p. 130-132.)

126 Bernard Silvester, *Comm. in Mart.* 8.772-787, p. 198-199.
    In addition to the examples quoted above about the wheel of *Fortuna*: Cuncta rotat fortuna rota, qua cuncta rotantur; / Sic tenui magnus orbis in orbe perit. (Henry of Settimello, *Elegia* IV.19-24, PL 204, col. 862.)

127 CB 16.3.7-8 (CB I.1, 34); Hecuba was the wife of Priam, the king of Troy, and as such, appropriately represented the fickleness of earthly luck. She was not however a common figure in the Middle Ages, and, unknown to other descriptions of *Fortuna* (see Hilka & Schumann 1930/1961, 28).

This *exemplum* may also be seen as a generic clue: while *Hecuba* is said to be rare in the context of *Fortuna* she is however an important tragic figure which was often mentioned in medieval generic definitions of tragedy.[128] The poem proceeds from prosperity to adversity as was said to be characteristic for tragedy.[129] On the other hand, it indeniably depicts private affairs. Perhaps the poem relates the most important genres, i.e. tragedy and satire, public and private affairs, dealing with the wordly fickleness personified by *Fortuna*. Thus it can be interpreted as "historical" poem which in its tropological level teaches the general nature of the world, and perhaps the fact that people wake up too late from the spell of *Fortuna* (to read exemplary tragedies about *Hecuba* and others alike - and learn the real nature of mortal life).

O Fortuna, velut luna: Should one seize the moment?

In the group of *Fortuna*-poems there is a thematic movement from general to particular in that the description in CB 14 remained general, and the caprices of *Fortuna* concerned first of all civilisations and, secondly, the great men of history. Moreover, CB 15 is a generalising collection of moral precepts *(praecepta)* and examples *(exempla)*. In CB 16, a personal subject, "I", then appears for the first time to relate his trial on the wheel of *Fortuna* - the depiction follows the conventional *topos* completely. In the *Fortuna* group, the next poem, CB 17, is the most personal, in the sense, that it presents a poetic *persona* who does not only complain his lot but wants, aims, and acts. It simultaneously opens a new topic, that is, the gambling which becomes an allegory of the sublunar life and the pursuit of happiness (or luck). *Fortuna* is also slightly different from her predecessors in the *Carmina Burana* since she not only has an impact on one's external lot but also "takes care of sharpness of mind in the game".

O Fortuna, velut luna (CB 17) proceeds as follows:

> 1. *O Fortuna, / velut luna / statu variabilis, / semper crescis / aut decrescis; / vita detestabilis / nunc obdurat / et tunc curat / ludo mentis aciem, / egestatem, / potestatem / dissolvit ut glaciem.*
> 2. *Sors immanis / et inanis, / rota tu volubilis, / status malus, / vana salus / semper dissolubilis, / obumbratam / et velatam / michi quoque niteris; / nunc per ludum / dorsum nudum / fero tui sceleris.*
> 3. *Sors salutis / et virtutis / michi nunc contraria, / est affectus / et defectus / semper in angaria. / hac in hora / sine mora / corde pulsum tangite; / quod per sortem / sternit fortem / mecum omnes plangite!*[130]

---

128 Kelly 1993, 33, 51, 75, 113, 187. A fifteenth-century portuguese author Johan Roiç de Corella (1440-97) associated the wheel of *Fortuna* and the fate of Hecuba (Kelly 1993, 211-214).
129 Kelly 1993, 78 and *passim*.
130 CB I.1, 35-36. The attribution and dating are obscure.

1. O Fortuna, like the moon you change your stature, you are constantly waxing or waning. Detestable life is trying me now - and then, she suddenly cures it and takes care of acuity of mind in the game. Like ice she dissolves poverty and power together.

2. The terrifying empty Chance *(Sors)*, you whirling wheel, in a bad position success (or: salvation) becomes vain, it is always dissolved, shaded and veiled even if it once shone for me. Now, due to the game I carry a naked back defamed by you.

3. The Chance *(Sors)* of salvation and virtue is now contrary to mine - mine is affected and perverted by constant anxiety. Immediately, at this moment, touch my heart's pulse for Chance *(Sors)* is knocking over the strong one - let all the people join my complaint.

The poem proceeds thematically from an overall depiction of *Fortuna* and her effects to individual anxiety: the *persona* in the poem is remarkably close to the description in Honorius Augustodunensis of those "whose liver is gnawed by the vulture of desire" – especially when the liver and desire (ultimately sexual lust) were associated with each other in the physiological theories of the time.[131] The presentation of personal anxiety – although possibly ironic – makes the poem an exception among the other *Fortuna* poems while it also resembles the erotic love-poems and some gambling-songs further on in the *Carmina Burana*.[132]

If the sublunar world, change and *Fortuna* were identified with each other, the moon was in itself an emblem and metaphor of transformation and dependence. According to the learned of the High Middle Ages, moon borrowed its light from sun (resembling in this the sublunar world which was insufficient in itself) and, furthermore, was constantly changing.[133] The first stanza also includes another allusion to the views of contemporary natural science, namely the theories of Bernard Silvester and others who had placed all irregular change in nature under the range of *Fortuna*. As an example he offered the transformation of water to ice *(ut cum aqua in glaciem vertitur)*. Bernard identified *Fortuna* with all temporal and mutable events *(Fortuna est temporalium eventus mutabilis)* - not however with regular change, such as the rotation of annual seasons which belongs to the sphere of determination of nature *(Natura)*.[134]

The second stanza identifies Chance *(Sors)*[135] with the wheel of *Fortuna*.

---

131 Honorius Augustodunensis, *Spec. Eccl.*, III Dom. xi post Pentecostem, PL 172, col. 1057; Bernard Silvester, *Cosmographia* II.xiv, tr. Wetherbee 1973/1990, 126; Alan of Lille, *De planctu Naturae* VI.pr.3, p. 824ff. The one whose liver was gnawed was Tityos (see Ovid, *Met.* IV.457, 460, X.43-44.)

132 See CB 122a, 156 (the first stanza), 199, 191, 195 (the second stanza) (CB I.2-3, *passim*).

133 The nature of the moon and its relation to the sun is explained in detail by William of Conches in his *Philosophia* which deal with the philosophy of nature. The moon, often personified as Diana, is cold and humid (as against the sun, i.e. Phoebus or Apollo) and borrows its light from her "brother", the sun *(Phil.* II.xiv.36, 37, xv.68, p. 54, 66-72).
See also Alan of Lille, *De planctu Naturae* IV.pr.2, p. 821.

134 Comm. in Mart. 8.600-615, p. 193.

135 The word *sors* means both destiny, man's lot, and an actual die or lottery ticket. There are also the unequivocal words *alea*, *tessera* and *decius* which have no special connotations

The description follows the normal conventions of the topic. The game *(ludus)* strips off the clothes and makes the *persona* naked. The game can also be understood here both as the play of *Fortuna* and as gambling proper.

The content of the third stanza is paradoxical: speaking of "the Chance of salvation and virtue" *(Sors salutis / et virtutis)* which is against the Christian doctrine – salvation and virtue are not in the power of *Fortuna*. The interpretation becomes even more complicated when one reads the poem in the context of the Stoic, Boethian and, then, of course Christian, views which all stressed the good effects bad luck had on the human when it taught him to appreciate true and constant values.[136] But the *persona* in the poem seems to think that for the loser there is but anxiety, and so he calls on all people to feel his pulse and to join in his complaint. The misfortunes do not seem to carry the expected effects: the *persona* cannot rid himself of mundane lusts which were described by Honorius Augustodunensis in connection with *Fortuna*. It is justifiable to ask what or who is treated ironically; the notion of the refining and educative effects of misfortunes (which do not bring "salvation and virtue"), or the "I" who does not seem to learn his homework. Perhaps the aim of the poem is to give an *exemplum* of the power of desire's vulture and the stubborness of human nature even when facing grave adversities.

The poem CB 17 is known only from the *Carmina Burana*, as is CB 16 (the two first poems, CB 14 and 15, do have other versions in some manuscripts, and CB 18 is a *versus cum auctoritate*, i.e. a text which is built around a few quotations from classical authors). Besides, the poem does not include any recognised allusions to authoritative poetry - except for the general connections to the Boethian interpretation of *Fortuna* and to the conceptions of scientific, cosmological and moral speculations in the twelfth century.[137] The most significant connection – together with Boethius – is another poem in the *Carmina Burana*, namely *Iste mundus furibundus* (CB 24), whose rhythmic metre and rhyme pattern is partly the same as in CB 17 although the line-pattern is different.[138] The poem runs as follows:

> *Iste mundus furibundus falsa prestat gaudia, / Quia fluunt et decurrunt ceu campi lilia. / Laus mundana, vita vana vera tollit premia, / Nam impellit et submergit animas in tartara. / Lex carnalis et mortalis valde transitoria / Fugit, transit velut umbra, que non est corporea. / Quod videmus vel tenemus in presenti patria, / Dimittemus et perdemus quasi*

---

about fate or destiny in medieval Latin.

136 Lady Philosophy argues in the second book of Boethius' *Philosophiae consolatio* to the complaint wordly success, i.e. the favours of *Fortuna*, is vain, and how bad luck is actually good for the progress of the human soul (especially *Phil. cons.* II.pr.viii, p. 224). Augustine also emphasized the educational and ennobling effects of adversities (for example *De civ. Dei* I.x, p. 220).

137 See Hilka & Schumann 1930/1961, 28-29; Bernt 1975, 461; Parlett 1986/1988, 205.

138 Parlett 1986/1988, 205-206.
    Only one other version of CB 24 is known, from a manuscript written in the early fourteenth century (CB I.1, 44; Walsh 1976, 142).

quercus folia. / Fugiamus, contemnamus huius vite dulcia, / Ne
perdamus in futuro pretiosa munera! / Conteramus, confringamus
carnis desideria, / Ut cum iustis et electis in celesti gloria / Gratulari
mereamus per eterna secula! Amen.[139]

This raging world appreciates false joys which flow and fade away
like the lilies in the meadow. Mundane praise, vain life, take away the
true reward. It just impels and submerges souls in hell. The law of
flesh and mortality is transitory, it flees and moves away like an
incorporeal shadow. What we see or touch in our present fatherland
we will throw away and lose like an oak losing its leaves. Let's fly
and contemn the charms of this life, so that we do not lose the precious
gifts of the future. We must exhaust and smash the desires of flesh so
that we can earn praise in celestial glory for eternal centuries among
the justified and elect. Amen.

The fervent preaching demanding the mortification of flesh and discarding
"the world" imposes itself as an counterbalance to CB 17 and its *persona*
driven by fleshly lust. The issue is not a simple dichotomy between the wordly
and spiritual lifestyle, since CB 24 with all its biblical allusions and hostility
against the world is an ardent monastic declaration, which is paradoxically
placed among those clerical texts which seak their inspiration from secular
and pagan literature. It represents an entirely different interpretation of
Christian spirituality. One has only to glance over the intertextual play which
CB 15 had with pagan authors and the Christian view, and the purely biblical
basis CB 24 is built upon.

In their commentary Alfons Hilka and Otto Schumann list allusions to
Isaiah *(velut quercus defluentibus foliis*, Is. 1:30), Matthew *(lilia agri*, Matt.
6:28), the Song of Songs *(flos campi et lilium convallium*, the Song of Songs
2:1), the Epistles *(lex carnalis*, Hebr. 7:15-16; *lex mortis*, Rom. 7:5-6; *in
presenti patria* vs. *patria caelestis*, Hebr. 11:16; *desideria carnis*, Gal. 5:16;
also Ephes. 2:3, 1. Petr. 2:11, 2. Petr. 2:18; *cum gloria caelesti*, 2. Tim. 2:10),
the Book of Job *(homo fugit velut umbra*, Job 14:2), and the Psalms *(arcum
conteret et confringet arma*, Ps. 45:10).[140]

The core of the poem is in its fifth and sixth verse: *lex carnalis et mortalis
valde transitoria / Fugit, transit velut umbra que non est corporea.* In the
manuscript the "law of the flesh" *(lex carnalis)* has tortuous emendations: *rex
carnalis* had originally been written in the manuscript, which a later medieval
corrector changed to *res carnalis*, and it was not until the modern editors that
this phrase was changed to its quite obvious form *lex carnalis*, alluding to
The Epistle to the Hebrews.[141] From the point of view of the entirety of the
poem all three variations give approximately the same result since the "king

---

139 CB I.1, 44. According to Hilka and Schumann the poem is probably composed in the latter
half of the 11th century or in the first half of the twelfth century. The authorship is obscure.
140 Hilka & Schumann 1930/1961, 37-38; see also Walsh 1976, 142.
141 CB I.1, 44; Schumann 1930/1961, 75*.

of the flesh or corporeality" is understandable even if a somewhat vague metaphor (it could refer either to the Old Adam or the devil); a similar interpretation follows from "thing or cause of flesh" but different readings are irrelevant in respect to the denial of the world. Nevertheless, overall allusions to the *Bible* in the poem and the meaning of this passage all justify the reading according to *The Epistle to the Hebrews*. Everything that is subjected to the law of flesh flees and changes like an incorporeal shadow.

The seventh chapter of *The Letter to the Hebrews* (verses 15-16):

> *Et amplius adhuc manifestum est, si secundum similitudinem Melchisedech exsurgat alius sacerdos, qui non secundum legem mandati carnalis factus est, sed secundum virtutem vitae insolubilis.*

> And it is yet far more evident: for that after the similitude of Melchisedec there ariseth another priest who is made, not after the law of carnal commandment, but after the power of an endless life.

The passage discusses the priesthood and the moral obligations imposed on consecrated priests *(sacerdotes)*. "Carnal law" or "law of the flesh" also appears in St. Paul's epistle to the Romans (7:5-6):

> *Cum enim essemus in carne, passiones peccatorum, quae per legem erant, operabantur in membris nostris, ut fructificarent morti. Nunc autem soluti sumus a lege mortis, in qua detinebamur; ita ut serviamus in novitate spiritus, et non in vetustate litterae.*

> For when we were in the flesh, the motions of sins, which were by the law, did work in our members to bring forth fruit unto death. But now we are delivered from the law, that being dead wherein we were held; that we should serve in newness of spirit, and not in the oldness of the letter.

"Carnal law" is a determining force, and only the grace of God can free the human from its subjection. At the same time, the carnal law is identified with "oldness of the letter" *(vetustate litterae)*, i.e. the Old Testament and Judaism.

The passage builds up a chain of meanings from the general "way of all flesh", that is the earthly human destiny, to the obligation of purity of the priesthood, and, ultimately to the allegorical interpretation in which the mortal letter and reviving spirit are set against each other. In this valley of sorrow everything is like a fleeting shadow and the true reality is hidden from the senses. Furthermore, the poem emphasizes that in its transitoriness the flesh like a shadow - a comparison which brings into mind a discussion of William of Conches about the similarities of tragedy and the world.[142]

The *Fortuna* poems of the *Carmina Burana* are dominated by the clerical,

---

142 Quid vita mundi non est nisi quoddam umbraculum preteriens. Cit. Kelly 1993, 72 n. 13, also 74, 79; see also Curtius 1948, 146-152.

secular and learned world which interprets Christian faith in the context of Boethius and Neoplatonism. It is certainly orthodox and does not attack any fundamental Christian teachings but, contrary to the monastic view, it only warns of a too strong attraction to earthly prosperity and does not deny the world in its entirety but, however, makes it dependant like moon depends from sun. In the collection there is side by side an older monastic layer which is openly hostile to this world (and, sometimes, to pagan learning). Its message is directed especially towards consecrated members of clergy *(sacerdotes*, not *clerici)* in a time when religious devotion was still primarily the limited vocation of a priest and a monk. It does not speak, at least to the same extent, to both layman and cleric. In the twelfth and early thirteenth centuries Christian theology and religious practices in the West were only on the way towards a religion which set the same demand of devotion for all Christians.[143]

The difference between the world leaning purely on the *Bible* and the world leaning also on pagan authors becomes apparent when we compare the *versus* completing the *Fortuna* group with the fervent denial of this world in CB 24. *O Fortuna levis* (CB 18) runs as follows:

> *I. O Fortuna levis! cui vis das munera que vis, / Et cui vis que vis auferet hora brevis.*
> *II. Passibus ambiguis Fortuna volubilis errat / Et manet in nullo certa tenaxque loco; / Sed modo leta manet, modo vultus sumit acerbos, / Et tantum constans in levitate manet.*
> *III. Dat Fortuna bonum, sed non durabile donum; / Attolit pronum, faciens de rege colonum.*
> *IV. Quos vult Sors ditat, quos non vult, sub pede tritat.*
> *V. Qui petit alta nimis, retro lapsus ponitur imis.*[144]

I. O light Fortuna, you have the power to give gifts as you please, and take them away at any moment.
II. Changeable Fortuna wanders abroad with aimless steps, abiding firm and persistent in no place; now she comes in joy, now she takes on a harsh mien, steadfast only in her own fickleness. (This verse transl. by A. L. Wheeler from *Tristia* of Ovid).
III. Fortuna gives a good but never a durable gift. She brings one up easily - and makes a serf of a king.
IV. The Chance *(Sors)* makes rich who she wills; those abandoned she treads on.
V. He who aims for the top will be pushed to the bottom by his error.

---

143 Chenu 1957/1976, 225-251; Foulon 1993, 49; Rapp 1993; see also Le Bras 1959; Little 1978/1983.
144 CB I.1, 36-37. The attribution and dating are obscure.

The tone of the poem is didactic and moralistic – as is the case in most of *versi* in the *Carmina Burana*. It lacks the fervour apparent in CB 17 and 24 which both hammer their message home with suggestive rhythmic goliardic-metre and rhymes.

The overtly didactic tone is not simply based on open and direct moralistic discourse and metric solutions, but also the poem being a fabric of quotations. It is not content only to allude various subtexts. Actually, it belongs to a common clerical genre, *versus cum auctoritate*.[145] The first strophe speaks in its "own words" and repeats a conventional description of the lightness and the fickleness of *Fortuna* and transitoriness of her gifts. The second strophe is a quotation from the *Tristia* by Ovid:

> *passibus ambiguis Fortuna volubilis errat / et manet in nullo certa tenaxque loco, / sed modo laeta venit (manet), vultus modo sumit acerbos, / et tantum constans in levitate sua est. (See the transl. by Wheeler above).*[146]

The strophe surely simultaneously echoed in the intertextual memory of medieval reader the verses by Boethius about the "aimless steps" of *Fortuna* – and in the context of the *Carmina Burana* it recalls the opening of second stanza of CB 15.[147] Obviously, strophes also bring to mind the teaching of Lady Philosophy about the stable instability of *Fortuna*.[148]

The final poem reiterates the characterizations already familiar from the poems above, the miniature in the *Carmina Burana*, and their sources from Antiquity and the Middle Ages. The *versus* functions as a kind of commentary which explains simply and openly the message of the earlier poems - if it ever was veiled for the poem's contemporary reader.

The miniature: *Fortuna cesarea* or omnipotent force in the sublunar world?

Unlike the *Fortuna* poems of the *Carmina Burana*, the miniature representing the wheel of *Fortuna*, originally placed in the end of the group has attracted some interpreters (see picture on page 95). Recently Ernst Kitzinger and Georg Steer have put forward their interpretations. In the Middle Ages *Fortuna* was not only a popular literary topos but a common motif in visual arts, as in a way Bernard Silvester hints also.[149] *Fortuna* and her wheel not appeared only

---

145 Cf. Schmidt 1974/1990, esp. p. 42.
146 Ovid, *Trist.* V.viii.15-18.
147 Boethius, *Phil. cons.* I.vs.i.22, p. 132; CB 15.2.1-2 (CB I.1, 33).
148 Tu fortunam putas erga te esse mutatam; erras. Hi semper eius mores sunt ista natura. Servavit circa te propriam potius in ipsa sui mutabilitate constantiam. (Boethius, *Phil. cons.* II.pr.1, ed. p. 176.)
149 Bernard Silvester, *Comm. in Mart.* 8.772-787, p. 198-199; Kitzinger 1973; Steer 1982.

in miniatures but were also popular in church art as well in mosaics as stained glass.[150]

All interpreters of the iconography of *Fortuna* share the view that her visual representations became common during the twelfth century. Moreover, scholars are unanimous that the twelfth-century representations presented the goddess as an active force rotating her wheel.[151] Although Boethius had been read already from Carolingian times,[152] the pictorial representations did not appear until during the eleventh century, when the basic iconographic concept seems to have been quickly established. The oldest representations handed down to us, depict only the wheel, four figures (kings) on its rim, a text *regnabo, regno, regnavi, sum sine regno*, but *Fortuna* herself is missing. Kitzinger assumes that the picture would have developed without being associated with Boethius (contrary to the claim of Courcelle). It would have been developed out of an image of the goddess standing on the wheel or globe which accords with the view of Alexander Murray about the development of this iconography. It was indeed wheels just like this that became common in church facades in the twelfth and thirteenth centuries.[153]

According to Kitzinger, H.R. Hahnloser has distinguished between two iconographical types in his studies of Villehard de Honnecourt. The first type from the twelfth century has *Fortuna* standing by the wheel actively rotating it and the other, dating from the early thirteenth century, has a more passive goddess in the centre of the wheel in the frontal position. The latter type would indicate a change in the idea of *Fortuna*, the earlier goddess dominating in the sublunar world being replaced by a goddess with restricted powers.[154] Kitzinger even thinks that the latter type would accord with the description of Honorius Augustodunensis quoted above, but when other textual proofs are lacking this seems to me unconvincing, since the Honorius's description points rather to the earlier monastic view.[155]

Ernst Kitzinger himself further develops his interpretation of a floor mosaic from the church of S. Salvatore in Turin from the late twelfth century. It presents *Fortuna* as a force influencing the sublunar world which is however subjected to the order of nature.[156] This interpretation resembles the description of *Fortuna* as a necessary agent of the cosmic order given by Alan of Lille which simultaneously points out the insignificance and transitoriness of this world.

According to Kitzinger, the miniature in the *Carmina Burana* pertains to

---

150 See Doren 1924, 71; Kitzinger 1973.
151 Patch 1927; Doren 1924; Kitzinger 1973; Murray 1978/1990; Steer 1982.
152 Courcelle 1967, 9, 241f.
153 Kitzinger 1973, 362-363; also note 132 in which K. lists the churches St. Étienne of Beauvais (1130-1140); Basel Cathedral (late 12th c.), S. Zeno of Verona (the turn of the 12th and 13th c.), Amiens Cathedral which had the wheel of *Fortuna* in their facades. In addition there was of course the mosaic of S. Salvatore of Turin.
154 Kitzinger 1973, 364-365, also note 133; see also Steer 1982, 184-186.
155 Kitzinger 1973, 364, 368-369; also Steer 1982, 186; see above p. 84-85.
156 Kitzinger 1973, 368-369 and *passim*.

the same type as the mosaic of Turin.[157] In the *Carmina Burana* majestic *Fortuna* has a crown and a robe, and sits in a frontal position with open book scrolls in her hands. Two of the kings on the rim, the one on the top and the descending one, have similar crowns and robes to *Fortuna*. Both the mosaic and the miniature of the *Carmina Burana* represent the transient nature of the sublunar world, connecting the notions of *mundus*, *orbis terrarum* and *Fortuna* with each other. The autonomous goddess has however lost some of her powers and no longer looks like the same independent and rebellious force as in earlier twelfth-century representations. She has become a part of cosmic order and rotation.[158]

While the miniature of the *Carmina Burana* is just one example among others for Kitzinger Georg Steer appears to be the only scholar who has concentrated on it and offered a thorough and carefully-argued interpretation. His point of departure is the majestic and royal nature of the figure of *Fortuna*. He sees the image as an independent representation of the goddess which does not illustrate any of the *Fortuna* poems in the collection, but represents same general theme as each of the poems, and adds to it one more aspect.[159]

To establish his interpretation, Steer adds to the iconographic types of Hahnloser (and Kitzinger) three different ideas of *Fortuna*. First he argues that there is the Boethian *Fortuna*, who acts as an agent of providence; secondly, there is Alan of Lille's *Fortuna* from *Anticlaudianus* which is necessary to the natural and moral order and distributes virtuous gifts (such as nobility, etc.); thirdly, there is *Fortuna imperatoris*, i.e. a personification of the success and prosperity of particular rulers.[160] However, one may doubt if these ideal types are really contradictory with each other. Rather it seems to list three complementary aspects of *Fortuna*. Nevertheless, Steer argues on the grounds of this division that the miniature of the *Carmina Burana* does not fit well with the two first notions. He claims on the other hand that a frontal representation which is god-like and similar to *Christos Pantokrator* images links it with iconographical conventions of depicting emperors and kings.[161] On this basis, Steer assumes that the miniature represents the *fortuna cesarea* of Emperor Frederick II or his successors, perhaps King Heinrich VII.[162]

Steer briefly analyses the differences between the miniature and the poems and argues that, for instance, the wheel of *Fortuna* in CB 16 is not the same as in the miniature.[163] Finally, he discusses why the miniature has been shifted from its original place to the beginning of the manuscript, suggesting that it

---

157 Kitzinger 1973, 365.
158 Kitzinger 1973, 368-369 and *passim*.
159 Steer 1982, 183, 193-194. See the picture on page 95 and the cover of this book.
160 Steer 1982, 187.
161 Steer 1982, 189.
162 Steer 1982, 190, 194; cf. Kelly 1993, 87-89 (Otto of Freising on the *fortuna cesarea* of Frederick Barbarossa).
163 Steer 1982, 192-193.

is to emphasise the nature of the whole manuscript, i.e. to point out its wordly nature, or simply to provide a decorative frontispiece.[164]

Even if painstakingly argued, Steer's interpretation is open to counter-arguments. First of all there is no indication in the manuscript that the miniature should be connected with some particular historical context. None of the rulers he mentions appear in the manuscript even if some other medieval kings, emperors and popes are mentioned.[165] The miniature is as general as the *Fortuna* poems themselves. On the other hand, the majestic image of *Fortuna* does not give any reasons to not interpret it as a representation of the nature of the sublunar world, indeed, it fits well within the descriptions of her power as in CB 14. Her majestic figure, the kings turning around on the rim, and the open scrolls in her hands (which Steer does not mention), can plausibly be interpreted as an allegory of the same historical change and the role of chance in human action as in CB 14. Moreover, it does not contradict the view of Alan of Lille and his contemporary interpreters – kings can be seen as a representation of the *conditio humana*, or *status vitae*, as Ralph of Longchamp explains *Fortuna* in Alan's work. Kingship is a human institution, and as such belongs to the sphere of *Fortuna*.[166] Further, it is rather difficult to imagine that *Fortuna* in the miniature could be identified with the description of Honorius Augustodunensis (as Kitzinger argues) - she is not tied to the wheel and does not seem to rotate with it. Thus, she rather seems to be a majestic (i.e. powerful) agent in human history whose open scrolls (or *sortes*, lottery tickets?) could contain exemplary tales (or perhaps tragedies) of the changing fortune of kings, princes, cities and dynasties.

Even Kitzinger's account of the Turinian floor mosaic would fit into this line of interpretation: the world, *orbis terrarum*, and human history both belong to the same sublunar world which *Fortuna* influences, and which has to be evaluated correctly in a Christian context. Of course, a medieval viewer could also interpret this general representation in connection with the destinies of contemporary rulers.

An interesting detail in Georg Steer's account is that he connects *Fortuna* and the king on the top in the miniature to justice *(iustitia)* to which the crossed legs of the king point.[167] This detail enforces the connection of the miniature and the CB 14 because the poem indeed begins with the unusual metaphor of *Fortuna*'s slippery court of justice *(O varium Fortune ... tribunal iudicium)*.[168] Hence it seems that the miniature is much more closely

---

164 Steer 1982, 195.
165 CB 41 (Pope Alexander III), CB 50 (Saladin), CB 51a *(Imperator rex Grecorum)*, CB 53 (Frederick Barbarossa and pope Alexander III), CB 122 (the death of Richard the Lionheart), CB 124 (the death of Philip of Swabia), CB 226 (the kings of France Louis VII, or possibly L. VI, VIII or IX).
166 Alan of Lille, *Anticlaudianus*; Ralph of Longchamp, *In. Al. Anticl. comm.* V.lxii, p. 167 (see above page 81-82, 92, 97f. and notes 29, 30 and 63).
167 Steer 1982, 189-190.
168 CB I.1, 31; see pages 97-103 above.

connected to the poems of the manuscript than Steer claims. There is good reason to assume that the primary meaning of the miniature is the same as in CB 14 which presents a general view of human history in the sublunar world. It is indeed the same poem that makes an allusion to the book of Samuel and compares the sublunar power of the goddess to the omnipotence of the Christian God.[169]

Fortuna, ethics and the sublunar world

Fortuna was a personification of sublunar fortuitousness and the transience of worldly prosperity. In the twelfth century, only a few secular learned followed St. Augustine in rejecting the sense to talk about randomness of the sublunar world represented by *Fortuna*. The group of *Fortuna* poems inclines towards the outlook of Boethius. In describing the sublunar world they do not appeal to the world beyond nor future salvation. This strategy resembles the Neoplatonic "natural theology" developed by Boethius when discussing the problem of good and evil, the caprices of destiny, divine providence and free will *(liberum arbitrium)* – Boethius left untouched the questions of divine revelation, salvation and grace.[170]

Providence in the first place ordered everything in superlunar, non-temporal and unchanging reality. The regularity in the sublunar world was established by God at the Creation, but he imposed natural laws and human free will to set the course of events.

In this context, the *Fortuna* poems of the *Carmina Burana* are a description of the sublunar world, and of forces influencing earthly human destiny. The allusions borrowed from classical and authors of late antiquity deepen the seeming truisms and stereotypes into a discussion of philosophico-religious themes which touches upon the freedom of will and the nature of human choice. The moral meaning or message of the group, its tropological level, emphasizes the narrow space of human choice and the relative unimportance of worldly prosperity (and the secondary status of that prosperity itself). One can throw oneself on the wheel of *Fortuna* or avoid it – that is *grosso modo* everything there is to be done. Strictly speaking human choice concerns destiny in the world hereafter: a correct moral choice now assures a favourable last judgement. While on the other hand, resolution and stability do not alone ensure the heavenly birthright at least according to some hints in CB 15, they do have an impact on one's worldly success.

Fortuna was an ambiguous force in the *Anticlaudianus* of Alan of Lille. When freed from the control of *Natura* she sent the world off its rails and inverted everything, but when she was under *Natura*'s regulation she divided

---

169 See page 99-100 above.
170 See Henry Chadwick's interpretation of *Philosophiae consolatio* (Chadwick 1981/1990, 247-253).

indispensable goods in the ideal order. Simultaneously *Fortuna* can be interpreted as a representation of sublunar human history as a tragic story ending in adversity – and, what is more important, as a process where confluent intentional lines of action cause apparently random and unintended events. Even if history follows the providential plan it is made by people but not controlled by them.

The *Fortuna* poems in the *Carmina Burana* can be placed without problems in the medieval category of ethical poetry. Evidently, they do give precepts by which to promote the good and just life and to avoid evil. This is made more than clear in the closing didactic *versus* (CB 18) which explains the message of the poems which was probably already open to the understanding of the contemporary medieval reader. If it is not an arbitrary question, one may ask which might have been their narrative genre in the view of their contemporary readers. The answer would undoubtedly be *historia* or *argumentum* because according to medieval notions these poems did not include untrue nor unprobable representations, rather to contrary. Among comedy, tragedy and satire, the last two seem to be possible genres (and then *argumentum*, that is, the probable and comic genre is dropped out). The poems are tragedies if we think in the words of Bernard Silvester that they teach us to bear adversities, but they are satires if they teach us to avoid the evil and to promote good. Both are possible characterizations. Other *Fortuna* poems handled common and public affairs such as kingdoms and the crimes of powerful, others dealt with private vices – at this level too, the *Fortuna* poems are according to their subject either tragedies or satires.[171]

The *Fortuna* poems do not contradict the clerical and Christian outlook. They apply *interpretatio christiana* to pagan materials and, are easily interpreted as the *integumenta* of the nature of the sublunar world. Neither would an expanded allegorical interpretation have to be forced through their literal (historical) meaning: allegory, a code, would tell how to interpret fickle destinies in the sublunar world, tropology (i.e. the level of moral meaning) would teach determination and the vanity of the pursuit of worldly prosperity. Anagogy, the eschatological sense, would be the same as it always necessarily is in a Christian context; the perfection of human life is possible only with the help of grace and it becomes real only in the life hereafter.[172]

Primarily, the *Fortuna*-poems of the *Carmina Burana* may be read as representing the turning-point of ecclesiastical worldview which also exist inside the collection, for example between the divergent views of *O Fortuna, velut luna* (CB 17) and *Iste mundus furibundus* (CB 24). The latter represents an earlier monastic denial of the world where mutability and change of luck are only evidence of the corrupt nature of this world – withdrawal into the

---

171 On tragedy and satire see among others Isidore of Sevilla, *Etym.* VIII.vii.5-7, ed. Lindsay 1911/1987; Bernard of Utrecht, *Comm. in Theod.* 85-107, p. 61-62. See also Kelly 1993, 36f., 73, 99, 92, 102.

172 On the exegetic allegorical interpretation see part I note 7.

monastery and permanent devotional exercise are the only sensible ways to survive the worldly adversity. The *Fortuna* poems share the same basic view of the transient and unreliable nature of this world, but their point of view is the world of the secular clergy and they try to conceptualize the change and to propose models which help to survive adversity caused by changing luck without withdrawing from the world.

It is quite understandable why Boethius was rediscovered and became so popular in the twelfth-century.[173] For a cleric participating in ecclasiastical and secular government, it was undoubtedly easy to identify himself with Boethius (whose career in the service of Theodoric, king of Goths, ended in imprisonment and execution), and his attempt to bring *vita activa* and *vita contemplativa* together.[174] The *Fortuna* in Boethius' work – as, in their own way, the *Fortuna* poems in the *Carmina Burana* - conceptualizes the changing world without urging withdrawal from it. It is a new kind of *contemptus mundi* which teaches remaining virtuous while acting in the world. According to this interpretation, the secular world was not simply despicable, but one had to keep his internal integrity in the face of it. Such a conception, compared to the monastic denial of the world, obviously offered a more sensible and meaningful approach for learned clerics who worked in towns and secular society.

Alexander Murray's thesis about *Fortuna* as a representation of the new social mobility is at least partly correct inasmuch as the new iconography of *Fortuna* and her wheel and the new abundant *Fortuna*-poetry were a reaction to the new socio-cultural situation. Nevertheless, it was not the same conservative reaction as the doctrine of three orders, which attacked the new social mobility,[175] but an attempt, leaning on authoritative sources, to build up an strategy for clerics acting in the secular world – a strategy which would compensate the monastic denial of the world with a clerical version of *contemptus mundi*. *Fortuna* was considered as a necessary element of the world order. One had to adapt oneself to her influence and, on the other hand, prevent it breaking loose and reversing the ideal moral order based on the order of *Natura*. However, Murray's thesis needs to be corrected. Although the wheel of *Fortuna* was related to the socio-cultural change it did not exactly represent the actual social rotation, but the idea of dynastic change, nature of sublunar history, and the unreliability of this world. As such it was a part of a clerical re-evaluation and reinterpretation of the relation of the men of the church to this world.

---

173 Chenu 1957/1976, 142-158; Courcelle 1967, *passim*.
174 Chadwick 1981/1990, 1-6, 46-66. The destiny of Boethius was well known in the Middle Ages, see Anon., *Saeculi noni auctoris in Boetii Cons. Phil. Comm.* I, p. 3-5.
175 Murray 1978/1990, 96-98; see Duby 1978; Little 1978/1983, 197-198 and *passim*.

Part III

The world upside down: The money-satires of the *Carmina Burana*

Dealing with money: *Nummus* in the *Carmina Burana*

The *Fortuna* poems of the *Carmina Burana* depict the general transitoriness and unreliability of the sublunar world. On the other hand, their allusions and themes show affinity with discussions of the conditions of human action following between *divina providentia* and the randomness, personified by *Fortuna*, reigning in the sublunar world. Ultimately the domain of free will (or decision) remains rather narrow; that is, mainly as a choice between concern for the soul's destiny in the afterlife, or giving in to the pursuit of good luck and prosperity in this world.

Other moral-satirical poems deal mostly with particular problems, such as *avaritia* (i.e. greed and ungenerosity), *simonia* (i.e. buying and selling the gifts of Holy Spirit; that is, ecclesiastical offices), real nobility, precepts for proper behaviour, the avarice of the papal curia in Rome, the crusades, etc. The most central theme is money, *Nummus*, and moral distortions caused by it among the clergy, in the ecclesiastical courts, and in the papal curia. Satire in general, and money satire in particular, was a distinctively twelfth- and thirteenth-century phenomenon in medieval Latin poetry.[1]

In the moral-satirical part of the *Carmina Burana*, *Fortuna* and *Nummus* form, couple in a certain sense even if not a symmetrical one. In the sublunar world they both have power to influence human destiny independently of people's own will and action, and this power seems to be comparable to divine power. *Fortuna* personifies the general principle in the sublunar world, but *Nummus* is a contingent social and historical force, although it is often treated as a general and suprahistorical feature. Both personifications are efforts to conceptualize the new and changing urban (clerical) world. The monastic contempt of the world was no longer a sufficient attitude, although the monastic views constitute a central layer in the moral-satirical poetry of the *Carmina Burana*. The collection is thus evidently located between two worlds; that is, between the old monastic one despising this world and the new urban world of cathedral schools, which was more affirmative of worldly

---

1   Yunck 1963, 1-13 *et passim*; Elredge 1970, 59-69; Witke 1970, 200-266; Schüppert 1972, 11-12; Thomson 1978; Kindermann 1978, 1-11; Mann 1980; Pepin 1988.

pursuits.

The satiric genre had a special position in the twelfth and thirteenth centuries as both the contemporary satirists and the works of Horace, Juvenal and Persius fitted well into the context of Christian conception of poetry. Some medieval writers even identified the composer of satiric poetry (*satiricus*) with the moral philosopher (*ethicus*).[2] One can argue on the one hand that satire, especially satire against the higher clergy and Roman curia, and on the other hand erotic poetry were the main genres of so-called *Vaganten Dichtung* or "goliardic poetry"; that is, the secular Latin poetry of the High Middle Ages.[3]

It has been claimed that satire has twice had a central position in the earlier Western literary scene: first, during early imperial Rome, and again in the twelfth and thirteenth centuries. However, the medieval popularity of the genre can hardly be explained merely through influence of Roman poetry and the genre's suitability as a means of Christian moral persuasion. The socio-cultural change going on during the centuries of the High Middle Ages and the fact that the clerical, literate and learned order was at the centre of this change undoubtedly influenced the new popularity of satire.[4] Satire is in itself a "social" genre, examining public and private *mores* and their relation to prevalent ethical views. The spread of the monetary economy, new social mobility, urbanisation, bureaucratisation of ecclesiastical government, and the new, growing clerical learned order formed the substrate for satiric literature. The viewpoint of satire was usually conservative appealing to an idealized Christian past, but it was at the same time one of the most central means of conceptually organizing the ongoing change. This twofold nature was supported by the models of the ancient poetry of the antiquity and by the Christian moral poetics.[5]

Satires dominate the first part of the *Carmina Burana*, modern editors calling it *Die moralisch-satirischen Dichtungen*. These poems attack *avaritia* and *simonia*, discussing the power of money in the world, especially in the ecclesiastical sphere, depicting the world upside down. Some of them are parodies of biblical and religious texts, expressly and aggressively attacking the Roman curia. There are also some openly satiric deviations later in the collection among the erotic poetry and drinking and gambling songs. The

---

2   Kindermann 1978, 41; see also Witke 1970; Yunck 1963; Schüppert 1972; Mann 1980.
      Bernard Silvester personified satire as *Satira* and called her a friend of philosophers (*Satira, philosophorum amica*; *Comm. in Mart.*, 4. 206-216, p. 90).
3   In this context the "genre" is to be understood as a loose division made on the basis of content especially in the case of erotic poetry. See Preminger 1972/1990, 324-325; also Raby 1934; Jackson 1960, 216-239; Rigg 1977a; Witke 1970, 267-275.
4   Alexander Murray explains the special popularity of satire both in early imperial Rome and in the High Middle Ages through an analogous social situation. New agitation caused by the spreading monetary economy and social mobility were characteristic of both ages. He claims that an analogous social state was behind this reaction in poetry, a similarity naturally strengthened by the strong influence that Roman literature had on medieval literary pursuits. (Murray 1978/1990, 75.)
5   Yunck 1963, *passim*; Schüppert 1972, *passim*; Murray 1978, 71-72.

erotic poetry includes *Dic Christi veritas* (CB 131) and *Bulla fulminante* (CB 131a) which has been attributed to the chancellor of Notre Dame of Paris, Philip the Chancellor (or de Grève; chancellor in 1218, d. 1236).[6] In the midst of the drinking and gambling songs are four satires on the theme of *vanitas* (CB 187-190), and at the end of the collection, before the religious plays, there is a group of more or less satirical poems on avarice and generosity (CB 220-226). Further, recent studies have indicated that several love-poems and parodies could have been intended as ironic and satiric.[7]

The moral-satiric part is divided into fourteen groups formed by one or more *rhythmi* and one *versus*.[8] The fourth group includes three complaints against *simonia* fortified by biblical allusions (CB 8-10), which are followed by an imposing leonine *versus In terra summus rex est hoc tempore Nummus* (CB 11).[9] The poem condenses the theme dominating the whole moral-satiric part as personified money, *Nummus*: money is king on the earth, and not only king but a force at least as remarkable as *Fortuna* in the sublubar world which determines the course of events independent of individual pursuits and moral correctness. Kings are subjected to money, money acts as judge in councils, it fights the wars, it concludes peace, and causes the quarrels. Money buys and sells, it lies. It is personified as *Fortuna*; it has a will of its own which exceeds the pursuits of those who rely and use it. One has to serve money as one serves God (cf. Matt. 6:24), to get into its favour. Thus, according to the poem, it is the god of the greedy, and its power is god-like in the sublunar world. In verses missing from the manuscript version of the *Carmina Burana* but known from other sources, money and the Almighty God of the Book of Samuel are equated, as is the case in CB 14 on *Fortuna*.[10] CB 11 is built on rhetorical repetition, most of the lines starting with the word *nummus*: *Nummus* leads women into errors, *Nummus* makes criminals nobles[11], and when *Nummus* speaks the poor have to fall silent. Nobody is respected if he does not have money.[12]

---

6   Schumann 1930/1961, 86*; Raby 1934, 227-235.
7   Robertson 1980, 131-138, 150; Elliott 1982, 353-368; Pelen 1988; Lehtonen 1996.
8   Schumann 1930/1961, 31*-32*, 41*-44*.
9   CB I.1, 10-29; Schumann 1930/1961, 42*; Hilka & Schumann 1930/1961, 17.
10   Erigit ad plenum de stercore Nummus egenum. (CB 11.9, CB I.1, 15-17; Hilka & Schumann 1930/1961, 24; I. Samuel 2:6-8).
11   The concept of nobility *(nobilitas)* is ambiguous in the *Carmina Burana*: in CB 11 it evidently denotes nobility as a class in feudal society but, on the other hand, CB 7 emphasizes that "true nobility" is identical with "nobility of spirit" independent of birth and standing (CB I.1, 8-9).
      In CB 11 a conservative idea which had in its background the static tripartite social division to clergy, chivalry and peasantry emphasized by the clerical learned is presented (see e.g. Duby 1978, 252-323; Murray 1978, 96-98).
12   I quote CB 11 in its manuscript order and vocabulary, and have left out the verses picked up from other versions by the modern editors. However, I am otherwise mostly following the ortography given by Hilka and Schumann:
      In terra summus rex est hoc tempore Nummus / Nummum mirantur reges et proceres venerantur / Nummo venalis favet ordo pontificalis / Nummus magnorum fit iudex conciliorum / Nummus bella gerit, nec si vult, pax sibi deerit / Nummus agit lites, quia vult deponere dites / Omnia Nummus emit venditque, dat et data demit / Nummus mentitur,

The *Nummus* in the *Carmina Burana* is even more than St. Augustine's *avaritia*, cupidity and greed and the root of all vices.[13] *Nummus* is not only the root of all vices and the object of lust *(cupiditas)* but one of the rulers of the sublunar world perverted from the correct moral order. It is one of the false gods, as Alan of Lille explains when he speaks about *Nummilatria*, the worship of money, as one of the forms of *idolatria*.[14]

The emergence of medieval Latin money satire in the twelfth century was naturally bound to the literary *topos* of the ancient authors, but the appearance of new satire cannot be reduced merely to its literary models. Even if "Queen Money" *(regina pecunia)*[15] was central to Roman satires, it did not acquire such an almost monolithic standing as in the High Middle Ages. In the twelfth century money was represented as a god-like power which destabilized the social relations based on feudal lordship *(Herrschaft, seigneurie)* and reciprocity. It was a false intruder which suddenly became a means of defining social value and action. Although conservative and sighing for the ideal state of the past, the point of view of money-satires was no longer monastic.

From monastic Christianity to the emergence of the secular clergy

The poems of the *Carmina Burana* on the state of the sublunar world are usually satires of which, in the world of medieval commentators, literal surface is open to understanding. However, the texts in the collection use also different ironic, parodic or concealed techniques. In such cases the moral meaning is practically always already explicit at the literal level. The interpretation of their deeper tropological-moral signification does not demand special interpretative efforts, even if the interpretation of single figures and

---

raro verax reperitur / Nummus periuros miseros facit et perituros / Nummus avarorum deus est et spes cupidorum / Nummus in errorem mulierum ducit amorem / Nummus venales dominas facit imperiales / Nummus raptores facit ipsos nobiliores / Nummus habet plures quam celum sidera fures / Si Nummus placitat, cito cuncta pericula vitat / Si Nummus loquitur, pauper tacet; hoc bene scitur / Nummus, ut est certum stultum docet esse disertum / In Nummi mensa sunt splendida fercula densa / Nummus habet medicos, blandos acquirit amicos / Nummus barbatos pisces comedis piperatos / Francorum vinum Nummus bibit atque marinum / Nummus dulce putat, quod eum gens tota salutat / Nummus famosas vestes gerit et pretiosas / Nummus adoratur, quia virtutes operatur / Vile facit carum quod dulce est, reddit amarum / Et facit audire surdos claudosque salire / De Nummo quedam maiora prioribus edam / Vidi cantantem Nummum, missam celebrantem / Nummus cantabat, Nummus responsa parabat / Vidi quod flebat, dum sermonem faciebat / Et subridebat, populum quia decipiebat / Nullus honoratur, sine Nummo nullus amatur / Quem genus infamat Nummus: "probus est homo!" clamat / Esse patet cuique, quod Nummus regnat ubique / Sed quia consumi poterit cito gloria mundi / Ex hac esse schola non vult sapientia sola / Nullus ei carus, nisi qui fore nescit avarus. (CB I.1, 15-29; CB facs. 46/47.) The dating and attribution are obscure.

13 Radix est omnium malorum avaritia, quam quidam adpetentes a fide pererraverunt et insuerunt se doloribus multis. (Augustine, *De civitate Dei* I.x.1; see also *De libero arbitrio* III.xviii.48; cf. St. Paul, *I.Tim.* 6:10: Radix omnium malorum est cupiditas.)

14 *De planctu Naturae* XII.pr.6, p. 852-857.

15 Horace *Epistulae* I.vi.36-38; Juvenal, *Saturae* I.109-114; see also Yunck 1963, 15-18.

tropes do make such demands.

Such moral-satirical poetry can be seen in the context of change that was going on in the clerical world. Many texts can still be reduced to the ways of thinking proper to monastic Christianity, and they continue the conventions of categorical contempt for the world.[16] On the other hand, several texts are already conceptualising problems which were hardly acute in the closed, static and hierarchically unambiguous monasteries. These texts pertain to the world of the new learned and urban clerical circles. This twofold situation is apparent when one compares the *Fortuna*-poems and *Iste mundus furibundus* (CB 24) discussed above. The sophisticated and learned description of the sublunar world is far from direct contempt of the world and emphasis on the theme of *vanitas*, although both share the same predominantly Christian distrust of the dubious nature of this world and look to the immutability of the world beyond. Change, mutability of luck and social movement were current topics which could not be conceptualized satisfactorily by simple rejection of this world. It is understandable at the same time that the poets of an urban world such as Horace, Juvenal and Persius provided tools for interpretation of the new situation.[17] Among the Christian authors the most "urban", Augustine and Boethius, also had a very influential position in the twelfth and early thirteenth century. For instance, the Augustinian rule written for a religious community in Hippo, became popular in the twelfth century precisely because it was intended for an urban order, and not for rural circumstances like the rule of St. Benedict and its later versions.[18] The birthplace of the *Carmina Burana* has also been ascribed to either to the cathedral school or the bishop See of Brixen (Bressanone), the Augustinian house in Neustift (Novacella) near it, or to the See of Seckau, also associated with Augustinians. The collection has affinities with the urban centres of the time, especially Paris.[19]

The clerical learned who earlier had emphasized static values faced a new social spectrum and change in towns and cities. In this context the concepts such as *Fortuna* seemed to be useful. Further it is in this context that the satires about *avaritia* and other vices arising from the appearance of money were composed. Not only was the surrounding urban society with its seemingly governing forces of money and fortuitousness, *Nummus* and *Fortuna*, in constant flux, but the clerical order was also part of that movement. Indeed, it was in the twelfth century that the new separate

---

16 Cf. e.g. Conrad of Hirsau, *Dialogus de contemptu mundi vel amore*; cf. Bultot 1969. On the change from monastic to secular Christianity see among others Chenu 1957/1976, 225-251; also Baldwin 1970; Luscombe 1971; Duby 1978, 252-265; Little 1978/1983; Stock 1983.

17 Yunck 1963, 1-45; Murray 1978/1990, 71-77, 81-109.

18 Heimbucher 1933, 398-469; Lawrence 1984, 17-35; Southern 1970/1983, 214-272; Little 1978/1983, 99-11; Sicard 1991, 7-21.

19 Dronke 1965, 564; Bischoff 1970a; idem 1970b; Lipphardt 1982, 211-221 Steer 1983, 34-36; Sayce 1992, 198-203; about Augustinians in general, see note 18 above. It is interesting that one of the best manuscripts of Conrad of Hirsau's *Dialogus super auctores* is found from the library of Neustift (Novacella) near Brixen (Bressanone) (Huygens 1970, 10).

professional and urban order of learned men emerged, opening completely new ways of meritocratic social mobility.[20] The Boethian moral teaching did not urge withdrawal from the world but accepting the change of fortune with Stoic serenity - one can assume that this attitude suited the men of the new clerical class who had to get used to the whims of *Fortuna* in their public offices in ecclesiastical and secular hierarchy particularly well.[21] The closed world of the monasteries did not have to deal similarly with rapid changes, whims of chance and social movement. The Benedictine monasteries were often exclusively aristocratic, their inner hierarchy beyond question and there were not the same possibilities for meritocratic movement as in the cities where intellectually able clerics could establish own schools, get into high offices both in ecclesiastical and secular government, and had constantly to deal with money.

However, the studies and advancement in the career of junior clerics ordinarily depended on their original bishop's generosity *(largitas)*.[22] Indeed, it was the episcopal financing that made it possible for clerics from a humble background to study in foreign schools and to advance their clerical career. The relation of a cleric and his bishop was based on mutual reciprocity and, as such, was typically a part of medieval system of lordship *(Herrschaft, seigneurie)*.[23] At the same time, money enabled the widespread use of study in distant cathedral schools since otherwise the income from ecclesiastical *prebenda* would not have been changeable into tranportable units (i.e. money) and studies in remote localities would not have been possible. On the other hand, money seemed to be an independent and strangely impersonal means in the web of lordship. New meritocratic and monetary elements shook the old system of feudal lordship.[24]

The historical dichotomy between monastic Christianity and the urban clerical world is naturally only a rough scheme which is, however, based on a contemporary medieval view, i.e. those who belonged to closed orders and those who lived in secular society. Contemporary authors repeatedly emphasized the difference between a monk and a cleric.[25] Of course, one has also to keep in mind that the monastic redemption of the world constituted a part of the clerical world view. Nevertheless, the theme of contempt of the world was treated in a new and more sophisticated way. The Christian basic themes constituted the assumptions of satires, and their criticism and demands of reform were constructed entirely on Christian moral dogma. Satires were

---

20 Le Goff 1957/1985; Southern 1970/1983, 208-211; Baldwin 1970, 150-157; *idem* 1982 138-172; Murray 1978/1990, 213-233.
21 Cf. the careers of several clerical learned in the twelfth and thirteenth centuries, e.g. Thomas à Becket, John of Salisbury, Walter of Châtillon, Philip the Chancellor.
22 Baldwin 1970, 117-130; Murray 1978, 213-233; Moulin 1991, 19-40. On this leading to the literary *topos*, see Betten 1976.
23 Brunner 1958/1984, 5-9, 53-64; Baldwin 1970, 117-149.
24 Murray 1978, 50-58; 81-109; Little 1978/1983, 3-41; Fossier 1982/1990, 305-314; Bisson 1994, 6-24.
25 Delhaye 1947, 211-216.

grounded on conservative and traditionalistic utopian views of an idealized past,[26] which derived their force from Christian moral dynamics. The different elements, both monastic Christian and clerical texts as well as satire against the Roman curia are intertwined.

The world upside down and the kinds of idolatry

In the *Carmina Burana* poems like *Iste mundus furibundus* (CB 24) represent the most open denial of the world with its direct reminder of transitoriness and power of the "law of the flesh" in this world.[27] There are also more complicated texts using the *topos* of the world upside down (e.g. CB 6 and 39) which vacillate between the monastery and cathedral school.[28]

Florebat olim studium (CB 6) complains about the degeneration of learning and behaviour:

> *Florebat olim studium, / nunc vertitur in tedium; / iam scire diu viguit, / sed ludere prevaluit. / iam pueris astutia / contingit ante tempora, / qui per malivolentiam / excludunt sapientiam. / sed retro actis seculis / vix licuit discipulis / tandem nonagenarium / quiescere post studium. / at nunc decennes pueri / decusso iugo liberi / se nunc magistros iactitant, / ceci cecos precipitant, / implumes aves volitant, / brunelli chordas incitant, / boves in aula salitant, / stive precones militant. / in taberna Gregorius / iam disputat inglorius; / severitas Ieronymi / partem causatur obuli; / Augustinus de segete, / Benedictus de vegete / sunt colloquentes clanculo / et ad macellum sedulo. / Mariam gravat sessio, / nec Marthe placet actio; / iam Lie venter sterilis, / Rachel lippescit oculis. / Catonis iam rigiditas / convertitur ad ganeas, / et castitas Lucretie / turpi servit lascivie. quod prior etas respuit, / iam nunc latius claruit; / iam calidum in frigidum / et humidum in aridum, / virtus migrat in vitium, / opus transit in otium; / nunc cuncte res a debita / exorbitantur semita / vir prudens hoc consideret, / cor mundet et exoneret, / ne frustra dicat 'Domine!' / in ultimo examine; / quem iudex tunc arguerit, / appellare non poterit.[29]*

Once learning flourished, now its turned to boredom; knowing used to be valued, but now playing is preferred.
Now boys are savouring astuteness before their time, and in their malevolence they exclude wisdom.

---

26 Brian Stock has drawn a distinction between traditional and traditionalistic: the first depicts activities based of inherited manners (e.g. orality, traditional customary jurisdiction etc.), and the latter denotes conscious orientation towards the past as was the case of several medieval "renaissances", and which is indeed one of the motors of the process of rationalization and modernisation (Stock 1990, 159-171).

27 See pages 112-115 above.

28 On the world upside down *topos* see Curtius 1948, 102-106; also Haavio 1959. See e.g. Eberhardus Alemannus, 340-341; also Alan of Lille, *Anticlaudianus & De planctu Naturae*. See also Lehtonen 1996.

29 CB I.1, 7-8. The dating and attribution are obscure.

Let us look back in the active centuries when disciples did not spare themselves - and not until in their eighties did they retire from their studies.

But now ten-year-old lads can free themselves from the yoke and boast as masters; the blind are leading the blind, and unfledged birds are flying, donkeys are plucking chords, bulls are dancing at the court, and ploughboys are acting as preachers.

Inglorious Gregory is now disputating down in the inn; austere Jerome is cavilling about the distribution of pennies; Augustine from the granary and Benedict from the wine-cellar are gathering together in a secret meeting and hurry from there to the shambles.

Mary is bored with listening and action does not please Martha; now the womb of Leah is sterile, and Rachel snivels with bleary eyes.

Stern Cato has turned to drink and feast, and the chaste Lucretia is lewdly serving lasciviousness.

All that earlier generations used to shun is now shining generally; now hot is turning cold, moist is dry, virtue is changing to vice, and work is translated into idleness; now all things of merit stray from the right path.

Now, prudent man, consider all this with care, clear and unburden your heart, so that you do not have to cry in vain 'Lord!' at the Last Judgement; the one who is then sentenced by the Judge cannot make a last appeal.

The world is really turned upside down; not only human society but also nature and, what is even worse, biblical characters act quite contrary to what is expected of them. The poem has a twofold structure: first, it depicts the prevailing state of affairs to which it turns again in the last lines. In the middle of this description there is a textual comparison with exemplary authoritative figures represented "falsely" as acting contrary to common expectations. In the terms of irony and satire as they were defined in medieval treatises, the presentation of the actual state of affairs thus becomes ironical. This is not how things ought to be, and this ironical treatment is confirmed by a comparison with falsely depicted authority figures. The poem plays with a tension between degradation of the world and the authoritative norm by using the topos of the world upside down.

The world upside down *topos* corresponds to the trope of irony among rhetorical concepts, a trope usually understood more broadly than simply transference of the meaning of a single word, that is, as a extended trope or a narrative which in its entirety meant something other than what was stated at the literal level.[30] Indeed, medieval theoreticians of literary genres thought that there could be ironic satire which at its literal level praised vices – the text ought to be read in this case for its contrary meaning.[31] *Florebat olim studium* and the *topos* of the world upside down can be understood as just this kind of satire but the poem's ironic structures are however different and

---

30   E.g. Diomedes, *Ars grammatica*, p. 456-462; see also Knox 1989.
31   Bernard of Utrecht, *Comm. in Theod.* 104-105, p. 62.

more complicated from mere praise of the vices. On the other hand, in the final verses it ensures that the moral message does not remain obscure - the prudent man considering the Last Judgement surely understands that the state of affairs presented earlier is wrong, and the model given by it should not be followed.

A satire praising vices trusts on the moral presumptions of the reader – thus the praise is turned into a warning about the perniciousness of vices. *Florebat olim studium* also builds up its irony on the prior knowledge of a probable reader but it proceeds differently. Firstly, it depicts the current state of affairs, and then gives some textual *exampla* which deviate from the authoritative sources. The literal meaning in the beginning does not become ironic but the actual state of affairs is itself presented as distorted into something that it ought not to be. The proper moral order does not reign in the sublunar world. The first fifteen lines describe schoolboys who esteem themselves too highly and call themselves masters, and confuse true knowing *(scire)* with playing *(ludere)*. The exaggerated contrasts at the beginning between the present ten-year-old masters and the past scholars not retiring until in their eighties already hints at present absurdities. These lines are followed by scornful similes of young masters who are like the blind leading the blind[32] and unfledged birds.[33]

If these similes already refer to the inverted state of affairs, another kind of ironic treatment begins in the twentyfirst line. Pope Gregory (the Great), St. Jerome, St. Augustine and St. Benedict all enjoy their stay in the tavern drinking and gorging themselves. The exemplary women of the *Bible*, i.e. Mary, Martha, Leah and Rachel behave or deviate from their description in textual authority. Cato has forgotten his famous asperity, and Lucretia has lost her chastity. Now the literal meaning of the text is apparently false, which means that the text has to be taken contary to its literal surface, i.e. "ironically".

A medieval reader might have understood the first part of the poem as a depiction of a real state of affairs in which exaggerations and absurd parallels indicate ridicule. However, its continuation does not describe an actual state of affairs but is openly at odds with the authoritative knowledge given by the Holy Scripture. A monk and a cleric knew well that the *divina pagina* and other authoritative ecclesiastical writings proved the blamelessness and the exemplariness of the Fathers of the Church; they also knew that Mary was a patient listener, that Martha was active, Leah fertile and Rachel witheld her tears and had flashing eyes.[34] The sternness of Cato was a commonplace, and the moral rigidity of the contents of whatever collections of moral precepts could be called *Disticha Catonis* regardless of their true origin was

---

32 Cf. Matt. 15:14; Luke 6:39.
33 Horace, *Epod.* 1.19.
34 On Leah and Rachel see Genesis 29:16-35; Jer. 31:15-17; on Mary and Martha see Luke 10:39-42. Cf. *vita contemplativa vs. vita activa*, e.g. Duby 1978, 111.

enough for them to be attributed to Cato.[35] Lucretia was also well-known for her chastity, for instance to Henry of Settimello.[36] If the state of affairs depicted in the rest of the poem is literally false, then the target of the description at the beginning appears in an ironic light: in the distant past learning flowered, but now against this morally and ideally correct state of affairs, the young lads are playing and toying in the name of learning.

The last lines explain that this degenerate state of affairs is caused by forgetting true, previously honoured values. Thus now nature as well as the human sphere becomes inverted and cold turns to hot, moist to dry, virtue to vice, and action to idleness. The order of nature and the moral order are analogous, the inversion of nature being a moral event, as it is in the long allegorical poems of Alan of Lille.[37] This kind of satire is "history" in Bernard Silvester's terms, that is, this depiction of the state of affairs is literally true and it is a warning about the vices prevalent. Indeed, the end of the poem urges the prudent man to consider this depiction (and what goes on in the world around him) and to think of his own destiny at the Last Judgement.

Florebat olim studium is a conservative complaint *(planctus)* about the degeneration of the times and *mores*. Its conservative point of view is based on the imagined flowering of past learning. The characteristics of this learning were gravity and lifelong toil. In the context of the twelfth and thirteenth centuries the claim of degeneration of learning is rather absurd, in fact learning was vigorous and deviated radically from the quiet life of earlier centuries. Indeed the poem is an attack on the new agonistic and passionate world of the cathedral schools. Its description of the flourishing of learning is a description of the static and contemplative learning proper to monasteries. The idealized learned men of the past in the poem did not pursue wisdom from secular learning but contemplated the *divina pagina*. *Florebat olim studium* is a manifestation of the monastic world taking sides against the new world of cathedral schools.[38]

Conservative *Florebat olim studium* used a false parapharase of a textual authority to prove the falsehood of the current state of affairs. It operates on levels of literal and tropological or moral meaning. The wordly degeneration is not regarded merely as general degeneration but as particular instance caused by the change in the nature of ecclesiastical studies and learning. It favours static monastery schools and is vehement against the new urban cathedral schools. A hybrid poem in the *Carmina Burana*, *In huius mundi patria*, which is according to modern editors a compilation of three separate poems (CB 39, 39a and 39b) is a reaction closer in outlook to the world of secular clerics. However, it is the hybrid nature of the poem that makes it an

---

35 Hilka & Schumann 1930/1961, 10.
36 *Elegia de diversitate Fortunae et Philosophiae consolatione* 717 ff.; Hilka & Schumann 1930/1961, 10.
37 See Wetherbee 1972; also Stock 1972.
38 Cf. Little 1978/1983, 174.

interesting intermediate form which combines apparent monastic *vanitas*-themes to more complex matters closer to the urban clerical class. There is a description of idolatry *(idolatria)*, particularly of the power of money (CB 39 *In huius mundi patria*), two stanzas about transitoriness and about the vanity of vanities (CB 39a *In huius mundi domo*) and some precepts for a priest about the celebration of the Mass (CB 39b *Cum vadis ad altare*). The order of stanzas in the manuscript is, in the numbers of the modern edition 39.1, 39a.1, 39b, 39.a2, 39.2-7. I will examine the text as it is appears in the manuscript.

Idolatry reigns in this world.[39] Spiritual gifts are openly for sale – the poem puts forward an argument about the spread of simony just as CB 8, 9 and 10 did earlier:

> *39.1. In huius mundi patria / regnat idolatria; / ubique sunt venalia / dona spiritalia. / custodes sunt raptores / atque lupi pastores, / principes et reges / subverterunt leges. / hac incerta domo / insanit omnis homo. / sed ista cum vento / transibunt in momento.*
>
> *39a.1. In huius mundi domo / miser qui vivis homo, / quod cinis es, memento: / transibis in momento. / post carnem cinis eris / atque morte teneris. / cinis et origo / sit tibi formido. / cum spiritus cadit / et ad Dominum vadit, / qui eum dedit. / miser, qui hoc non credit.*
>
> *39b. Cum vadis ad altare / missam celebrare, / te debes preparare, / vetus expurgare / de corde fermentum; / sic offers sacramentum: / invoca Christum, / psalmum dicas istum: / "Iudica", / teque ipsum preiudica, / Israel et Iuda / cordis mala denuda.*
>
> *39a.2. Vanitatum vanitas / et omnia vanitas! / est animalis homo / in huius mundi domo. / cuncta, que sub sole, / assimilantur mole. / nam omnia volvuntur, / quedam dissolvuntur, / quedam ad vitam crescunt / et omnia decrescunt. / sed spiritalis homo / Dei regnat in domo.*
>
> *39.2. Lia placet lipposa, / sed Rachel flet formosa, / que diu manens sterilis / ob immanitatem sceleris / generat an(i)cilla; / nam Raab ancilla / navem mundi mersit, / discordia dispersit / mortis seminaria, / et mundi luminaria / luminant obscure; / pauci vivunt secure.*
>
> *39.3. Doctores apostolici / et iudices katholici / quidam colunt Albinum / et diligunt Rufinum, / cessant iudicare / et student devorare / gregem sibi commissum; / hi cadunt in abyssum. / si cecus ducit cecum, / in fossam cadit secum. / hi tales subsannantur / et infra castra cremantur.*
>
> *39.4. Episcopi cornuti / conticuere muti, / ad predam sunt parati / et indecenter coronati; / pro virga ferunt lanceam, / pro infula galeam, / clipeum pro stola / – hec mortis erit mola – / loricam pro alba / – hec occasio calva –, / pellem pro humerali / pro ritu seculari.*
>
> *39.5. Sicut fortes incedunt / et a Deo discedunt, / ut leones feroces / et ut aquile veloces, / ut apri fredentes / exacuere dentes, / linguas ut*

---

39 Alan of Lille considered the disappearance of ideal moral order and its restoration in the sublunar world in his *Anticlaudianus*. The degeneration of nature and perverted language of poets are interconnected (VIII.pr.4, p. 832-842). The sublunar world has turned upside down, and the worship of the true God is displaced by idolatry. The forms of idolatry are *Nummilatria*, the worship of money, and *Bacchilatria*, the worship of Bacchus, i.e. gluttony and drunkenness (XII.pr.6, p. 852-857).

serpentes / pugnare non valentes, / mundo consentientes / et tempus redimentes, / quia dies sunt mali, / iure imperali.

39.6. Principes et abbates / ceterique vates / ceteri doctores / (...?) / iura deposuerunt / canones ac decreta. / sicut scripsit propheta, / Deum exacerbaverunt / et Sanctum Israel blasphamaverunt.

39.7. Monachi sunt nigri / et in regula sunt pigri, / bene cucullati / et male coronati. / quidam sunt cani / et sensibus profani. / quidam sunt fratres / et verentur ut patres. / dicuntur Norpertini / et non Augustini. / in cano vestimento / novo gaudent invento.[40]

39.1. In the fatherland of this world idolatry reigns; everywhere the spiritual gifts are for sale. Custodians are robbers, and shepherds turn out to be wolves, princes and kings subvert the laws. These uncertainties make everyone insane in the house. But all these are wiped in a moment by the wind.

39a.1. In the house of this world you live in misery, remember that you are ash: at any moment you will die. From flesh you turn to ashes, when death takes you away. Ash is the origin of your fear. When the spirit leaves you, it goes to Lord who gave it. You are miserable, who do not believe this.

39b. When you are going to altar to celebrate the Mass, you should prepare yourself and expel old ferment from your heart. This is how you offer the Sacrament: make an appeal to Christ by pronouncing this psalm: "Judge me" and pre-judge yourself, Israel and Judah, and expunge evil from your heart.

39a.2. Vanity of vanities, and all is vanity! Man is an animal in the house of this world. Everything under the sun is made similar in the mill. For everything is revolved, some are dissolved, others grow towards life, and everybody withers away. For it is the spiritual man that reigns in the House of God.

39.2. Blear eyed Leah pleases, but beautiful Rachel is crying, (because she) has stayed so long sterile, because of dreadful crimes, the maid is giving birth. For Rahab the maid is sinking the ship of world, discord is spreading in the nursery garden of death, and the light of the world is lighting obscurely. Only a few live securely.

39.3. Some of the apostolical doctors and catholical judges are cultivating Albinus (Silver) and honour Rufinus (Gold). They cease to judge and are studious to gorge the flock commissioned to them; they are falling into the abyss. If the blind leads the blind they both fall into a pit. Beneath they are grimacing, and in the military camp they are cremated.

39.4. Mitred bishops stay mute, they are prompt to booty and are shamefully enthroned. Instead of a staff they carry a lance, instead of a mitre a helmet, instead of a stole a shield – this will be the mill of death – instead of an alb they wear armour – this is a bald occasion – instead of humeral veils they wear furs, and instead of sacred offices they take care of secular affairs.

39.5. Thus the strong ones are on the march and distancing themselves from God, as ferocious lions and fast-flying eagles, as teeth-grinding wild boars, with serpents' tongues, fighting unhealthily, consenting

---

40   CB I.1, 62-64; CB facs. 7^r/7^v.

with the world and buying time, because the days are bad under imperial rule.

39.6. Princes and abbots and other seers (or poets), other doctors (***) displaced justice, canonical laws and decretals. As the prophet wrote, they made God angry and blasphemed sacred Israel.

39.7. Monks are black and lazy in their rule, well-clothed and badly tonsured, some are grey and their senses are profane. Some are brethren but let themselves be venerated as fathers. They call themselves Norbertines, not Augustinians, and are rejoicing over this innovation in grey habit.

The beginning of the poem is a general complaint about the inverted moral order in the sublunar world. The next stanza (39a.1) is an even sterner *memento mori* and as such its spirit is thoroughly monastic. The third stanza (39b) moves suprisingly to precepts for a priest who should take care of his own heart's purity before judging others. The poem then turns again to the theme of vanity with the words of Ecclesiastes (39a.2). It then (39.2-7) gives a description of inverted ideal order proceeding from false authoritative references to actual states of affairs - basically the same ironic technique as in CB 6 with a different order of procedure. Now, the textual references are presented first[41] and a more particular description of different ecclesiastical offices and orders follows. Money has replaced the true values and true God when bishops and doctors run after silver and gold.[42] The shamefully crowned bishops remain silent and are ready to rob their flocks. Instead of a priestly habit they clothe themselves in armour, and instead of sacred offices they take care of secular affairs. All this seems to be caused by imperial rule.[43]

The poem proceeds thus from the general description of the degenerate state of the sublunar world to a reminder for the transitoriness, and to precepts of celebration of the Mass in an inwardly correct state. Then it returns to general vanity, transitoriness and to the fact that "everything is revolved in the same mill". Now, the revolver is not *Fortuna* who distributed wordly success and adversities, but a more powerful force which grinds all animal and corporeal into nothingness. This mill resembles more inevitable fate, "the law of the flesh", which knows no exceptions, than chance.[44] Only the "spiritual man" survives the mill: this ellipsis signifies both the spiritually

---

41 In the *Bible* it was the beautiful Rachel and not blear-eyed Leah who pleased Jacob (Genesis 29:16-35). Hilka and Schumann suppose that in the poem it could be an allegory of the Church (Rachel) and the secular world (Leah) (1930/1961, 66).

42 Saints *Albinus* and *Rufinus* meant usually silver and gold, although sometimes white and red wine (Hilka & Schumann 1930/1961, 67). This pair is very common in medieval satirical literature (Lehmann 1922-23/1963, 25-30, 38; Yunck 1963, 71-75; Thomson 1978, 74-75).

43 The dating and target of CB 39 remains rather uncertain according to Hilka and Schumann. The Premonstratensian or Norbertin order was founded in 1121 which gives a *terminus a quo* for the poem. The critique against fighting bishops might point to Reinald of Dassel (archbishop of Cologne 1159-67) and Christian of Mainz, and thus to the rule of Frederick Barbarossa (1152-1190) which seems to be a rather late date to criticize the *novum* of the Norbertins. (Hilka & Schumann 1930/1961, 64-68, esp. 68).

44 See Cioffari 1935, *passim*; Chadwick 1986/1987, 61-67, 105.

inclined human believing in God, following his orders, and the soul which remains when flesh is turned to ashes. The poem then presents the conventional exemplary women of the *Bible*, Leah and Rachel, again in a state contrary to the revelation, clearly indicating the perverted state of affairs. Rahab, identified with the church, is sinking.[45] The rest of the poem then enumerates all the faults of the ecclesiastical hierarchy and secular princes.

The description of the unreliable nature of this world and the prevailing moral degeneration includes several stages. CB 39, separated by modern editors as a poem on its own, is not, despite its stern attack on wordly decadence, purely committed to the monastery: rather, its point of view is close to that of a poor and religiously rigid cleric who criticizes the decadence of the powerful and all the orders of the church. The sympathy of the poem might be for the collegial Augustinian order because it mocks the grey brothers who call themselves Norbertins instead of Augustinians in the last stanza.[46] In the *Carmina Burana*, however, the poem has a *mise en abyme* which presents the theme of *vanitas* (CB 39a) and resembles the absolute denial of the world already presented in *Iste mundus furibundus* (CB 24). This sequence is evidently closer to monastic withdrawal from the world than the reformistic CB 39, which demands the correction of *mores*. CB 39b does not lean clearly to either side but its demand for inner purity and self-judgement could be put forward for the clergy of the cathedral or collegial church as well for monks.

Change and uncertainty: the crisis of reciprocal relations

In the world of personal seigneurial relations, there was no conceptual means of analysing the ongoing structural change. This change was especially clearly visible in the church, and it brought the clerical ideology emphasizing reciprocity into crisis.[47] The problem had to be personalized.

Several modern scholars have emphasized that during the twelfth century a new specialised and professional learned "class" emerged.[48] The competition, both intellectual and economic, was intense. Despite the fact that at the same time both in the ecclesiastical hierarchy and in secular government new possibilities for advancement opened to learned clerics and that the scholarly institutions themselves grew and absorbed the members of this new

---

45 Hilka & Schumann 1930/1961, 67.
46 quidam sunt cani / et sensibus profani. / quidam sunt fratres / et verentur ut patres. / dicuntur Norpertini / et non Augustini. / in cano vestimento / novo gaudent invento. (CB 39.7.5-12; CB I.1, 63.) The "grey brothers" have secular instincts although they venerate themselves as "fathers", that is consecrated priests. The grey monks were premonstratensians who called themselves after their founder Norbert. See above note 42. See also Little 1978/1983, 104-105; about the *Carmina Burana* and Augustinians, Sayce 1992, 201-202.
47 See Little 1978/1983; Murray 1978; Duby 1978; Vance 1986.
48 Delhaye 1947, 211-268; Le Goff 1957/1985, 7-69; Baldwin 1970, *passim*; Mundy 1973/1980, 463-484; Murray 1978/1990, 213-233.

"class", many clerics saw the situation as menacing and contradictory in respect to original Christian ideals. When the clergy dependent on the favours of a single bishop multiplied, and when the lower clergy had to pay tribute to both bishop and pope in addition to reciprocal service, it was quite natural that satires reminiscent of CB 39 accusing the ecclesiastical shepherds of devouring their flocks instead of tending them should appear.[49] On the other hand, learned and half-independent clerical order were no longer humble servants of bishops, but challenged them both in the throes of their own intellectual hubris[50] and on the grounds of Christian moral obligations. Latin clerical poetry was not any more supported solely by ecclesiastical patrons – a new learned audience in the environments of schools and ecclesiastical courts had emerged. This literary publicity, half-detached from the consistorial and ecclesiastical control, was undoubtedly one precondition for the satire's inner freedom and its popularity. The change probing reciprocal obligations is a natural context for the profusion of accusations of avarice and simony.

The manuscript of the *Carmina Burana* in its present state begins with attacks on simony and avarice and attacks the disappearance of generosity *(largitas)*. The first poem in the collection *Manus ferens munera* (CB 1)[51] castigates venality and the power of money. The following poems continue the same theme. CB 3 *Ecce torpet probitas* complains of the paralysing of honesty and the burial of virtue. Now the stingy person is generous; that is in sharing his stinginess. *Regnat avaritia* – greediness reigns. Truth is made a lie, and all rights are violated. The rich refuse to know the words I give, you give, he gave, to give.[52]

Avaritia leads to the rejection of honesty *(probitas)*, generosity *(largitas)* and truth *(veritas)*. Avarice is the real root of all evil – *avaritia radix omnium malorum* as Augustine stated, or as in the inverted word-order used in Walter Map's acrostic *ROMA (radix omnium malorum avaritia)*.[53]

The money satires first reveal their close connection with the schools by

49 Cf. Baldwin 1970, 117-149; Yunck 1963, 130.
50 Cf. Peter Abelard, *Historia calamitatum*.
51 The original order of pages in the manuscript was different from the order of the *codex* in its present state. *Folium* 43 is the first leaf of the original version handed down to us. CB 1 edited by Hilka & Schumann is mainly a compilation from other manuscripts. Only the end of the sixth stanza is from the *Carmina Burana*. (CB I.1, 1-2; CB facs. 43; Schumann 1930/1961, 5*-13*, 31*-39*.)
52 In the manuscript there are the three first stanzas of the modern edition - the two last (4 and 5) are an addition picked up from other sources by Hilka & Schumann. I quote the text according to the manuscript version, following however the ortography and punctuation of the modern editors:
    1. Ecce torpet probitas, / virtus sepelitur; / fit iam parca largitas, / parcitas largitur; / verum dicit falsitas, / veritas mentitur. / Omnes iura ledunt / et ad res illicitas / licite recedunt.
    2. Regnat avaritia, / regnant et avari; / mente quivis anxia / nititur ditari, / cum sit summa gloria / censu gloriari. / Omnes iura ledunt / et ad prava quelibet / impie recedunt.
    3. Multum habet oneris / do das dedi dare; / verbum hec pre ceteris / norunt ignorare / divites, quos poteris / mari comparare. / Omnes iura ledunt / et in rerum numeris / numeros excedunt. (CB I.1, 3-5; CB facs. 43.)
53 *De civ. Dei* I.x.1, p. 222. See Yunck 1963, 93.

combining the forms of grammatical exercises and the requests for generosity. The first lines in the manuscript (CB 1.6.5-10) already toy with grammatical terminology: *nostrum fedus hodie / defedat et inficit / nostros ablativos, / qui absorbent vivos, / moti per dativos / movent genitivos.*[54] Later *Est modus in verbis* (CB 20)[55] reminds the reader the antonyms 'I give, you give' *(do, das)* and 'I hold' *(teneo)*.

The poems summarize in simple grammatical cases and semantic opposites the core of reciprocal thinking in which the basis of exchange are presents, return presents and services. This exchange was not based on measurable units but on reciprocity in which material and immaterial exchange were confused, the principle of just prices was followed, and the value of a present was rather determined according to the potential of the giver and to the standing of the receiver than according to actual value. The principle of generosity was naturally emphasized both by Christian moral dogma and the classical tradition of the virtues, but in the case of the grammatical play of clerical poetry, it is hard not to see in its case at least partial reference to reciprocity and the seigneurial system regulating the actions of the clerical order.[56]

The last poems of the collection before the church plays close the circle and return to the opening themes. *Artifex qui condidit hominem ex ludo* (CB 224) begs the noble bishops, the learned men *(viri litterati)*, the high legates *(legati)* of kings and the blessed presbyters to notice the poverty of the *persona* of the poem.[57] Similarly *Sacerdotes et levite* (CB 225) urges the priests, doctors and *litterati* to remember the central Christian virtue of charity *(caritas).*[58]

The last *rhythmus* of the collection, *Mundus est in varium sepe variatus* (CB 226), has its own title *De mundi statu*, i.e. concerning the state of the world,[59] which drifted away from an ordered state *(a statu ordine)* from which the old are withdrawing and the ancient (good) habits are disappearing. The new generation is inexperienced and wild: *Saturnus* reigned before, now *Ludowicus* reigns, that is, following the golden age, people have fallen into decadence. The *Ludowicus* in the poem may refer to Louis VII of France (1137-1180).[60] The poet wishes that someone could still remain pure and

---

54 CB facs. 43ʳ; CB I.1, 1. I am following the manuscript version.
55 CB I.1, 39.
56 On medieval hierarchical reciprocity Little 1978/1983, 3-18; see also Duby 1973/1985, 60-69; *idem* 1978, 57, 81, 93-94, 192, 198-203, 305, 321-323, 381; also Gurevich 1970/1979, 74f.; *idem* 1972/1983, 213f.; Baldwin 1970, 117f.; Vance 1986, 111-151. For ancient ideas based on reciprocity see Aristotle, *Eth. Nic.* 1132b21-1134a16, 1158b1-33, 1162b1-4, 1162b16-1163a24; also Finley 1954/1979; *idem* 1974; Mauss 1950/1993. On lordly domination *(Herrschaft)* see Brunner 1958/1984; Hietaniemi 1992, 146-151.
57 O prelati nobiles, viri litterati, / summi regis legati, / o presbyteri beati, / genus preelectum, / me omnibus abiectum / consolans despectum / virtutis vestre per effectum, / pauperie mea conteste / patet manifeste, / quod eo sine veste / satis inhoneste. / si me vultis audire: / contestor me scire / viro probitatis mire. (CB 224.2; CB I.3, 83.)
58 CB 225.2; CB I.3, 84.
59 CB facs. 98ʳ; CB I.3, 85-86.
60 Thus argues Bischoff on the basis of poem's form and the age of the manuscript (CB I.3, 86). At the time of Louis VII the Capetian dynasty had indeed become wealthier and it

would support this fallen world with giving and would offer presents from a full cornucopia. He would be honoured with the title generous, and he would achieve something which is worth more than ownership.

The first-person narrator in the poem regards the fulfilment of his wish as highly improbable since a generous person is rarer than the phoenix, and may well be compared to the chimera, a non-existent creature. Thus the world sinking without support, rushes, falls down and collapses when nobody turns to the virtuous paths of generosity. The open complaint about the disappearance of generosity turns halfway through the poem to ironic allegory – there is indeed one species of generosity characteristic of clerics, that which was practised by the famous Thais in the baths of Cumae and Baiae. The clerics are generous like Thais in cheating and emptying the purses of others.[61]

The structure of the poem resembles the structure of the poems at the beginning of the collection which complain about the decadence of the world. First the poem tells explicitly what is wrong, and this statement is confirmed with an *exemplum* which may ironically be a false exemplary tale (an inversion of textual authority) or *integumentum* in which the target of the criticism – now the clerical order in general - is compared to a figure borrowed from the authorities of antiquity. The latter kind of use of exemplary tales and the poetry of antique authors was common in so-called moral encyclopedias and sermons.[62] On the other hand this text can also be seen as to the common twelfth-century topos of begging poetry.[63]

---

had begun its expansion (Duby 1978, 403).

61 1. Mundus esti in varium sepe variatus / et a status ordine sui degradatus: / ordo mundi penitus est inordinatus, / mundus nomine tenus stat, sed est postratus.
2. Transierunt vetera, perit mos antiquus; / inolevit nequior mos et plus iniquus. / nemo meus, quilibet suus est amicus; / non Saturnus regat nunc, immo Ludowicus.
3. Sperabamus, quod adhuc quisquam remaneret, / mundum qui precipitem dando sustineret, / pleno cornu copie munera preberet, / nomen largi, sed et rem, quod plus est, haberet.
4. Avem raram nondum hanc potui videre, / est Phenice rarior, hircocervus vere. / hanc quesivi sepius; felix, tu iam quere! / ei nomen interim dabimus Chimere.
5. Mundus ergo labitur, nullus hunc sustentat; / currit, cadit, corruit, quis eum retentat? / largitatis semitas nemo iam frequentat, / actus largi strenuos nemo representat.
6. Unam tamen video formam largitatis, / quam vos specialiter, clerici, libatis; / hanc edicam nudius, si vos sileatis, / si cum patientia me sustineatis.
7. Dicet quis: "enuclea! quid est hoc quod ais?" / dicam: "larga munera vestra sentit Thais, / Thais illa celebris thermis, Cumis, Bais, / illa Troie pestilens et damnosa Grais.
8. Hec dum nudo nudam se propter hoc iniungit, / manu, lingua, labiis palpat, lingit, ungit; / at Venus medullitus scalpit, prurit, pungit: / Pamphilum dupliciter sic Thais emungit.
9. Tamen est, qui Thaidem ut cadaver odit, / ab hac ut a bestia cavens se custodit; / sed dum Ganymedicum pusionem fodit, / inguen ei loculos pari dente rodit.
10. Nullum hic est medium: quivis clericorum, / si non in Glycerium, largus est in Sporum. / licet ambidextri sunt multi modernorum, / uni tamen prefero iocos geminorum.
11. Restat adhuc alterum largitatis genus, / sed hoc totum ventris est, nil hic capit Venus. (...). (CB I.3, 85-86.)
Thais was a *hetaira* from Athens who is mentioned e.g. by Plutarch (Pauly-Wissowa II.5, 1183-1184).

62 E.g. *Distinctiones monasticae et morales*; *Moralium dogma philosophorum*; Honorius Augustodunensis, *Speculum Ecclesiae*. See Lehmann 1922.

63 Latzke 1970, 109-131; Betten 1976, 143-150.

The manuscript of the *Carmina Burana* closes the circle: it begins with poetry dealing with greed, bribery and neglect of generosity,[64] while at the end it returns to avarice and expressly to lack of generosity. Thus the collection defines its own socio-cultural place in the world of the lower clerical order, an order whose action was based on the support of higher ecclesiastical hierarchy and "generosity"; that is, on approval of scholarly pursuits, their promotion and financing.

The texts dealing with reciprocity and the reign of *avaritia* are clearly situated in the world of cathedral schools, and do not simply reject "this world" but consider the cause of its depravity. The causes of the unhappy state now reigning is described even more specifically in the poems attacking the Roman curia.

The Roman curia and the monetary economy

The versions of the first poem of the *Carmina Burana* known from other sources present a simple explanation of the contemporary state of affairs in the world: *Hec est causa curie* – the cause of all this is curia.[65] The growth of the government of the Roman curia and its consequences, primarily increased taxation, had already provoked angry criticism in the eleventh century.[66] In the satires of the twelfth and thirteenth centuries the greed of the Roman curia was established as a literary *topos*, and it remained so independently of who the pope was and what his actual actions were.[67] The establishment of this literary *topos* was however not completely independent of the real state of affairs, R.W. Southern among others arguing that the popes remained prisoners of burgeoning bureaucracy and taxation apparatus and that their personal intentions and actions had little effect on it. Once the apparatus had been established it became more or less autonomous.[68] However, satire attacking the pope and the curia had clearcut limits, never questioning the existence of the institutions themselves, and criticizing only those who held the offices or merely levelling rather unspecific accusations of deviation from Apostolic ideal at the curia.[69]

The poems criticizing the decadence of the Roman curia form the thirteenth group in the manuscript of the *Carmina Burana* (CB 41-45).[70] Some poems (i.e. CB 131, 131a and 187-190) return to this theme later.

---

64 One can justifiably assume that the missing *folia* from the beginning did not deviate radically from the contents of the present collection. For example, the original headings in the collection do indicate thematic continuity - the first groups are titled only with *item* or *item eodem* (Schumann 1930/1961, 41*-43*.).
65 CB 1.6.1; CB I.1, 1-2.
66 Yunck 1963, 47-117; Thomson 1978.
67 Yunck 1963, 184.
68 Southern 1970/1983, 109-111.
69 Schüppert 1972, 76; Thomson 1978, 74.
70 Schumann 1930/1961, 44*.

I have already analysed the irony applied in the satires which were structured on false reference to or quotation of textual authority. The textual source is in such cases understood as "falsified" or ironic and thus the level of the moral meaning becomes a negative warning. The *exemplum*, a description of the state of affairs, is prooved to be opposite to the norm by comparing it to the falsified authority. In the *Carmina Burana* there are also other kinds of parodic and ironic techniques – often those which have been subsequently interpreted as sliding into blasphemy of the original subtext of the parody.[71]

Propter Sion non tacebo

Propter Sion non tacebo (CB 41) is a longer poem based on biblical allusions, mythological allusions to antiquity, and commentaries explaining them. It attacks Rome's prevailing decadence and the power struggle in the church. In its own time the poem was popular and widely read.[72] The version in the *Carmina Burana* deviates from the version thought to be˙ the correct and original one written by Walter of Châtillon (ca. 1135-1180/90). However, the central theme of Rome being caught as a stage in a power-struggle, and as its consequent falling into decadence is common both to the "correct" version reconstructed in the modern edition of the *Carmina Burana* and the version in the manuscript. Only in the final part of the poem is there a slightly different emphasis. I will follow the manuscript version in my analysis, but I am also going to examine the differences in the endings, i.e. the one thought to be correct by the editors, and that in the manuscript.

The poem is partly obscure in having allegories grounded on topical allusions, whose historical significance has remained unknown or at least highly speculative.[73] The text combines biblical and ancient materials, and treats them according to two generic conventions: on the one hand the poem uses the forms of prophecies and apocalyptic and dream visions, and on the other, it plays with the models of commentary literature. One can argue that this apocalyptic tone, the combination of *integumenta* and commentaries explaining them relates to the conventions of sermon-literature – indeed the poem associates itself at one point with a sermon.[74] Despite its ecclesiastical and religious echoes, it however uses primarily figures borrowed from ancient authors (e.g. Scylla and Charybdis), which the text itself interprets as allegorical representations of contemporary persons.

The poem opens with four stanzas in which the the first-person narrator

---

71   E.g. Jackson 1960, 237; Morris 1970, 128-130.
72   Hilka & Schumann enumerate fourteen manuscript versions (CB I.1, 68-69).
73   See Hilka & Schumann 1930/1961, 70-79; Elredge 1973; Walsh 1976, 125-131.
74   The eleventh stanza begins: Nunc rem sermo prosequatur - Now the sermon follows the subject-matter (CB 41.11.1, CB I.1, 66). Cf. Häring 1982, 173 (note 1); Witke 1970, 254-255.

offer a moral and religious obligation as motivation for his satire. He cannot remain silent when he is crying over the ruins of Rome. When was the last time righteousness illuminated the church like a burning lamp? Worthlessness reigns, Rome is abandoned and damaged. The *persona* says that he has seen the "head of the world" *(caput mundi)* and the "deep throat of the Sicilian glutton". In the world surrounded by two seas (i.e. in Sicily) Crassus (i.e. the Fat Man) is devouring gold and silver, Scylla is barking and Charybdis is susceptible to gold. The galleys of the pirates, that is, of the cardinals *(id est cardinalium)* are at war.[75]

Isaiah is cited in support: *Propter Sion non tacebo, et propter Jerusalem non quiescam, donec egrediatur ut splendor justus ejus, et salvator ejus ut lampas accendatur* (Is. 62:1: For Zion's sake will I not hold my peace, and for Jerusalem's sake I will not rest, until the righteousness thereof go forth as brightness, and the salvation thereof as a lamp that burneth). There is also another passage from Isaiah in the first stanza: *Rorate, caeli, desuper, et nubes pluant Justum; aperiatur terra, et germinet Salvatorem, et justitia oriatur simul: ego Dominus creavi eum* (Is. 45:8: Drop down, ye heavens, from above, and let the skies pour down righteousness: let the earth open, and let them bring forth salvation, and let righteousness spring up together; I the Lord have created it). The poem gets a sounding board which refers to the long tradition of defending the honour of the heavenly Jerusalem from the biblical allusion. Augustine's dichtomy between the heavenly and terrestrial cities was continued in the twelfth century among others by Otto of Freising in his world history, and also in an apocalyptic religious play at the end of the *Carmina Burana*.[76] The heavenly city was not confined to the world beyond, the church being its representative in the sublunar world, and this fact made the decadence of the head of the church especially grave. The problem became even more critical because the ecclesiastical decadence was seen in the context of the Apocalypse of St. John as a signal of the millennium.

The visionary of the *Carmina Burana* was however not a monastic preacher declaring the decadence of this world or an apocalyptic popular demagogue but a learned cleric, Walter of Châtillon, who had a remarkable career in the church.[77] In the poem, the Isaiah reference is immediately followed by a classical allusion, not affirming earthly degeneration, but siding with reform of the church. Thus the poem pursues change in this world even if only in

---

75   1. Propter Sion non tacebo, / sed ruinas Rome flebo, / quousque iustitia / rursus nobis oriatur / et ut lampas accendatur / iustus in ecclesia.
2. Sedet vilis et in luto / princeps facta sub tributo; / quod solebam dicere: / Romam esse derelictam, / desolatam et afflictam, / expertus sum opere.
3. Vidi, vidi caput mundi, / instar maris et profundi / vorax guttur Siculi. / ibi mundi bithalassus, / ibi sorbet aurum Crassus / et argentum seculi.
4. Ibi latrat Scylla rapax / et Charybdis auri capax / potius quam navium; / ibi cursus galearum / et conflictus piratarum, / id est cardinalium. (CB I.3, 65.)

76   *Ottonis episcopi Frisingensis Chronica sive historia de duabus civitatibus*; CB I.3, 104-111. See Manitius 1931, 376-388; 1048-1056.

77   Manitius 1931, 920; Witke 1970, 233; Pepin 1988, 90-91.

the sphere of the representatives of the heavenly city, that is, the church. The second stanza still leans on the old testament words, but there is a slight allusion to Ovid as well.[78] The third and fourth stanzas clearly alluded to the *Metamorphoses* of Ovid: *quid, quod nescio qui mediis concurrere in undis / dicuntur montes ratibusque inimica Charybdis / nunc sorbere fretum, nunc reddere, cinctaque saevis / Scylla rapax canibus Siculo latrare profundo?* (But what of certain mountains, which, they say, come clashing together in mid-sea; and Charybdis, the sailor's dread, who now sucks in and again spews forth the waves; and greedy Scylla, girt about with savage dogs, baying in the Sicilian seas?, transl. by F.J. Miller).[79] In the *Carmina Burana*, however, not only do Scylla and Charybdis appear in the next stanza, but also the *caput mundi ... vorax guttur Siculi*, i.e. the Sicilian throat of the head of the world. Thus the verses of Ovid are fused with an allusion to the pope and his curia devouring everything at hand.

The vision of the poet identifies the dogs of Scylla with the lawyers of Roman curia, and Charybdis is explained as the chancery of the pope. The first bark out their fabrications *(fingunt)* and break down the hull, the latter watches to see that nobody slips in without paying.[80]

Who are *Syrtes* and *Sirenes* who attract Byzantian gold coins with their smooth talk?[81] They speak to incoming people in a mixture and French and Latin: *"Frare ben je te cognosco, certe nichil a te posco, nam tu es de Francia"* (Brother I know you to be a good person, surely I demand nothing from you, because you are from France). The speaker continues: "Your country has well begun, and led us kindly to the harbour of a council. Ours are you, ours. Whose? The trustworthy sons of the most holy see." The stanza refers to the contemporary events (ca. 1171-1175), when there was a schism following the death of pope Hadrian IV (1159). The "well-begun" affair by the French refers probably to the councils and synods held during the reign of Pope Alexander III (1159-1175) in Toulouse (spring 1160), Montpellier (May 1162) and Tours (May 1163). In the background lay the struggle and intrigues in which Emperor Frederick Barbarossa (1152-1190) and Pope Alexander III faced each other. This struggle ended in the meeting between pope and emperor in Venice in 1177.[82] *Syrtes* and *Sirenes* are explained in

---

78 Jer. 2:36; Sap. 15:10; Is. 47:1; Ezech. 26:16; Ovidius, *Fasti* 1.218; see Hilka & Schumann 1930/1961, 71.

79 *Metamorph.* VII.63-65; Hilka & Schumann 1930/1961, 71-72.

80 Canes Scylle possunt dici / veritatis inimici, / advocati Curie, / qui latrando falsa fingunt, / mergunt simul et confringunt / carinam pecunie. (CB 41.9; CB I.1, 66.)
     Nunc rem sermo prosequatur: / hic Charybdis debacchatur, / id est cancellaria, / ubi nemo gratus gratis / neque datur absque datis / Gratiani gratia. (CB 41.11; CB I.1, 66.)

81 *Byzantium* (Fr. *besant*) meant a gold coin in medieval Latin (Hilka & Schumann 1930/1961, 75). The name of the Byzantine gold coin was established as a general name for gold pieces although it did was no longer in use in the Western market in the twelfth century (Fossier 1982/1990, 305-311).

82 13. Qui sunt Syrtes vel Sirenes? / qui sermone blando lenes / attrahunt byzantium; / spem pretendunt lenitatis, / sed procella parcitatis / supinant marsupium.
     14. Dulci cantu blandiuntur / ut Sirenes, et loquuntur / primo quedam dulcia: / "Frare, ben

other versions of the poem as cardinals - and the same interpretation is also implied in the *Carmina Burana* version.[83]

The poem differentiates between the pope and the papal bureaucracy whose chancery, ushers, curia and cardinals rob, grasp and plot, both praising Alexander III and accusing his adversaries. The pope is remembered as a patron of scholars or *litterati*.[84] Among other details this fact makes the poem more sophisticated than the most other conventional satires since it does not put the blame on the pope for all misdeeds, and even recognizes Alexander's achievements. It was he who advanced scholarly pursuits and reorganized the ecclesiastical school system. Under his guidance the Third Lateran council ordered that teachers to be paid a salary by the bishoprics in order that poor students should have an opportunity of schooling at the time when teachers were paid by their students.[85]

The version edited by Alfons Hilka and Otto Schuman ends with the poetic *persona* optimistically finishing his sermon, when the ship of the church reaches a harbour (CB 41.8) where Alexander should stop the favouring the sellers of ecclesiastical offices *(Elisei Giezi*, CB 41.29).[86] The 'I' is anyhow secured in 'Him' (i.e. Christ), so that he may finish his sermon. In the *Carmina Burana* manuscript the last five stanzas are 29, 8, 18, 19 (verses 1-3), and 17 – the ship (of the church) reaches the harbour where the sin of simony lurks earlier (CB 41.29). The poem then speaks about the ruthless franc (CB

---

je te cognosco, / certe nichil a te posco, / nam tu es de Francia."

15. Terra vestra bene cepit / et benigne nos excepit / in portu concilii. / nostri estis, nostri! cuius? / sacrosante sedis huius / speciales filii. (CB I.1, 66.)

    The dating is based particularly on the 27th stanza which is included also in the *Carmina Burana* manuscript (Hilka & Schumann 1930/1961, 75, 78). See note 84 below.

83   CB 41.17, CB I.1, 66 (the seventeenth verse ends up the manuscript version).

84   27. Petrus enim Papiensis, / qui electus est Meldensis, / portus recte dicitur. / nam cum mare fluctus tollit, / ipse solus mare mollit, / et ad ipsum fugitur.

28. Est et ibi maior portus, / fetus ager, florens ortus, / pietatis balsamum: / Alexander ille meus, / meus, inquam, cui det Deus / paradisi thalamum.

29.Ille fovet litteratos, / cunctos malis incurcatos, / si posset, erigeret. / verus esset cultor Dei, / nisi latus Elisei / Giezi corrumperet.

30. Sed ne rursus in hoc mari / me contingat naufragi, / dictis finem faciam, / quia, dum securus eo, / ne submergar, ori meo / posui custodiam. (CB 41.27-30; CB I.1, 67.) According to Hilka & Schumann Petrus Papiensis (Peter of Pavia) was probaly the cardinal-priest of San Grisogono (in 1173) and later cardinal-bishop of Frascati (in 1179). He was elected in 1171 as the bishop of Meaux but he was never consecrated to this office. Alexander III made him renounce his claims to the See of Meaux in 1175. Thus the poem date probably between 1171-1175 (Hilka & Schumann 1930/1961, 78).

85   ne pauperibus, qui parentum opibus iuvari non possunt, legendi et proficiendi opportunitas subtrahatur, per unamquamque ecclesiam cathedralem magistro, qui clericos eiusdem ecclesiae, et scholares pauperes gratis doceat, competens aliquod beneficium assignetur quo docentis necessitas sublevetur et discentibus via pateat ad doctrinam. *(Sacrorum conciliorum Nova et Amplissima collectio* 22, Mansi 1778, 227-228; see Delhaye 1947, 240; Baldwin 1970, 117-120; *idem* 1982).

86   Simony was both buying and selling ecclesiastical offices, i.e. the gifts of Holy Spirit. Sometimes they were separated, selling was referring to Gehazi, the servant of Elisha *(Elisei Giezi)* from the Second book of Kings, who was willing to sell prophetic abilities (5:19-27). Simony derives from Simon Magus who tried to buy the gifts of Holy Spirit from apostle Peter (Acts 8:14-20). See also Yunck 1963, 25-26, 47-48; Schüppert 1972, 46-57, 60, 169-173.

41.8), and about cardinals who have sold the patrimony of Christ Crucified (CB 41.18). Such are the possessors of the ship of St. Peter, who have the power to bind (CB 41.19.1-3). The final stanza mentions cardinals who are accustomed to enticing the credulous and emptying their purses (41.17). The manuscript version is more incoherent, and the first-person narrator is more pessimistic. The optimistic expectations raised by Alexander III are derailed by the unreliable cardinals, and the poetical *persona* is not rescued through trust in his own salvation. The disillusion seems to be much more complete.

Laurence Elredge's analysis of Walter Châtillon's poem *Propter Sion non tacebo* emphasizes critique of the disappearance of actual exchange of grace as the new canon law emerged during the twelfth century. Elredge contextualises Walter's poem, reading it as a critical commentary on the effects of Gratian in the papal government. He deviates from the interpretation of the poem's editor, Karl Strecker, by claiming that the meanings of details in the text are not really vague, as Strecker argues, but their connections with each other, and thus the overall meaning of the poem, is rather obscure (contrary again to what Strecker thinks).[87] However, Elredge's claim does not concern the poem's general moral meaning (as indeed does Stecker's interpretation), but its exact contextual and textual connections. The moral indignation caused by distortion of values in the papal curia is evident even without exact interpretation of the details. Instead, the relevance of details to their context makes the critique more acute, and thus sets the satire in its proper historical context.

The main lines of Elredge's interpretation which divides the poem in two parts of which the first (stophes 1-8) is an old testament prophecy, and the second is an interpretative commentary utilising classical imagery are the same as I proposed above. The target of the critique is *avaritia*.[88] The interpretative part is twofold. First comes the commentary proper (strophes 9-19), complemented by an anagogic part (strophes 20-29).[89] Gold-swallowing Charybdis is identified with lawyers, and the word-play *gratus – gratis – Gratiani gratia* in the eleventh strophe explicitly attacks Gratian's reform of canon law. Law has intruded into the domain of theology, and the freely-given grace of God is replaced by purchasable mercy. Money has become a unit of exchange, and the actual exchange of grace has turned to something else. Canon law has brought new contractual practices into the church.[90] Material values have taken the place of immaterial, and ideal reciprocal order has broken down.

---

87 Elredge 1970, 59-60; Strecker 1929, 17-18.
88 Elredge 1970, 60-63.
89 Elredge 1970, 63; see Strecker 1929, 18-30.
90 Elredge 1970, 64. Gratian's influence on papal jurisdiction was not profound until in the 1180s and 1190s (Robinson 1990/1993, 207). According to this the poem should be dated to late years of Walter of Châtillon - and perhaps after the papacy of Alexander III who died in August 1181 which however seems to be a rather late date comparing to other references to the contemporary events, see page 145-146 (n. 82) and note 84 , also Hilka & Schumann 1930/1961, 75, 78.

Thus the allegorical or interpretative commentary (strophes 9-19) explains the actual state of affairs presented in the initial part with the help of classical imagery. The final part from the nineteenth strophe onwards is an anagogy which moves the focal point to the ship of St. Peter *(Petri navem)*, i.e. the church, and elevates the poem from historical facts to the general level describing the sailing of the ship of church in this world steered by money.[91] Elredge writes:

> It is here, ... that the climax of the poem lies. Walter has already noted that the intrusion of legal formulas has transformed the church into an economic enterprise. Here he makes clear the secular nature of church economics: the church is no longer the type of Noah's ark, a bulwark against the threatening environment; it has now become part of secular world, and as such, dependent upon secular economics for its continued existence.[92]

Elredge interprets the seeming incoherence in the imagery of the poem, e.g. that cardinals are called pirates, and later Syrtes and Sirens, as an ironical switch of roles. Walter wants to show that the corrupted curia not only hurts others but the church itself. The critique turns on the ecclesiastical institution itself, and is not standard anti-clerical attack.[93]

It is obvious that detailed and contextual analysis supports to a reformist interpretation of Latin clerical satire.[94] However, Elredge leaves this point more or less open, and furthermore, does not follow the allegorical scheme very closely. Thus, he does not explicate the moral level of meaning, rather presenting the first part as an historical (or "literal") statement which is then allegorically interpreted, and finally completed with anagogic significance. However, according to the standard allegorical reading he should have also stated the moral level – especially because during the twelfth century it was given special emphasis. It is true that the poem does not present it separately if one does not take the final statements as such (Elredge takes them rather as ironic withdrawal). It is this moral level that is the most clear and apparent: indeed it is a general demand for moral reform both at the individual level and the church as a whole. In certain sense, the moral message needed no separate treatment because it is written into the ethical paradigm of satire, a paradigm which the poem clearly recognizes.

Utar contra vitia

The next satire in the *Carmina Burana*, *Utar contra vitia* (CB 42) is also one of the best-known and in its own time one of the most widely disseminated

---

91   Elredge 1970, 63, 66-67.
92   Elredge 1970, 67.
93   Elredge 1970, 67-68; see also Pepin 1988, 98-94.
94   Contrary to what Thomson (1978) argues.

poems of the collection. This time the manuscript version is not in a "degenerated" state. The only deviations from the version considered as the correct one is one extra stanza (5a), and the missing last stanza. The first one the editors have printed in the commentary following the poem, and the latter one they have added to their edition.[95] Perhaps the most remarkable allusion to the poem is a well-known passage about Golias by Gerald of Wales (ca. 1147-1220) in his *Speculum Ecclesiae*.[96]

The opening of the poem is rhetorically similar to the previous one. The speaker of the poem declares himself an utterer of the truth, as in the previous poem the speaker spoke of his obligation to tell the truth "for the sake of Zion":

> *1. Utar contra vitia carmine rebelli. / mel proponunt alii, fel supponunt melli, / pectus subest ferreum deaurate pelli / et leonis spolium induunt aselli.*
>
> *2. Disputat cum animo facies rebellis, / mel ab ore profluit, mens est plena fellis; / non est totum melleum, quod est instar mellis, / facies est alia pectoris quam pellis.*
>
> *3. Vitium in opere, virtus est in ore, / tegunt picem animi niveo colore, / membra dolent singula capitis dolore / et radici consonat ramus in sapore.*[97]

1. I will use rebellious songs against vices. Others propose honey - hiding poison in it. Under a golden cover they have an iron chest, and little donkeys clothe themselves with lion's armour.

2. The rebellious figure disputes with the soul: honey pours from his mouth while his mind is filled with poison. Not all is honeyed which looks like honey. The appearance of the chest is different from its real skin *(pellis)*.

3. The deeds are vicious while their speech is virtuous. They cover the colour of the magpie of their soul with the whiteness of snow. The individual members suffer from an aching head, and the taste of branches is same as that of roots.

The poem presents itself as an open reprehension of vices, that is, it generically declares itself a satire in its opening lines. The openness of its literal surface is programmatic the speaker announcing he will use rebellious

---

95   CB I.1, 78-81.
96   Gerald of Wales wrote that the times of the popes Alexander III (1159-1181) and Lucius III (1181-1185) were critisized in songs similar to the songs of a certain Golias to whom he attributes a part this poem: Item parasitus quidam, Golias nomine, nostris diebus gulositate pariter et lecatitate famisissimus, qui Golias melius quia gulae at crapulae per omnia deditus dici potuit, literatus tamen affatim sed nec bene morigeratus nec bonis disciplinis informatus, in papam et curiam Romanam carmina famosa pluries et plurima, tam metrica quam ridicula (ridmica?), non minus impudenter quam imprudenter evomuit *(Spec. Eccl.* IV.xv, p. 291-292). The passage includes stanzas 4-7 and 12-15 printed in the modern edition of the *Carmina Burana* and two stanzas from CB 191; see also Mann 1980, 63-66; Cairns 1984, 159-161. On this basis Hilka & Schumann date the poem immediately after the IV Lateran Council in 1215 (1930/1961, 86).
97   CB I.1, 76.

songs against vices, declaring himself to be different from those who cover their inner poison under a honeyed surface. Things which seem one thing on their surface conceal their opposites beneath it. The poem uses the opposite of the surface and the hidden content in a twofold fashion: on the one hand, it claims to be direct and literally true speech (when compared to the poison covered with honey) and, on the other hand, it satirizes those who dress up as lions or hide an iron chest under a golden cover; that is, those whose deeds and words are not compatible.

What follows is as direct as announced. The poem extends the metaphor of the relation of head and other members, the aching head being the *caput mundi*, Rome.

> *4. Roma mundi caput est, sed nil capit mundum, / quod pendet a capite, totum est immundum; / trahit enim vitium primum in secundum, / et de fundo redolet, quod est iuxta fundum.*
> *5. Roma capit singulos et res singulorum, / Romanorum curia non est nisi forum. / ibi sunt venalia iura senatorum, / et solvit contraria copia nummorum.*
> *5a. Si te forte traxerit Romam vocativus / et si te deponere vult accusativus, / qui te restituere possit ablativus. / vide quod ibi fideliter presens sit dativus.*
> *6. In hoc consistorio si quis causam regat / suam vel alterius, hoc inprimis legat: / nisi det pecuniam, Roma totum negat; / qui plus dat pecunie, melius allegat.*
> *7. Romani capitulum habent in decretis, / ut petentes audiant manibus repletis. / dabis, aut non dabitur, petunt quando petis, / qua mensura seminas, et eadem metis.*[98]

4. Rome is the head of the world, but it does not embrace purity. On the contrary, what hangs out of its head is totally impure. The first vice leads to the second, and that which is close to the bottom, stinks like the bottom.
5. Rome reaches individuals and their concerns, and the Roman curia is nothing else than a marketplace. There the judgments of the senators are for sale, and conflicts are solved there with the copiousness of money.
5a. If by chance vocative have attracted you to Rome, and if accusative wants to give you up, then can ablative restore you. See how faithfully dative is present there.
6. If in this consistory someone pleads his own cause as he pleads others', he will lead this party. If one does not give money, Rome will deny everything; the one who gives more gets more advancement.
7. The Romans have a clause in their decretals that petitioners have to listen with full hands. Give, or you are not given; they beg you when you beg. Whatever measure you sow, that is the measure you reap.

---

98   CB I.1, 76-77, 81; CB facs. 9ᵛ-10ᵛ.

Everything that can be sold is on sale in the Roman curia. The first vice leads to the second. The stanza included in the manuscript version (5a) is a typical grammatical parody which evidently affinities with the world of schools. It parodies Roman decretals, utilizing biblical orders and precepts. In the same way as in the poems about the inverted world, biblical and ecclesiastical figures are presented in a situation which contradicts their proper nature, and inverts the message of biblical precept. The passages in New Testament "give, and it shall be given unto you" and "with what measure you mete, it shall be measured to you again" appear in several contexts (e.g. Matt. 7:2; Marc 4:24; I Cor. 9:6). In Luke: *Date et dabitur vobis: mensuram bonam, et confertam, et coagitatam, et supereffluentem dabunt in sinum vestrum. Eadem quippe mensura, qua mensi fueritis, remetietur vobis. Dicebat autem illis et similitudinem: Numquid potest caecus caecum ducere? nonne ambo in foveam cadunt?* (Lk. 6:38-39: Give, and it shall be given unto you; good measure, pressed down, and shaken together, and running over, shall men give into your bosom. For with the same measure that ye mete withal it shall be measured to you again. And he spake a parable unto them. Can the blind lead the blind? shall they not both fall into the ditch?).

At Rome the rule of giving has been perverted into taking. People arriving there are hypocritically urged with the biblical words to give, and urging turns out to be threatening: give, or you shall not be given; rather than: give, and it shall be given you. The passage in Luke continues with the parable of Jesus about the blind leading the blind which was extremely popular in the Middle Ages in general, and in the *Carmina Burana* in particular (e.g. CB 6, CB 39.3). It is not impossible that this parable is also intertextually connected with the poem, and that Rome should be compared with "the blind leading the blind" (cf. also the fourth strophe of the poem, in page 150 above).

The poem goes on to mock the greed of the curia, while disputing, one does not have to be scared of Cicero because money takes care of eloquence, for it pleases the Romans when money speaks and law remains silent.[99] Money surpasses learning; it starts to speak itself. For the penniless it is vain to seek justice. In its following stanzas the poem anticipates the *Carmina Burana*'s "Gospel according to Marks of Silver" (CB 44), and it derives the word *papare*, referring to the pope from a quasi-etymology from the French words *paies, paies* (pay, pay)[100]:

> *11. Solam avaritiam Rome nevit Parca: / parcit danti munera, parco non est parca, / nummus est pro numine et pro Marco marca, / et est minus celebris ara cum sit arca.*
> *12. Cum ad papam veneris, habe pro constanti: / non est locus pauperi,*

---

99 Tullium ne timeas, si velit causari / Nummus eloquentia gaudet singulari. (CB 42.8.3-4; CB I.1, 77).
   ... et Romanos placet, / ubi nummus loquitur, et lex omnis tacet. (CB 42.9.3-4; CB I.1, 77.)
100 On the word *papare* see Hilka & Schumann 1930/1961, 80.

soli favet danti, / vel si munus prestitum non sit aliquanti, / respondet:
"hec tibia non est michi tanti."
13. Papa, si rem tangimus, nomen habet a re: / quicquid habent alii,
solus vult papare, / vel si verbum gallicum vis apocopare, / "paies,
paies" dist li mot, si vis impetrare.
14. Porta querit, chartula querit, bulla querit, / papa querit, etiam
cardinalis querit, / omnes querunt, et si des - si quid uni deerit, / totum
mare salsum est, tota causa perit.[101]

11. Parca (the goddess of fate) has gathered only avarice in Rome,
which is favourable to those who give gifts; it does not spare the stingy
one. Money replaces divinities, and so does mark instead of Mark.
The altar is less revered than the coffer.
12. When you come to the pope, keep this always in your mind: this
is not a place for the poor, it favours only givers. If the present offered
is not remarkable, he responds: 'These bones are not much to me'.
13. The pope, if we touch upon these things, has got his name from
this: whatever others have, he wants always to be a pope *(papare)*
alone, or if you want to express it in a Gaulish word: you utter the
word 'pay, pay' *(paies, paies)*, if you want to get permission.
14. The gate demands, the charter demands, the letter demands. The
pope demands, the cardinal demands, everybody demands. And if you
give, beware: if some one remains unbribed, its throwing good money
after bad, and whole cause will perish.

The translation does not do full justice to the original because the poem is
based on word-plays, which were characteristic of Goliardic poetry.[102] At
Rome you had to bribe everybody, until *magna, maior, maxima preda fit*
gradatim; that is, the robbery increases from step to step.[103] The poem ends
up in the manuscript conclude with the following: the world has turned upside
down, the divinity of the Underworld is in Heaven and the divinity of Heaven
is in the Underworld – this inverted state of affairs was represented by the
figures from classical Pantheon:

> *18. Redeunt a curia capite cornuto; / ima tenet Iupiter, celum habet*
> *Pluto, / et accedit dignitas animali bruto / tamquam gemma stercori*
> *vel pictura luto.*[104]

18. They are returning from Rome with crowned heads, the
Underworld is held by Jove, Pluto has Heaven, and dignity has gone
to an ugly animal as a jewel to filth and pictures to dirt.

Hilka and Schumann have added a final stanza from other versions, according
to which the rich give to the rich, and gifts fly to relatives. On the earth there

---

101 CB I.1, 77.
102 Dobiache-Rojdestvensky 1931, 65-70; Lehmann 1922-23/1963, 1-24; Jackson 1960,
      228-230.
103 CB 42.16.2; CB I.1, 78.
104 CB I.1, 78.

is a law that if you give to me, I give to you.[105] Generosity *(largitas)* has disappeared, greed, simony and nepotism rule with no betterment in sight.

Evangelium secundum marcas argenti

Roma, tue mentis oblita (CB 43) is a strictly biblical cry of distress for the church. The Apostolical see ought to repent: there remain only the dregs in the church and it is orphaned from the Fathers of the Church. The poem is a simple *vox clamans in deserto,*[106] a complaint about the state of the world and the church, which resembles the monastic denials of this world.[107] The next text is a prose mock-Gospel (CB 44) which is one of the best known exemplar from the collection. I will quote it in its entirety both in the English translation given by Jill Mann, and the Latin original. In the latter I have emphasized the biblical allusions and indicated in parantheses their originals in the *Bible* (see Paul Lehmann, Hilka and Schumann and Jill Mann for a more comprehensive list of the allusions).[108]

The beginning of the Gospel according to the Mark of Silver.
   In those days the pope said to the Romans: "When the son of man shall come to the throne of our glory, first say to him: 'Friend, wherefore art thou come?' But if he shall continue knocking without giving you anything, cast him out into outer darkness." And it came to pass that a certain poor cleric came to the court of the lord pope and cried out, saying: "Have pity upon me, O ye ushers of the pope, for the hand of poverty hath touched on me. I am poor and needy, and so I ask you to relieve my calamity and misery." But when they heard it they were greatly moved with indignation and said: "Friend, thy poverty perish with thee. Get thee behind me Satan, for thou savourest not the things that money savours. Verily, verily, I say unto thee, thou shalt not enter into the joy of thy lord till thou hast paid the uttermost farthing." And the poor man went and sold his cloak and his tunic and all that he had, and gave to the cardinals and the ushers and the chamberlains. They however said: "But what is this among so many?" And they cast him out before the doors, and he went out and wept bitterly and had no comforting. Afterwards there came to the court a certain rich cleric, waxen fat, grown thick, covered with fatness, who on account of the insurrection had committed murder. He gave

---

105 Divites divitibus dant, ut sumant ibi, / et occurrant munera relative sibi. / lex est ista celebris, quam fecerunt scribi: "si tu michi dederis, ego dabo tibi." (CB 42.19; CB I.1, 78.)
106 This phrase does not occur in the poem but does in CB 10 (CB I.1, 14). Isaiah (40:3) from where it is borrowed in several passages in the New Testament (e.g. Matt. 3:3) stands in the background.
107 CB I.1, 84-85.
108 The allusions are recognized by Lehmann (1922-23/1963, 183-184), Hilka & Schumann (1930/1961, 90-91), Thomson (1978, 78-79) and Mann (1980, 75-76). Thomson claims that he presents the complete list of biblical allusions for the first time but actually his list is not even as complete as that of Lehmann and Hilka & Schumann. The most comprehensive account is in Mann although I have made some less important amendments. I have quoted the translation by Jill Mann (1980, 75-76).

first to the usher, secondly to the chamberlain, thirdly to the cardinals. But they supposed that they should have received more. But when the lord pope heard that the cardinals and ministers had received many gifts from the cleric, he fell sick nigh unto death. But the rich man sent him a medicine of gold and silver and immediately he was made whole. Then the lord pope called the cardinals and ministers unto him, and said to them, "Take heed, brethren, that no man deceive you with vain words. For I give you an example, that as I extort, you should extort also."

Initium sancti evangeli secundum marcas argenti.
In illo tempore (various Gospel passages and liturgy) dixit papa Romanis: *"Cum venerit filius hominis ad sedem maiestatis nostre* (Matt. 25:31 *et al.*), primum dicite:*'Amice, ad quid venisti?'* (Matt. 26:50) At *ille si perseveravit pulsans* (Luke 11:8) nil dans vobis, *eicite eum in tenebras exteriores* (Matt. 25:30 *et al.*)." *Factum est autem* (Luke 1:8 *et al.*), ut quidam pauper clericus veniret ad curiam domini pape, et *exclamavit dicens* (Matt. 15:22; Luke 18:38): *"Miseremini mei saltem vos,* hostiarii pape, *quia manus pauperitas tetigit me* (Job 19:21). *Ego vero egenus et pauper sum* (Ps. 69:6 *et al.*), ideo peto, ut subveniatis *calamitati et miserie mee* (Zeph. 1:15 *et al.*)." Illi autem *audientes indignati sunt valde* (Matt. 20:24; Dan. 14:27 *et al.*) et dixerunt: "Amice, *paupertas tua tecum sit in perditione* (Act. 8:20). *Vade retro, satanas, quia non sapis ea, que sapiunt nummi* (Mark 8:33, Matt. 16:23). *Amen, amen, dico tibi* (Matt. 5:26): *non intrabis in gaudium domini tui* (Matt. 25:23), donec dederis novissimum quadrantem." *Pauper vero abiit et vendidit pallium et tunicam et universa que habuit* (Matt. 13:44, 46, 19:21; Luke 18:22, 12:33, 22:36; Mark 10:21 *et al.*) et dedit cardinalibus et hostiariis et camerariis. At illi dixerunt: *"Et hoc quid est inter tantos?"* (John 6:9) *Et eiecerunt eum ante fores* (John 9:34), *et egressus foras flevit amare* (Matt. 26:75; Luke 22:62) *et non habens consolationem* (Lam. 1:9; Jer. 31:15). *Postea venit ad curiam quidam clericus dives* (Matt. 27:57), *incrassatus, impinguatus, dilatatus* (Deut. 32:15), qui *propter seditionem fecerat homicidium* (Mark 15:7; Luke 23:19). *Hic primo dedit hostiario, secundo camerario, tertio cardinalibus* (Matt. 25:15). At illi *arbitrari sunt inter eos, quod essent plus accepturi* (Matt. 20:10). *Audiens autem* (various biblical passages) dominus papa cardinales et ministros *plurima dona* (Prov. 6:35) a clerico accepisse, *infirmatus est usque ad mortem* (Phil. 2:27; John 11:4). Dives vero misit sibi electuarium *aureum et argenteum* (cf. Act. 3:6), *et statim sanatus est* (John 5:9; Matt. 8:13). Tunc dominus papa ad *se vocavit cardinales et ministros et dixit eis* (Matt. 20:25; Mark 9:34 *et al.*): *"Fratres, videte, ne aliquis vos seducat inanibus verbis* (Hebr. 3:12; Eph. 5:6, 15; Col. 2:8; Matt. 24:4). *Exemplum enim do vobis* (John 13:15), ut, quemadmodum ego capio, ita et vos capiatis."[109]

The Gospel according to the Mark of Silver is a biblical parody whose satirical effect is based on the contradiction between the tale and the intertextual

---

109 CB I.1, 86; see also Lehmann 1922-23/1963, 32-36, 183-184.

background formed by the *Bible*. Its allusions, paraphrases and quotations are for the most part from the Gospels. Contrary to some modern interpreters' assumptions it does not blaspheme the Sacred Scriptures,[110] but skilfully turns the textual authority upside down to demonstrate the moral falseness of prevailing state of affairs. Neither can this text – or others of its kind – be understood as the "laughter culture of the people of marketplace" or anti-clerical mockery.[111] The text is thoroughly scholarly, based on the clerical view of true morals and the relation between textual authority and this world. The biblical parody was comprehensible only to the audience who knew its *Bible* well. In this sense the text corresponds to the characterization given by Rodney M. Thomson of satire as a literature of advanced and highly literate cultures.[112]

The text uses a simple form of didactic tale *(exemplum)*:[113] at the beginning the pope gives some instructions to his staff. Two contrary cases appear, poor and rich, to test these instructions, and through dramatic peripety (the pope's falling sick and his miraculous recovery) the tale completes its lesson and the improvement of the instructions given at the beginning. In terms of medieval generic theory, the text is an ironic satire since it does not directly reprehend vices, but in a Christian context even a less sophisticated receiver surely understands that the way of the pope and his curia is false - in this sense the satire is morally *nuda et aperta*. Unlike the other satires of the *Carmina Burana*, open and pointed attacks on named vices are lacking. Criticism of avarice, the power of money, simony and bribary of justice is however incorporated into the structure of the tale (the rich cleric accused of murder succeeds in freeing himself with the help of money) or beneath ambiguous intertextual references. *The Gospel according to the Mark of Silver* leaves its moral lesson implicit and trusts to the obvious nature of its parody and satire. At the same time its parodic techniques are multilevelled; being in certain aspects comparable to medieval ecclesiastical pictorial programs which addressed themselves to their interpreters as definitely as they knew their subtexts.

The mock-Gospel makes its biblical source recognisable from the title, its familiar biblical phrases and the exemplary tale form, which resembles the parables of Jesus. At the same time it includes exact quotations which either follow their sources literally or are ironically transformed with some strategic changes. Some of the quotations also set the original context of the quotation as a subtext or rather a counter-text for the mock-Gospel – either so that the parody has behind biblical typologies (and thus a cluster of texts) or so that a single biblical passage is set as a direct counter-text. Thus the biblical

---

110 E.g. Jackson 1960, 237; Morris 1972, 128.
111 Bakhtin 1965/1984, 4-18; *idem* 1940/1994, 68-82; cf. Cook 1986, 172-173, 180-182; Höfner 1988.
112 Thomson 1978, 76.
113 Le Goff 1985, 99-102; Lehtinen 1993.

sources of parody are evident and as such they set general reading expectations in relation to the content of the text. It is sufficient from the point of view of moral understanding that the receiver perceive the contradiction between biblical teachings and the tale. However, in the clerical context the text acquires much more exact pertinence when its textual background is revealed.

The mock-Gospel openly attacks the pope and the curia. Through the textual references the accusation becomes even more grave because the pope is compared to Judas the betrayer of Jesus, and to Gehazi of Elisha who tried to sell divine gifts (i.e. the counterpart of Simon Magus, see note 86 in page 146). Generosity and reciprocity are forgotten when money and Mammon displace genuine Christian charity and reciprocity. Money and multiple bureaucracy hinder the ideal direct contact between clerics and pope.

The different parodic allusions and quotations are compatible with different stages of interpretation. In the text there are several sayings proper to the *Bible*, especially to the Gospels, which do not establish any specific passage as a subtext for the mock-Gospel, including phrases like *in illo tempore*, *factum est autem, audiens autem*, etc. Secondly, there are references which either quote literally their sources more or less literally, or paraphrase or allude to them, but do not lead to any further comparison between the parody and its source. These include the saying *exclamavit dicens*, for which there are several biblical counterparts e.g. when the Canaanite woman (Matt. 15:22) and the blind man (Luke 18:38) beg mercy from Christ. Similar references to Job (19:21), Psalms (69:6), Zephaniah (1:15), Matthew (20:24) etc. are found. These allusions create the ground for the relation between the mock-Gospel and the *Bible*; making the moral contradiction between *The Gospel according to the Mark of Silver* and actual Gospels obvious. This general function is also carried out by more precise quotations as far they are recognized as biblical only generally, but their original exact context is not recognized.

In several cases allusions of the first and second group have comic function arising from the disparity between the biblical words and the contents of the tale; this is the comic effect of general citation in the wrong context *(in illo tempore)*, but it applies the poor cleric asks for mercy quoting Job, and when he declares his poverty in the words of Zephaniah originally describing the day of wrath, *dies irae*.[114] The comic apogee follows from the combination of intertextual allusions and the structure of the narrative when pope suddenly falls sick (cf. Phil. 2:27 and John 11:4) and is then miraculously cured (cf. John 5:9; Matt. 8:13). In the typology of allusions it anticipates the third type

---

114 Dies irae illa, dies tribulationis et angustiae, *dies calamitatis et miserie*, dies tenebrarum et caliginis, dies nebulae et turbinis, dies tubae et clangoris super civitates munitas, super angulos excelsos. In English: That day is the day of wrath, a day of trouble and distress, a day of wasteness and desolation, a day of darkness and gloominess, a day of clouds and thick darkness, a day of the trumpet and alarm against the fenced cities, and against the high towers. (Zepaniah 1:15; cf. also Job 30:3; Is. 47:11.)

of ironical reference.

The third type is formed by those allusions and references which refer to a precise biblical passage and which adapt the original passage ironically. The emphasis of these allusions varies according to their intertextual setting. On the other hand there are allusions which can be assigned to a particular biblical passage. In such cases the passage alluded to functions in the mock-Gospel as such and does not draw upon its original context or any larger biblical typology.[115] The allusions usually refer to the original passage, slightly altering it. It can be called ironic variation by which the strategic changes in vocabulary or their position in the parodic tale often changes the meaning of quotation to juxtapose its original meaning. In the mock-Gospel this leads to an ironic comparison between the biblical passage and the person or situation in the narrative, as when the pope recovers with the help of valuable presents and money – in the biblical context it is Christ who cures the sick who put their faith in him. The question: *Amice, ad quid venisti?* which Christ poses to Judas (Matt. 26:50) employs a different ironic technique. Now it is asked by the pope who himself seems to have renounced his faith in Christ in favour of the worship of money. The pope seems to be identified with Judas. Other ironic allusions based on false quotation include the wish of the ushers for the poor cleric: *paupertas tua tecum sit in perditione*. These words are from Acts (8:20) where Peter says to Simon Magus, who attempted to buy the gifts of the Holy Spirit with money: *pecunia tua tecum sit in perditionem, quoniam donum Dei existimasti pecunia possideri!* (Thy money perish with thee, because thou hast thought that the gift of God may be purchased with money). The distorted quotation turns against the ushers themselves, and the mock-Gospel mounts an attack on simony hidden in the intertextual play which is stated openly in other poems of the *Carmina Burana*.

There are plenty of ironic quotations and allusions. The most essential are those relating to the pope himself in the latter part of the mock-Gospel. The Pope speaks to the cardinals and ministers in the same words as Christ uses his disciples (e.g. Matt. 20:25; Mark 9:35), where He, St. Paul and the author of the Epistle to the Hebrews warn about "vain words" and deception (Matt. 24:4; Mark 13:5; Eph. 5:6, 15; Col. 2:8; Hebr. 3:12), and Christ says that he himself will give an example (John 13:5). The example given by the pope is of course false as is the state of affairs in the whole tale and its *exemplum*.[116] The quotations may also be ironical fusions of several passages like the warning about deception above. Similarly the papal ushers say mockingly to

---

115 Biblical typology meant that the events of Old Testament were interpreted as anticipation of the New Testament. Biblical characters and events are further transformed as a typology for world history which could be interpreted as the word of God. See Smalley 1952/1984, 1-36; Frye 1983, 78-101, 105-138; Auerbach 1959/1984, 37-43; Todorov 1978, 112-120. See also de Lubac 1959-64/1993; Chydenius 1960; Brinkmann 1980; Pépin 1987.

116 The Gospel parody is not only comparable to the *Bible* but also to the genre of didactic exemplary tales *(exempla)*. See e.g. Le Goff 1985, 99-102; Lehtinen 1994.

the poor supplicant: *Amen, amen dico tibi: non intrabis in gaudium domini tui, donec dederis novissimum quadrantem.* (Verily, verily. I say unto thee, thou shalt not enter into the joy of thy lord till thou hast paid the uttermost farthing.) This is a quotation from the Sermon on the Mount in which Christ threatens those who do not settle their quarrels: *Amen dico tibi non exies inde, donec reddas novissimum quadrantem.* (Verily I say unto thee, Thou shalt by no means come out thence, till thou hast paid the uttermost farthing; Matt. 5:26.) Another source is a parable of Jesus where a master speaks to his faithful servant: *Euge serve bone, et fidelis, quia super pauca fuisti fidelis, super multa te constituam; intra in gaudium domini tui.* (Well done, good and faithful servant; thou hast been faithful over a few things, I will make thee ruler over many things: enter into the joy of thy lord; Matt. 25:23.) One can now enter into the "joy of the lord" only by effecting sufficient payment. In the mock-Gospel Christ's metaphor of the last farthing has changed to a literal utterance in the mouth of the ushers. In the papal curia literal meanings and material values have deposed spiritual understanding and Christian charity.

From the interpretative point of view the most important quotations and allusions are those which are attuned to the background of the gospel-parody as a biblical typology, or set precise counter-texts to it. Some ironic comparisons already function as typological attuners: both greedy Judas and Simon Magus, who offered money for the gifts of the Holy Spirit, are biblical "types". The central counterpair of the text, the poor and rich cleric, also refer obviously to an important biblical pair. The pope's advice begins with the words *Cum venerit filius hominis ad sedem maieastatis nostre. Filius hominis* in the Gospels is a euphemism for Christ: he comes in his glory and he shall sit upon the throne of his glory (cf. Matt. 25:31).[117] The poor supplicant of the parody is compared to Christ himself. In addition there is a warning in the Gospel according to St. Matthew (26:24): *Filius hominis vadit, sicut scriptum est de illo; vae autem homini illi, per quem Filius hominis tradetur! bonum erat ei, si natus non fuisset homo ille.* (The Son of man goeth as it is written of him: but woe unto that man by whom the Son of man is betrayed! it had been good for that man if he had not been born.) Is the pope the betrayer? And who has ascended the throne? Is it Antichrist, as in the religious play ending the collection (CB 228)?[118]

Who then is the rich, fat and thick cleric? Who had commited a murder in the insurrection? *Qui in seditione fecerat homicidium?* – it was Barabbas (Mark 15:7).[119] *Qui erat, propter seditionem quamdam factam in civitate et homicidium, missus in carcerem.* (Who for a certain sedition made in the city,

---

117 cum autem venerit Filius hominis in maiestate sua ... tunc sedebit super sedem maiestatis suae. (Cf. also Matt. 19:28; Luke 9:26; 21:27 etc.)
118 CB I.3, 104-110.
119 And there was one named Barabbas, which lay bound with them that had made insurrection with him, who had committed murder in the insurrection.

and for murder, was cast into prison. Luke 23:19). The text suggests a parallel typological setting, Christ and Barabbas, between whom the pope and his curia make their decision. The pope seems to abandon Christ as the Jewish people did during the trial, and he is, like Judas, ready to sell his Lord for gold and silver.

The fifth type of intertextual reference is passages which establish a precise counter-text to the mock-Gospel of the *Carmina Burana*. This kind of setting is realized when not only the quoted passage but also its surrounding text is extensively posed as a counter-text to the whole satirical tale.

The most central counter-text is already contained in the instructions given by the pope when he says: "But if he shall continue knocking without giving you anything". It intertwines into the tale a passage from Luke (11:5-10). The quotation is from the eighth verse but it is a part of a longer passage on charity and generosity:

> *Et ait ad illos: Quis vestrum habebit amicum, et ibit ad illum media nocte, et dicet illi: Amice, commoda mihi tres panes, quoniam amicus meus venit de via ad me et non habeo quod ponam ante illum; et ille deintus respondens dicat: Noli mihi molestus esse, jam ostium clausum est, et pueri mei mecum sunt in cubili, non possum surgere, et dare tibi.* Et si ille perseveravit pulsans, *dico vobis, etsi non dabit illi surgens eo quod amicus ejus sit, propter improbitatem tamen ejus surget, et dabit illi quotquot habet necessarios. Et ego dico vobis: Petite, et dabitur vobis; quaerite, et invenientes; pulsate, et aperietur vobis. Omnis enim qui petit, accipit; et qui quaerit invenit: et pulsanti aperietur.*

> And he said unto them, Which of you shall have a friend, and shall go unto him at midnight, and say unto him, Friend, lend me three loaves; For a friend of mine in his journey is come to me, and I have nothing to set before him? And he from within shall answer and say, Trouble me not: the door is now shut, and my children are with me in bed; I cannot rise and give thee. I say unto you, Though he will not rise and give him, because of his importunity he will rise and give him as he needeth. And I say unto you, Ask, and it shall be given you; seek, and ye shall find; knock, and it shall be opened unto you. For every one that asketh receiveth; and he that seeketh findeth; and to him that knocketh it shall be opened.

The passage concludes with a striking echo of the eighth verse *(et si ille perseveravit pulsans)* quoted in the *Gospel according to the Mark of Silver*: *et pulsanti aperietur* (and to him that knocketh it shall be opened). The mock-Gospel tells a short tale like the parables of Jesus, but in this tale the poor end up in misery and the needy get no relief. Only by buying does one get what one needs. The reciprocal charity is seriously disrupted when the exchange does not occur according to the resources of each, but the rich man buys whatever he needs (including justice) and the poor is left without a thing even having given all he had. It turns out to be even more serious crime because what is bought is justice. The disappearance of reciprocity and charity thus ends in the collapse of moral order. In Luke Jesus is teaching something quite different; that the mercy of God falls upon the importuning beseecher. For the clerics the exemplary tale mediated by Luke in the *Carmina Burana* not only taught how to pursue divine blessing but it also provided a model for correct earthly behaviour since ecclesiastical lords should open their doors to suppliant clerics and give them what they need.

The hints about simony and bribing justice are not modern accusations about corruption. Such accusations have no sense in a society in which political and economic activity was still organized through reciprocal exchange, present and counterpresent.[120] The point was what was exchangeable and, how it was exchangeable. At the same time the general problems of livelihood justified begging poetry and accusations against the avarice of the higher clergy, the appearance of money and bureaucratic relations validated claims about the imbalance of material and immaterial exchange. Simony and the selling of the gifts of the Holy Spirit were crimes against generosity and immaterial presents. The pope was accused of handing over ecclesiastical office (and its incomes) for monetary payment, when ultimately the bestowal an immaterial state (consecration) was at stake.

In the *Gospel according to the Mark of Silver* there is a parallel between material values, first of all, money, and literal meanings in that the papal curia has taken the side of the dead letter of the law and put itself under the command of law of the flesh. It appreciates the goods of this world. The spiritual meanings and immaterial values are perverted into literal meanings and material values. The relation between immaterial and material has turned upside down. Literal meanings ought to lead to spiritual understanding, but on the contrary, the metaphors and parables of Jesus are turned from spiritual to literal. Similarly the priorities of ecclesiastical government itself have been inverted and material values are overpowering immaterial ones. Judas, Barabbas, Simon Magus and Gehazi of Elisha flourish when Christ is thrown outside the walls. The world is really turned upside down.

Jill Mann, in her otherwise sophisticated and illuminating analysis of the *Evangelium secundum marcas argenti*, has proposed that the

> present cruelty of papal officers is set against the final cruelty of God which will judge them. ... And the transferral into an obviously cruel human situation of biblical texts which, even in their proper context, challenge and perplex us with their apparent ruthlessness and cynicism, re-awakens our sense of the problems presented by these texts in their original form. The Goliards challenge their readers with what might be called the 'problem parables'... If we are to say that the pope 'mis-interprets' the Bible, how then is it to be properly interpreted?

---

120 Cf. Mauss 1950/1993, 145-157, 250-255, 258-279; Gurevitch 1970/1979; *idem* 1972/1983; Duby 1973/1985, 60-69; *idem* 1978, 57, 81, 93-94, 198-203, 321-322, 381; Little 1978/1983, 3-18; Vance 1986, 111-151. See also note 56 above.

Don't these texts 'provide for' cruelty in the same way as language provides for disorder? The satirists, however, do not merely challenge their readers; they also challenge themselves... It (the mock-Gospel, TMSL) is also confronting the cruelty involved in its own judgements. It is thus opening up the question of judgement, of the satirist's right to 'play God', of the possibility of appealing to a text as a kind of impersonal judge... – and this makes it a ... more serious work of literature. It re-creates the biblical sense of suffering... In that sense it pays homage to the texts, but it also questions whether such texts provide in reality the fixed standard of judgement, the stable point of reference, that we seek to find in them. Our interest here, then, is no longer primarily absorbed by the clerical misdemeanours which constitute the satiric object; it is also attracted towards the problem of interpreting the texts which are performing the act of judging, and which here occupy the position of a satiric subject.[121]

It might well be that the mock-Gospel will "challenge and perplex *us*" in the way Jill Mann claims. However, *we* are modern readers. Mann does not base her argument on anything else than her own impression, her own reaction to the cruelty of biblical texts. At the same time, she revealingly sees the complicated relation of satiric subject and object as a proof about the "literariness" of the text, and puts the modern assumptions of "literature" and "fiction" (or, belles-lettres) into the medieval world. Nothing in the text itself or in its context indicates that the author of the *Evangelium secundum marcas argenti* did not think it possible to deem that pope and his curia misinterpret the *Bible*. The virtuosity of the textual play in the mock-Gospel is in the subtle identification of spiritual understanding and immaterial exchange and its contrast with literal misreading and material values, not in its doubting of biblical exegesis and the cruelty of biblical texts themselves.

Money and clerical morals: reformation *sub cathedra*

The emergence of the monetary economy is a conventional explanation for great social changes especially in the Middle Ages. It has become all-explaining *deus ex machina* as Alexander Murray has pointed out.[122] Obviously, the spread of the use of money alone does not explain the great economic, social, political and cultural transition which took place in the central regions of Western Europe during the eleventh and twelfth centuries. The causes and elements of this transition were multiple, from growth in the efficiency in agriculture and changes in feudal seigneurial relations to the emergence of towns and long-distance commerce.[123] On the other hand, it is evident that in the clerical world the appearance of money did attract special

---

121 Mann 1980, 77-78.
122 Murray 1978/1990, 26.
123 See e.g. Anderson 1974/1992, 147f.; Cipolla (ed.) 1972/1981; Duby 1973/1985.

attention among contemporaries. One may state with T.N. Bisson that as administrative accountability slowly overturned "prescriptive" accountability in the feudal world of knights, lords and princes, in the ecclesiastical sphere the appearance of monetary imputation, contractual canon law and bureaucratic relations started to replace reciprocal relations.[124] The new literary and learned clerical class reacted to this change with money satires. It can be regarded as one utopian-conservative reaction among others.[125]

Satire is – together with erotic and love poetry – the most studied genre of Latin clerical poetry. In modern scholarship satire has been commonly interpreted in relation to administrative and economic change, for instance by John A. Yunck, Helga Schüppert and Alexander Murray. On the other hand, satire has been frequently put into the context of Latin satirical tradition, starting with Roman poets (Charles Witke, Rodney M. Thomson, Ronald E. Pepin). Thirdly, a more recent point of view is a structural and allusive textual analysis of satire (Laurence Elredge, Paul Gerhart Schmidt, Jill Mann). These different points of view are not mutually exclusive, and, in fact, Laurence Elredge (1970) and Paul Gerhard Schmidt (1974/1990) among others have expressly combined these different approaches, and have provided even more detailed idea-historical and socio-cultural context in their analyses. Perhaps the most neglected aspect in the scholarship of satire, as well as other medieval Latin poetry, has been its relation to its contemporary notions of poetry and generic theory, although Udo Kindermann and Paul S. Miller have inquired into the generic conceptions of satire.[126]

In the scholarship prevails a consensus that Latin clerical satire became common from the turn of eleventh and twelfth centuries, and that money satire can be expressly understood as a reaction to new economic and administrative reality in the Church. Money satires not only continue the old Christian critique of the worship of Mammon but are a reaction to a change perceived by contemporaries, a change which determined social relations anew. The interpretative disagreements primarily concern whether if satire should be understood as reformistic aspiration or disillusioned reaction to the weakness of human nature.[127] Furthermore, Jill Mann (1980) for instance has interpreted satires as a critique or more or less cautious questioning of Christian teachings. The reformist line of interpretation can at least partly be connected with the optimistic new secular Christian view that despite the forces overpowering the human sphere of influence like *Fortuna*, the essential moral choice is in the hands of individuals, and it does not require a retreat from the world. One has just to understand the real nature of the sublunar

---

124 Bisson 1994, 34-42; cf. Elredge 1970, 59-69.
125 Cf. the theory of the three orders, see Duby 1978; Murray 1978/1991, 96-98; see also Little 1978/1983.
126 Kindermann 1978; *idem* 1982; Paul S. Miller 1982 (unpublished), see Minnis & Scott 1988/1991, 116-117, notes 14 and 15.
127 Cf. the difference between Yunck (1963) and Witke (1970) offering reformative interpretation and Thomson (1978) who sees satire essentially as a genre of disillusion.

world to gain *Fortuna*'s true benefits, primarily her daughter *Nobilitas*. The new man has to understand what is worth seeking on the earth, and what is not. The disillusioned intrepretation is thus either Manichean or monastic. The first possibility makes satire an affirmation of the evil of flesh, and thus the perceivable world in general. The second would be tied to the conservative monastic view which sees withdrawal as the only possibility for a genuinely Christian virtuous life and sees no possibilities of change in secular society. Only restraint and contemplation would free humanity from the power of evil. However, the medieval notion of satire is clearly contrary to the disillusioned view because it states the moral (and to some extent, political) persuasion to improvement as the fundamental function of satiric poetry. In practice, different satires are bound to either the monastic or secular Christian views, or in some cases both, as I have demonstrated above.

Thus satire addressed itself explicitly to its contemporary society, first of all towards the problems of the clerical world. For instance, Laurence Elredge has clearly shown in his detailed analysis of Walter of Châtillon's *Propter Sion non tacebo* that alludes to the *Decretum* of Gratian – in fact he shows that the poem is a critique of Gratian's influence. Elredge's study shows that the poem presents the rise of regulated contractual relations (based on Roman law) and monetarised accountability as a menace to ideal exchange of grace.[128]

Rodney M. Thomson especially has criticised the John A. Yunck's reformist interpretation of satire (and without mentioning him, Charles Witke's). He grounds his argument on the relation between *festa stultorum* and satire pointed out by Paul Gerhard Schmidt and dismisses any idea of satire persuading or changing society.[129] However, Thomson leans only on general essentialistic statements that satire appears only when all hope has been lost, emerging only as a symptom of general disillusion with human nature. He gives no further arguments as to why the actual context of the feasts of fools should turn the satirical texts into anti-reformist manifestations of general disillusionment. On the contrary, the analysis of the contents of satires and their intellectual context, namely medieval ethical poetics and generic satiric theory, point to the opposite interpretation. The generic theory of satire indeed makes satirical poetry a part of ethical poetics, even defining the satire not only as correction of individual morals but making it possible to read it as "political" moral science concerning human communities and their rulers.[130] Thus Thomson's interpretation seems to contradict the self-awareness of medieval contemporaries.

Paul Gerhard Schmidt's interpretation of satire is based on textual analysis, i.e. authoritative quotations in the so-called goliardic (or vagant) poetry, and on the other hand, their performance context, i.e. the feasts of fools *(festa stultorum)*. Schmidt emphasises, as several other scholars, the literary and

---

128 Elredge 1970, 64 and *passim*.
129 Thomson 1978, 81.
130 See Kindermann 1978 and part I (The notion of satire).

intertextual (without using the term) background of goliardic satire. Despite their seeming spontaneity satires were skilfully composed fabrics of allusions and quotations. They were the poetry of schools and clerics dominated by a learned element. Quotation was the intended structural principle of these poems. Schmidt indeed takes it as his project to scrutinize closely the functions and significations of *Vagantenstrophe cum auctoritate*, a concept introduced to scholarship by Wilhelm Meyer.[131]

Schmidt puts satirical poetry, principally the works of Walter of Châtillon, in the context of feast of fools, *festum stultorum*, to which Walter openly refers. These feasts of the lower clergy offered an opportune occasion to perform learned allusive poetry and, what is even more important, a favourable context to criticize the upper ecclesiastical hierarchy, especially the lack of *largitas* and the power of *avaritia*.[132] However, it is difficult to see why this performance context would show that the satires were intended as a demonstration of the incorrigible nature of man, as Thomson argues. On the contrary, instead of general corruption and degeneration in the sublunar world and its people, the poems handle actual problems and sought a change in the wretched state of morals.

Nevertheless, Schmidt's remarkable analysis does not explain the use of different types of allusions and quotations. The differences of literal and ironical quotations particularly remain vague. Schmidt draws only a chronological distinction between two phases, i.e. the earlier, in which the quotation was preceded by announcement of the quotation or/and its source, and the later, in which the quotations were incorporated in the text by the *mise en abyme* technique without revealing its source or its nature as quotation. Often they were even arranged into a new metrical structure.[133] In the light of the evidence offered by the *Carmina Burana* the standing of quotations seems to be more nuanced.[134] Firstly, there are simple texts underlying didactic and normative authority, as are the most of the *versi* ending the groups in the moral-satirical part of the *Carmina Burana*. On the other hand, a single *versus* could also use metre as an indicator of its authority although there were less quotations and allusions or they were at least less apparent. Futhremore, the quotations and allusions often had an ironic function, especially when the quotation originated from the *Bible*.[135] Thus, one can argue that the intertextual references were a central technique which could be used for several purposes and manners – ambiguous ironic intertextuality, often veiled to a modern reader becomes an essential means of critique, as does elevation of the authoritative status of texts.

Despite the scholarship on medieval Latin satire, all the relevant aspects

---

131 Schmidt 1974/1990, 39-42.
132 Schmidt 1974/1990, 44-49; cf. also Hood 1994, 195-216.
133 Schmidt 1974/1990, 42-43, 49.
134 Cf. Mann 1980; Elliott 1982; Höfner 1988; Smolak 1986; *idem* 1987.
135 See e.g. Schüppert 1972, 140f.; Mann 1980.

have not yet been combined, even if most them have been dealt with separately in different studies. The notion of satire as a conservative-utopian reaction to economic and social change is today a commonplace, although the differences between monastic and secular Christian overtones have not attracted wider attention.[136] Futhermore, the connection of satire and its generic theory to classical tradition and the use of classical imagery as its allusive background are well-known. Elredge and Schmidt had gone furthest in putting together the textual connections and historical context. Nevertheless, central generic self-awareness of poetry's general moral function and of satire as a paradigmatic case of ethical poetics have not yet had their effect on scholarship. Yet from this viewpoint it is possible to distinguish both the reformist tones, the openness of moral meaning and the relation of hidden messages, and this poetry's obvious position in ecclesiastical discursive hierarchy as discourse *sub cathedra* with paradoxically authoritative stance.

This thesis is a continuation of Schmidt's interpretation about the specific performance context to a more extensive interpretation of the nature of satires (and secular Latin poetry in general) as poetry *sub cathedra* when the most other Latin discourse was *ex cathedra*. Poetry and *festa stultorum* offered a voice for the lower clerical orders. In a way, one can see the feast of fools as an instance free of the control of episcopal courts and higher clergy of cathedrals, in which the new "literary community" emerging at the fringes of schools could produce and receive critical clerical poetry.[137] It was here that there was room for poetry composed *sub cathedra* which formed conceptual tools for describing the contemporary society and presenting an ethical view slighty deviating from the normative or "official" ethics. In its morally receptive stance the satire had a hidden internal multilayered allusive apparatus beneath the quotations which made it possible to direct, and strengthen its critique from below with an appearance of authority.

The clerical theory of morals found its special expression in satires. The weight of this special expression was increased by the understanding of satire as a sub-branch of history, i.e. a literally true narrative, and by twining the biblical and classical authorities into the structure of texts. This structure, analysed by Schmidt, can be interpreted as programmatic strengthening of a persuasive gravity of discourse that is, stregthening its moral-authoritative status. Thus satirical poetry can also be opened up to modern interpreter as a critique of contemporary medieval society which did not content itself merely with affirming the contempt of this world from the monastic view, but tried to influence on the ecclesiastical hierarchy and individuals within it, by appealing to a utopian reciprocal order. There were possibilities of betterment even in the sublunar world governed by *Fortuna*. Her arbitrary

---

136 There are some exceptions, e.g. Schüppert 1972.
137 See Schmidt 1974/1990; Stock 1983; *idem* 1990.

rule had to be restrained by resisting her temptations, and by letting her positive gifts have effect in the emergence of the new man as Alan of Lille proposed.[138] *Nummus* was obviously a negative force which had to be kept in check to restore the moral order of nature; indeed *Nummilatria* was one of the forms of idolatry which had derailed the ideal order.

---

138 Alan of Lille, *De planctu Naturae* XII.pr.6, p. 852-857.

Conclusion

■ Speculum clericorum

The texts of the *Carmina Burana* with all their learned allusions belong to the context of cathedral schools and learned centres. Both the internal elements of the texts and the manuscript interrelations attest to this fact. Institutionally, the collection may well have been associated with the feasts of fools *(festa stultorum)* of the lower clergy. It is thus appropriate to interpret the texts in the context of the clerical schools and the learned world, whether economic, social or intellectual context in which the poetry of the *Carmina Burana*, especially its moral-satirical poems, are apparently an attempt to conceptualise and define the transition which was going on during the twelfth and early thirteenth century among the learned orders. This transition affected not only the ecclesiastical and clerical world. Latin poetry transmitted however a special clerical reaction to this change in the economic and social order.

An intellectual context for this conceptual effort was formed by the Christian-Platonic theory of signs, a view of the world as a book written by God, a hierarchical cosmology based on it, an indisputable authority of Holy Scripture, a tradition of allegorical-tropological interpretation, and a system of sciences inherited from Antiquity, part of which the poetry was understood as moral discourse.

Thus it is certainly justifiable to read the *Carmina Burana* as a kind of *speculum clericorum*, a discursive mirror emerging from its intellectual and social context. As *speculum* it is a poetical moral anthology compiled from different sources whose heterogenous elements are unified by a scrutiny of the preconditions and moral nature of human action in the sublunar world.[1] The collection treated these facts in a way relevant and understandable to clerical learned.

As a matter of fact, it seems that Latin secular poetry formed a more flexible and subtle way of managing the problems in the moral order of the sublunar world than normative moral encyclopedias and even sermon literature. It was characterised by the *sub cathedra* point of view of the lower clerical orders. Whereas moral encyclopedias and collections of distiches presented simple normative precepts *(praecepta)*[2], the *Carmina Burana*, and Latin secular poetry in general, did explore the preconditions of human action, represented

---

1   Cf. Lehmann 1922; Bischoff 1970a, 19; Lehtonen 1996.
2   E.g. *Distinctiones morales et monasticae*; *Moralium dogma philosophorum*; Honorius Augustodunensis, *Speculum Ecclesiae*; cf. also Lehmann 1922.

different ways of action and certainly offered also precepts for righteous action. Adapting Mikhail Bakhtin, secular Latin poetry was based on polyglossia:[3] both formally (its metrical solutions were borrowed from vernacular)[4], linguistically (the poetry was often macaronic or plurilingual, mixing authoritative Latin and vernacular, which brought in the lower registers)[5], semantically (irony, parody, double-entendres and puns were typical)[6], and also morally in mixing monastic views with more secular interpretations and presenting heterogenous elements without always giving precepts by which to evaluate them.[7] It seems possible to argue that the emergence and flourishing of Latin secular poetry from the turn of the eleventh and twelfth centuries for the next hundred years was at least partly a consequence of its being the central means by which the learned clerics, oriented towards secular society, could handle its complex new situation, and criticise the upper level of society and Church from below. The special suitability of poetry for this task was partly due to its greater freedom (e.g. the *festa stultorum*), and partly because a semi-public and relatively independent "literary" audience which built institutional conditions for this freedom had emerged on the fringes of ecclesiastical schools.

The marginalisation of poetry from the early thirteenth century onwards also, seems to relate to institutional changes in the ecclesiastical school system. The centralisation of the learned institutions and their emergence as universities at same time as with the revival of Aristotelian logic is probably one element in the dissolution of the central cultural position of Latin poetry. It is likely that the synchronous tightening of Christian dogma (the IV Lateran council), a crack-down on heretics (the Cathars) and the intensification of ecclesiastical government narrowed the living-space of ideologically vacillating and heterogenous poetry.[8] The freedom of *festa stultorum* also became limited.[9]

* * *

The initial question about the special nature of the *Carmina Burana* led me to study medieval strategies of interpretation[10], the standing of poetry[11], and to a hypothesis about this collection as an inverted allegory of the sublunar

---

3   See Bakhtin 1940/1994, 41-83, 431; *idem* 1965/1984, 1-58; see also Kristeva 1969/1978, 82-112.
4   Beare 1957, *passim*; Bakhtin 1940/1994, 75.
5   Beatie 1967, 16-24; Sayce 1992.
6   Cf. e.g. Lehmann 1922-23/1963, *passim*; Cairns 1980, 87-103; Mann 1980, 63-86; Elliott 1982, 353-368; Wehrli 1985.
7   This is obvious e.g. in the love-poetry and drinking songs in the *Carmina Burana* (CB I.2-3).
8   Curtius 1948, 61-65, 475-478; Vauchez 1982/1990, 385-421; Baldwin 1970, 80.
9   Baldwin 1970, 131-133; Schmidt 1974/1990, 49.
10 10. Lehtonen 1989; *idem* 1991.
11 Lehtonen 1992; *idem* 1993.

world according to the topos of the world upside down.[12] Meanwhile, it had become evident that the problems of interpretation of the *Carmina Burana* and secular Latin poetry in general demand detailed contextualisation, tracing the intertextual network and analysis of intellectual history – and that such an effort would certainly be an exhaustive undertaking for a single scholar. Thus this study, which concentrates on the moral-satirical poetry only saw daylight. It became a study of the standing of poetry among the various branches of knowledge, of *Fortuna* as an effort to outline the preconditions of human action, and satires as representations of acute socio-cultural problems. The analyses of texts are at the same time analyses of the textual strategies of the clerical culture – or of the adaptation of authorities, intertextual structures and ironic means in poetical moral-discourse *sub cathedra*.

It is obvious that the exploration of these elements offers a comprehensive ground for wider studies of the historical significance of Latin secular poetry and its place in clerical culture. Poetry was not, of course, a simple mirror of social or cultural "reality" – it was itself one discursive element which formed and created this "reality".

This two-way interaction between the discursive level and socio-cultural practices forms the central problem in this study. The analysis of medieval views of poetry thus has twofold significance. Firstly, examining the notions of poetry maps the its contemporary discursive sphere, and naturally the role that poetry plays in it. Secondly, it is the medieval ethical poetics itself, the discussions of the truthfulness of poetry and the nature of its representations that directs one towards the twelfth-century social sphere. Furthermore this direction is emphasized by the moral-tropological interpretation employed in ethical poetics. Poetry is defined first of all as a persuasive instrument guiding action, i.e. as a discursive means of working up the extra-linguistic reality.

Means such as the *Fortuna* poems and money satires have seemed to be the most crucial. The *Fortuna* poems represent the nature of human action and the historical course of events. Freely willing human agents are indeed a cause of sublunar history (together with natural events), but these agents are not able to control the course of events. This is because randomly crossing intentional lines of action cause consequences which do not follow the intentions of individual agents. The fortuitousness personified by *Fortuna* is finally a providential agent which instructs people of the unstable and transient nature of the sublunar world and directs their pursuits towards the stability of the world beyond. However, because of people's short-sighted liability to apprehend her true nature, *Fortuna* has had a tendency to overthrow the sublunar moral order.

This is what happens when such influences as *Nummus*, money, have appeared on the historical stage. The satires propose a primitive theory of

---

12 Lehtonen 1989; *idem* 1996.

money according to which liquidity dethrones kings and is like a riotous *Fortuna* which whirls communities and individuals. As a matter of fact, neither groups of poems discuss proper social mobility even though money or *Fortuna* would raise a poor man up from the dust or make a rhetor a consul. These seem rather to be *exempla* of the arbitrary power of money and the usurpation of the moral order as exemplified by an inverted textual authority and order of nature. *Fortuna* rather revolves human communities randomly (like Troy, Athens, or Rome) and dynasties (kings on the rim of the wheel) than is causing proper social mobility. At most, it causes unexpected events, i.e. sometimes it may happen that even a poor man becomes rich and powerful. Thus these poems do not react to the monetary economy alone, but rather to a complex new social organisation. The appearance of the monetary economy is rather a part of this change, although the most visible one. Indications of this are the money satires' concern with the disappearance of *largitas*, and with it reciprocal lordship and, on the other hand, the role of *iustitia* (or its lack) both in the context of *Fortuna* and *Nummus*. The reign of *Fortuna* deposes justice, and *Nummus* makes it a purchasable commodity equal to grace or other immaterial features.

■ Bibliography

PRINTED SOURCES

Carmina Burana

Carmina Burana. Mit Benutzung der Vorarbeiten Wilhelm Meyers kritisch herausgegeben von Alfons Hilka und Otto Schumann.

CB I.1. *I Band: Text 1. Die moralisch-satirischen Dichtungen.* Hrsg. von Alfons Hilka und Otto Schumanna. Zweite, unveränderte Auflage. Heidelberg 1930/1978.

CB I.2. *I Band: Text 2. Die Liebeslieder.* Hrsg. von Otto Schumann. Zweite, unveränderte Auflage. Heidelberg 1941/1971.

CB I.3. *I Band: Text 3. Die Trink- und Spielerlieder - Die geistlichen Dramen - Nachträge.* Hrsg. von Otto Schumann und Berhard Bischoff. Heidelberg 1970.

CB faks. *Faksimile-Ausgabe der Handschrift der Carmina Burana und der Fragmenta Burana (Clm. 4660 und 4660a) der Bayerischen Staatsbibliothek.* Hrsg. von Bernhard Bischoff. München 1970 (1967).

SCHMELLER 1847 *Carmina Burana. Lateinische und deutsche Lieder und Gedichte einer Handschrift des XIII. Jahrhunderts aus Benedictbeuern auf der K. Bibliothek zu München.* Hrsg. von Johann Andreas Schmeller. Bibliothek des Literarischen Vereins in Stuttgart XVI. Stuttgart.

See also Bernt 1975, Parlett 1986/1988, Walsh 1976 and Wolff 1995 in literature.

Primary materials

ALAN OF LILLE *Anticlaudianus de Antirufino.* Éd. R. Bossuat. Textes philosophiques du moyen âge 1. Paris 1955.
- *Anticlaudianus or the Good and Perfect Man.* Tr. J. J. Sheridan. Pontifical Institute of Mediaeval Studies. Toronto 1973.
- *De planctu Naturae.* Ed. N. M. Häring.

Studii Medievali 3 serie 19.2, 1978, p. 797-879.
- *Plaint of Nature.* Tr. J.J. Sheridan. Pontifical Institute of Mediaeval Studies: Mediaeval Sources in Translation 26. Toronto 1980.

ANONYMOUS *Accessus ab auctore incerto.* In William of Conches, *Glosae in Iuvenalem,* ed. Wilson 1980. Paris 1980, p. 89-91.

ANONYMOUS *Accessus ad auctores.* In *Accessus ad auctores. Bernard d'Utrecht; Conrad d'Hirsau, Dialogus super auctores.* Éd. R. B. C. Huygens. Leiden 1970, p. 19-54.
- idem. In *Collection Latomus* XV. Éd. R.B.C. Huygens. Berchem & Bruxelles 1954.

ANONYMOUS *Appendice in Anticlaudiano Alani ab Insulis.* In Alan of Lille *Anticlaudianus,* p. 199-201.

ANONYMOUS *Distinctionum monasticorum et moralium.* In *Spicilegium solesmense* III. Ed. J. B. Pitra. Parisiis 1855, p. 452-487.

ANONYMOUS *Moralium dogma philosophorum. Das Moralium dogma philosophorum des Guillaume de Conches* (sic!). Hrsg. J. Holmberg. Uppsala - Paris 1929.

ANONYMOUS *Rhetorica ad Herennium. Cicero in Twenty-Eight Volumes I: [Cicero] Ad C. Herennium de ratione dicendi (Rhetorica ad Herennium).* Ed. & tr. H. Caplan. The Loeb Classical Library 403. Cambridge, Mass. & London 1954/1981.

ANONYMOUS *Saeculi noni (sic!) auctoris in Boetii Consolationem Philosophiae commentarius.* Ed. E.T. Silk. Papers and Monographs of the American Academy in Rome. Vol. IX. Rome 1935.

ARCHIPOETA *Die Gedichte des Archipoeta.* Kritisch bearbeitet von H. Watenpuhl. Hrsg. von H. Hrefeld. Heidelberg 1958.
- *Hugh Primas and the Archpoet.* Tr. & ed. by F. Adcock. Cambridge Medieval Classics 2. Cambridge 1994, p. 69-127.

ARISTOTLE *Rhetorica.* Rhétorique I-III. Éd. & tr. M. Dufour & A. Wartelle. Collection des universités de France (G. Budé). Paris 1931-1973/ 1967-1989.
- *Physica. Aristotle in Twenty-Three Volumes 4-5: The Physics.* With an Engl. tr. by P. Wicksteed & F.M. Cornford. The Loeb Classical Library 228, 255. London

1968-1970.
- *Metaphysica. Ibid. 17-18: The Metaphysics.*
  With an Engl. tr. by H. Tredennick. The
  Loeb Classical Library 271, 287.
  Cambridge, Mass. 1933-35/1977-80.
- *Ethica Nicomachea. Ibid. 19: The
  Nichomachean Ethics.* With an Engl. tr.
  by H. Rackham. The Loeb Classical
  Library 73. Cambridge, Mass. 1968.
AUGUSTINE *De libero arbitrio. Oeuvres de
  Saint Augustin* 6. Éd. & tr. G. Madec.
  Bibliothèque Augustinienne. Paris 1976,
  p. 157-529.
- *De doctrina christiana. Oeuvres de Saint
  Augustin* 11. Éd. Bénédictine & tr. G.
  Combès et J. Farges. Bibliothèque
  Augustinienne. Paris 1949.
- *De civitate Dei I-V, VI-X. Oeuvres de Saint
  Augustin* 33-34. Éd. B. Dombart, A. Kalb
  & tr. J. Combès. Paris 1959/1981.
BEDE *De arte metrica et de schematibus et
  tropis.* Ed. C.B. Kendall & M.H. King. In
  *Beda Venerabilis opera. Pars IV: Opera
  didascalica 1.* Corpus christianorum s.l.
  123 A. Turnhout 1975.
BERNARD SILVESTER *Commentum in
  Martianum.* Ed. Haijo J. Westra.
  Pontifical Institute of Mediaeval Studies:
  Studies and Texts 80. Toronto 1986.
- *Commentum super Eneidos sex libros.
  Commentary on the First Six Books of the
  Aeneid of Virgil Commonly Attributed to
  Bernardus Silvestris.* Ed. J. W. Jones &
  E. F. Jones. Lincoln & London 1977.
- *Commentary on the First Six Books of
  Virgil's Aeneid by Bernardus Silvestris.*
  Tr. E.G. Schreiber & T.E. Maresca.
  Lincoln & London 1979.
- *Bernardi Silvestris Cosmographia.* Ed. by P.
  Dronke. Textus minores 53. Leiden 1978.
- *The Cosmographia of Bernardus Silvestris.*
  Tr. W. Wetherbee. Records of Western
  Civilization. A Series of Columbia
  University Press. New York 1973/1990.
BERNARD OF UTRECHT *Commentum in
  Theodulum.* In *Accessus ad auctores.
  Bernard d'Utrecht, Conrad d'Hirsau,
  Dialogus super auctores.* Ed. R.B.C.
  Huygens. Leiden 1970, p. 55-69.
Biblia sacra juxta vulgatam Clementinam.
  Denuo ediderunt complures Sacrae
  Professores Facultatis Parisiensis et
  Seminarii Sancti Spiriti. Romae - Tornaci
  - Parisiis 1947.
BOETHIUS, ANICIUS MANLIUS SEVERI-
  NUS *De Trinitate.* In Boethius, *Tractates,
  De consolatione Philosophiae.* Ed. & tr.
  H. F. Stewart, E.K. Rand, & S.J. Tester.
  The Loeb Classical Library 74.
  Cambridge, Mass. & London 1918/1978,
  p. 2-31.
- *Contra Eutychen et Nestorium. Ibidem,* p.
  72-129.
- *Philosophiae consolatio.* Ed. E.K. Rand &
  tr. S.J. Tester. Ibidem, p. 130-435.

- *Commentarii in librum Aristotelis* Peri
  hermeneias I-II. Rec. C. Meiser. Lipsiae
  1877-1880.
CASSIODORUS, FLAVIUS MAGNUS
  AURELIUS *Institutiones divinarum et
  saecularum litterarum.* Ed. R.A.B.
  Mynors. Oxford 1937.
CICERO, MARCUS TULLIUS *De
  inventione.* In Cicero, *Cicero in
  Twenty-Eight Volumes II: De inventione,
  De optimo genere, Oratorum topica,* Ed.
  & tr. H.M. Hubbell. The Loeb Classical
  Library 386. Cambridge, Mass. & London
  1949/1976.
CONRAD OF HIRSAU *Dialogus super
  auctores.* In *Accessus ad auctores.
  Bernard d'Utrecht, Conrad d'Hirsau,
  Dialogus super auctores.* Ed. R.B.C.
  Huygens. Leiden 1970, p. 71-131.
- *Dialogus de mundi contemptu vel amore.* Éd.
  R. Bultot. Analecta mediaevalia Namur-
  censia 19. Louvain - Lille 1966.
DIOMEDES *Ars grammatica.* In *Scriptores
  grammatici Latini* I. Ed. H. Keil. Leipzig
  1855, p. 297-529.
DOMINICUS GUNDISSALINUS *De
  divisione philosophiae.* Hrsg. L. Baur.
  Beiträge zur Geschichte der Philosophie
  des Mittelalters. Texte und Unter-
  suchungen Bd. IV H. 2-3. Münster 1903.
EBERHARDUS ALEMANNUS *Laborintus.*
  In Faral 1924, p. 336-377.
GERALD OF WALES *Speculum Ecclesiae.*
  In *Giraldi Cambrensis Opera* IV. Ed. J.S.
  Brewer. Rerum Britannicarum Medii
  Aevi scriptores. London 1873, p. 1-354.
GREGORY THE GREAT *Expositio in
  Canticis canticorum.* Grégoire Le Grand,
  *Commentaire sur le Cantiques des
  cantiques,* Éd. & tr. R. Belanger. Paris
  1984.
GUIBERT OF NOGENT *De vita sua, sive
  Monodiae.* Guibert de Nogent,
  Autobiographie. Éd. & tr. E.-R. Labande.
  Les Classiques de l'histoire de France au
  Moyen Age 34. Paris 1981.
HENRY OF SETTIMELLO *Elegia de
  diversitate Fortunae et Philosophiae
  consolatione.* In *Patrologia Latinae* 205.
  Ed. J.-P. Migne 1855, col. 840-868.
Holy Bible. The King James Version.
  Nashville: Thomas Nelson Publishers
  1977/1984
HONORIUS AUGUSTODUNENSIS
  Speculum Ecclesiae. In *Patrologia
  Latinae* 172. Ed. J.-P. Migne. Parisiis
  1854, col. 813-1108.
HORACE *Carmina, Epodi.* In *The Odes and
  Epodes.* Ed. & tr. C. E. Bennett. The Loeb
  Classical Library 33. Cambridge, Mass. &
  London 1914/1978.
- *Epistolae et Ars poetica.* In *Satires, Epistles
  and Ars poetica.* Ed. & tr. H.R.
  Fairclough. The Loeb Classical Library
  194. Cambridge, Mass. & London

1926/1978.

HUGH PRIMAS OF ORLÉANS *The Oxford Poems of Hugh Primas and the Arundel Lyrics*. Ed. by C.J. McDonough. Toronto Medieval Latin Texts 15. Toronto 1984.

- *Hugh Primas and the Archpoet*. Ed. and transl. F. Adcock. Cambridge Medieval Classics 2. Cambridge 1994, p. 1-67.

HUGH OF SAINT VICTOR *Didascalicon: de studio legendi*. Ed. C.H. Buttimer. The Catholic University of America: Studies in Medieval and Renaissance Latin X. Washington, D.C. 1939.

- *The* Didascalicon *of Hugh of St. Victor*. Tr. by J. Taylor. Records of Western Civilization. A series of Columbia University Press. New York 1961/1991.

ISIDORE OF SEVILLE *Etymologiae*. Isidore of Seville, *Etymologies. Book II: Rhetoric*. Ed. & tr. by P. K. Marshall. Collection Auteurs Latins du moyen âge. Paris 1983.

- *Isidori Hispaliensis Episcopi Etymologiarum sive Originum libri XX*. Ed. W. M. Lindsay. Scripta Classicorum Bibliotheca Oxoniensis. Vols. 1-2. Oxford 1911/1987.

JOHN OF HAUVILLA *Architrenius*. (Johannes de Hauvilla) Hrsg. P.G. Schmidt. München 1974.

- *idem*, tr. & ed. by W. Wetherbee. Cambridge Medieval Classics 3. Cambridge & New York 1994.

JOHN OF SALISBURY *Metalogicon*. Ed. C.C.I. Webb. Oxford 1929.

- *Policraticus* I-II. Ed. C.C.I. Webb. Oxford 1909.

JUVENAL *Saturae*. In *Juvenal and Persius*. Ed. & tr. G.G. Ramsay. The Loeb Classical Library 91. Cambridge, Mass. & London 1918/1979, p. 1-307.

MATTHEW OF VENDOME *Ars versificatoria*. In Faral 1924, p. 106-193.

OTTO OF FREISING *Chronica sive Historia de duabus civitatibus*. Übersetzt von A. Schmidt und hrsg. W. Lammers. Berlin 1961.

- *Gesta Frederici I Imperatoris. Die Taten Friedrichs oder richtiger cronica*. Bischoff Otto von Freising und Rahewin. Übersetzt von A. Schmidt & hrsg. von F.-J. Schmale. Darmstadt 1986.

OVID *Ars amatoria*. In *Ovid in Six Volumes II: The Art of Love, and Other Poems*. Ed. & tr. J.H. Mozley. The Loeb Classical Library 232. Cambridge, Mass. & London 1929/1985, p. 11-175.

- *Metamorphoses*. In *Ovid in Six Volumes III-IV: Metamorphoses*. Ed. & tr. F.J. Miller. The Loeb Classical Library 42-43. Cambridge, Mass. & London 1916/1984.

- *Fasti*. In *Ovid in Six Volumes V: Fasti*. Ed. & tr. J.G. Frazer. The Loeb Classical Library 253. Cambridge, Mass. & London 1931/1989

- *Tristia & Ex Ponto*. In *Ovid in Six Volumes*

VI: Tristia. Ex Ponto. Ed. & tr. A.L. Wheeler. The Loeb Classical Library 151. Cambridge, Mass. & London 1924/1975.

PETER ABELARD *Historia calamitatum*. Éd. J. Monfrin. Paris 1959/1978.

QUINTILIAN *Institutio oratoria. The Institutio Oratoria of Quintilian in Four Volumes*. Ed. Halm & tr. H. E. Butler. The Loeb Classical Library 124-127. Cambridge, Mass. & London 1920-1922/1979-1989.

RABAN MAUR *De institutione clericorum*. Hrsg. A. Knoepfler. Veröffentlichen aus dem Kirchenhistorichen Seminar München Nr. 5. München 1901.

RALPH OF LONGCHAMP *In Anticlaudianum Alani commentum*. Ed. J. Sulowski. Polska Akademia Nauk. Zaklad Historii Nauki i Techniki. Zródla do dziejów nauki i techniki. Tom XIII. Wroclaw, Warszawa, Kraków & Gdánsk 1972.

Sacrorum Conciliorum Nova, et Amplissima Collectio. Edidit Joannes Dominicus Mansi et Dominicus Passioneus. Tomus XXII. Venetiis 1778.

THIERRY OF CHARTRES *The Latin Commentaries by Thierry of Chartres*. Ed. by K.M. Fredborg. Pontifical Institute of Mediaeval Studies: Texts and Studies 84. Toronto 1988.

THOMAS OF CAPUA *Ars dictandis. Die Ars dictandi des Thomas von Capua*. Hrsg. E. Heller. Sitzungsberichte der Heidelberger Akademie der Wissenschaften, philosophisch-historische Klasse. Jhrg. 1928/29, Abh. 4. Heidelberg 1929.

THOMAS AQUINAS *S. Thomae Aquinitatis doctoris angelici Summa theologiae. Pars prima et prima secundae*. Cura et studio Sac. P. Caramello cum textu ex recensione Leonina. Torini 1952/1963.

WALTER OF CHATILLON *Die Gedichte Walters von Châtillon. 1. Die Lieder der Handschrift 351 von St. Omer*. Hrsg. von K. Strecker. Berlin 1925.

- *Moralisch-satirische Gedichte Walters von Châtillon (2.) aus deutschen, englischen, französischen und italienischen Handschriften*. Hrsg. von K. Stracker. Heidelberg 1929.

WILLIAM OF CONCHES *Glosae super Platonem*. Éd. E. Jeauneau. Textes philosophiques du moyen âge 13. Paris 1965.

- *Glosae in Iuvenalem*. Ed. B. Wilson. Textes philosophiques du Moyen Age 18. Paris 1980.

- *Glossa super Macrobium*. In Dronke 1974, p. 68-78.

- *Philosophia*. Ed. G. Mauruch. University of South Africa: Studia 16. Pretoria 1980.

LITERATURE

ALLEN, JUDSON B. 1982 *The Ethical Poetic of the Later Middle Ages: A decorum of convenient distinction*. Toronto.

ANDERSON, PERRY 1974/1992 *Passages from Antiquity to Feudalism*. London & New York.

Antiqui und Moderni. Traditionbewußtsein und Fortschittsbewußtsein im späten Mittelalter. Hrsg. von A. Zimmermann. Miscellanea medievalia. Veröffentlichungen des Thomas-Instituts der Universität zu Köln. Bd. 9. Berlin & New York 1974.

AUERBACH, ERICH 1958 *Literatursprache und Publikum in der lateinischen Spätantike und im Mittelalter*. Bern.

- 1959/1984 "Figura". Tr. R. Mannheim. In E. Auerbach, *Scenes from the Drama of European Literature*. Theory and History of Literature 9. Minneapolis, p. 11-76.

BAGNI, PAOLO 1968 *La costituzione della poesia nelle artes del XII-XIII secolo*. Universitá degli studi di Bologna facoltá di lettere e filosofia. Studi e ricerche n.s. XX. Bologna.

BAKHTIN Mihail 1940/1994 From the Prehistory of Novelistic Discourse. In *The Dialogic Imagination by M.M. Bakhtin. Three Essays*. Ed. by M. Holquist. Tr. by C. Emerson & M. Holquist. Austin, p. 41-83.

- 1965/1984 *Rabelais and His World*. Transl. by H. Iswolsky. Bloomington 1984.

BALDWIN, JOHN W. *Masters, Princes, and Merchants. The Social views of Peter the Chanter & his circle*. Vols. I-II. Princeton, N.J. 1970.

- 1982 Masters at Paris from 1179 to 1215: A Social Perspective. In *Renaissance and Renewal in the Twelfth Century*, p. 138-172.

BARTHÉLEMY 1990 *Nouvelle histoire de la France médiévale 4: L'Ordre seigneurial (XIe-XIIe siècle)*. Paris.

BEARE, WILLIAM 1957 *Latin Verse and European Song. A Study in Accent and Rhythm*. London.

BEATIE, B. A. 1967 Macaronic Poetry in the Carmina Burana. In *Vivarium* 5, p. 16-24.

BECHTUM, MARTIN 1941 *Beweggründe und Bedeutung des Vagantentums in der lateinischen Kirche des Mittelalters*. Beiträge zur mittelalterlichen, neueren und allgemeinen Geschichte 14. Jena.

BERNT, G. 1975 Anmerkungen und Nachwort. In *Carmina Burana. Die Lieder der Benediktbeurer Handschrift in vollständiger Übertragung*. Übersetzung der lateinischen Texte von Carl Fischer, der mittelhochdeutschen Texte von Hugo Kuhn nach der von B. Bischoff abgeschlossenen kritischen Ausgabe von A. Hilka und O. Schumann, Heidelberg

1930-1971. Darmstadt, p. 427-571.

- 1978 'Carmina Burana' Sammlungen lat. (und dt.). Dichtungen um 1225/30. Teoksessa *Die deutsche Literatur des Verfasserlexikon Bd 1*. Hrsg. von W. Stamper et alii. Berlin & New York.

BETTEN, ANNE 1976 Lateinische Bettellyrik: Literarische Topik oder Ausdruck existentieller Not? Eine vergleichende Skizze über Martial und Archipoeta. In *Mittellateinisches Jahrbuch* 11, p. 143-150.

BISCHOFF, BERNHARD 1970a Carmina Burana. Einführung zur Faksimile Ausgabe der Benediktbeurer Liedeshandschrift. In *CB faks.*, p. 5-17.

- 1970b Vorwort. In *CB I.3*, p. VII-XVI.

BISSON, T.N. 1994 The "Feudal Revolution". In *Past and Present* 142, p. 6-42.

BLACK, D.L. 1990 *Logic and Aristotle's Rhetoric and Poetics in Medieval Arabic Philosophy*. Leiden 1990.

BLOCH, MARC 1939-40/1980 *La société féodale*. Paris.

BLOCH, R. HOWARD 1983/1986 *Etymologies and Genealogies. A Literary Anthropology of the French Middle Ages*. Chicago and London.

BOSSUAT, R. 1955 Introduction. In Alan of Lille, *Anticlaudianus*, p. 7-53.

BOUREAU, ALAIN 1993 Hypothèses sur l'émergence lexicale et théorique de la catégorie de séculier au XIIe siècle. In *Le clerc séculier au moyen âge. XXIIe Congrés de la S.H.M.E.S.* (Amiens, juin 1991). Société des Historiens Médiévistes de l'Enseignement Supérieur Public. Série Histoire Ancienne et Médiévale 27. Paris, p. 35-43.

BRINKMANN, HENNIG 1980 *Mittelalterliche Hermeneutik*. Darmstadt.

BRUNNER, OTTO 1958/1984 *Sozialgeschichte Europas im Mittelalter*. Göttingen.

BULTOT, R. 1969 *Grammatica$_k$ ethica et contemptus mundi aux XIIe et XIIIe siècles*. In *Arts libéraux et philosophie au Moyen Age*. Actes du quatrième conrès internationale de la philosophie médiévale, 1967 Montréal. Montréal & Paris 1969, p. 815-827.

CAIRNS, FRANCIS 1980, The Archpoet's Confession: Sources, Interpretation, and Historical Context. In *Mittellateinisches Jahrbuch* 15, p. 87-103.

- 1984 The addition to Richard of Poitiers 'Chronica' and 'Hugo Primas of Orléans'. In *Mittellateinisches Jahrbuch* 19, p-159-161.

CERQUIGLINI, BERNARD 1989 *Éloge de la variante. Histoire critique de la philologie*. Paris.

CHADWICK, HENRY 1981/1990 *Boethius. The Consolation of Music, Logic, Theology, and Philosophy*. Oxford.

- 1986/1987 *Augustin*. Tr. A. Spiess. Paris.
CHATILLON, FRANÇOIS 1951 *Flagello sepe castigatus vitam terminavit*. Contribution à l'étude des mauvais traitements infligés à Gautier de Châtillon. In *Révue du Moyen Age Latin* VII:2, p. 151-174.
CHENU, MARIE-DOMINIQUE 1957/1976 *La Théologie au douzième siècle*. Études de Philosophie Médiévale XLV. Paris.
CHYDENIUS, JOHAN 1960 The Theory of Medieval Symbolism. In *Commentationes Humanarum Litterarum* XVII:2. Helsinki, p. 1-42.
CIOFFARI, VINCENZO 1935 *Fortune and Fate from Democritus to St. Thomas Aquinas*. New York.
- 1940 *The Conception of Fortune and Fate in the Works of Dante*. Cambridge, Mass.
CIPOLLA, CARLO M. (ed.) 1972/1981 *The Fontana Economic History of Europe: The Middle Ages*. Glasgow.
CLANCHY, M. T. 1983 *England and its Rulers 1066-1272*. Glasgow.
CLOGAN, PAUL 1990 The Ethical Poetic in the Thirteenth and Fourteenth Centuries. In *Knowledge and the Sciences in Medieval Philosophy*. Proceedings of the Eighth International Congress of Medieval Philosophy (S.I.E.P.M.). Helsinki 1987. Vol. III. Ed. R. Työrinoja, A.-I. Lehtinen & D. Follesdal. Annals of the Finnish Society for Missiology and Ecumenics 55. Helsinki, p. 193-204.
COOK, JON 1986 Carnival and the Canterbury Tales: 'Only equals may laugh' (Herzen). In *Medieval Literature. Criticism, Ideology and History*. Ed. D. Aers. Brighton, p. 169-191.
COULTER, JAMES A. 1976 *The Literary Microcosm. Theories of Interpretation of the Later Neoplatonists*. Leiden.
COURCELLE, PIERRE 1967 *La consolation de philosophie dans la tradition littéraire*. Paris.
COURTENAY WILLIAM J. 1984a Nature and the Natural in Twelfth-Century Thought. In W. J. Courtenay *Covenant and Causality in Medieval Thought. Studies in Philosophy, Theology and Economic Practice*. Variorum Reprints. London, p. 1-26.
- 1984b The Dialectic of Divine Omnipotence. *Ibid.*, p. 1-37.
CRAIG, WILLIAM L. 1988 *The Problem of Divine Foreknowledge and Future Contingents from Aristotle to Suarez*. Brill's Studies in Intellectual History Vol. 7. Leiden.
CULLER, JONATHAN 1981/1983 *The Pursuit of Signs. Semiotics, Literature, Deconstruction*. London, Melbourne and Henley.
CURTIUS, ERNST ROBERT 1948 *Europäische Literatur und lateinisches Mittelalter*. Bern.

DAHAN, GILBERT 1980 Notes et textes sur la Poétique au Moyen Age. In *Archives d'histoire doctrinale et littéraire du Moyen Age* 47, p. 171-239.
- 1990 Les classifications du savoir aux XIIe et XIIIe siècles. In *L'enseignement philosophique. Revue association des professeurs de l'enseignement public* 40:4, p. 5-27.
DAHIYAT I.M. 1974 *Avicenna's Commentary on the Poetics of Aristotle*. Leiden.
DELHAYE, PHILIPPE 1947 L'organisation scolaire au XIIe siècle. In *Traditio* 5, p. 211-268.
- 1949/1988 L'Enseignement de la philosophie morale aux XIIe siècle. In P. Delhaye *Enseignement et morale au XIIe siècle*. Vestigia 1. Fribourg & Paris, p. 59-81.
- 1958/1988 "Grammatica" et "Ethica" au XIIe siècle. *Ibid.*, p. 83-134.
- 1966 La nature dans l'oeuvre de Hugues de Saint-Victor. In *La Filosofia della natura nel medioevo*. Atti del 3° congresso internazionale di filosofia medioevale 1964. Milano, p. 272-278.
DOBIACHE-ROJDESTVENSKY, OLGA 1931 *Les poésies des Goliards*. Les textes du christianisme 9. Paris.
DOREN A. 1924 Fortuna im Mittelalter und in der Renaissance. In *Vorträge der Bibliothek Warburg* I:1922-23. Leipzig, p. 71-144.
DRONKE, PETER 1962 A Critical Note on Schumann's Dating of the Codex Buranus. In *Beiträge zur Geschichte der deutschen Sprache und Literatur* 84, p. 173-183.
- 1965-66 *Medieval Latin and the Rise of European Love-Lyric. Vol. I: Problems and Interpretations. Vol. 2: Texts newly edited from the manuscripts and for the most part unpublished*. Oxford.
- 1974 *Fabula: Explorations into the Uses of Myth in Medieval Platonism*. Mittellateinische Studien und Texte 9. Leiden & Köln.
- 1975 Poetic Meaning in the Carmina Burana. In *Mittellateinisches Jahrbuch* 10, p. 116-137.
- 1976 Peter of Blois and Poetry at the Court of Henry II. In *Medieval Studies* 38, p. 185-235.
DUBY, GEORGES 1973/1985 *Guerriers et paysans. VIIe-XII siècle: Premier essor de l'économie européenne*. Paris.
- 1978 *Les trois ordres ou l'imaginaire du féodalisme*. Paris.
- 1988 *Mâle Moyen Age. De l'amour et autres essais*. Paris.
EHLERS, JOACHIM 1974 Monastische Theologie, historischer Sinn und Dialektik. Tradition und Neuerung in der

Wissenschaften des 12. Jahrhunderts. In *Antiqui und Moderni. Traditionbewußtsein und Forschrittsbewußtsein im späten Mittelalter*. Hrsg. von A. Zimmermann. Miscellanea medievalia Bd. 9. Berlin & New York, 58-79.

ELREDGE, LAURENCE 1970 Walter of Châtillon and the *Decretum* of Gratian: An analysis of "Propter Zion non tacebo". In *Studies in Medieval Culture*. Ed. J.R. Sommerfield. The Medieval Institute, Western Michigan University. Kalamazoo, p. 59-69.

ELLIOTT, A. G. 1982 The Art of Inept 'exemplum': Ovidian Deception in 'Carmina Burana' 117 and 178. In *Sandalion* 5, p. 353-368.

FARAL, EDMOND 1924 *Les arts poétiques du XIIe et du XIIIe siècle. Recherches et documents sur la téchnique littéraire du môyen âge*. Paris.

FICHTNER, EDWARD G. 1967 The Etymology of Goliard. In *Neophilologus* 51, p. 231-237.

FINLEY, MOSES I. 1954/1979 *The World of Odysseus*. Rev. ed. Harmondsworth.

- 1974 Aristotle and Economic Analysis. In *Studies in Ancient Society*. Ed. M.I. Finley. London, p. 26-52.

FOSSIER, ROBERT 1982/1990 Le bond en avant. In R. Fossier, *Le Moyen Age. L'éveil de l'Europe 950-1250*. Paris, p. 267-314.

FOULON, JEAN-HERVÉ 1993 Le clerc et son image dans la prédication synodale de Geoffrey Babion, archevêque de Bordeaux (1136-1158). In *Le clerc séculier au moyen âge. XXIIe Congrés de la S.H.M.E.S. (Amiens, juin 1991)*. Société des Historiens Médiévistes de l'Enseignement Supérieur Public. Série Ancienne et Médiévale 27. Paris, p. 45-60.

FREDBORG, KARIN M. 1988 Introduction. In Thierry of Chartres, p. 1-43.

FRIIS-JENSEN, KARSTEN 1988 Horatius liricus et ethicus. Two twelfth-century school texts on Horace's poems. In *Cahiers. Institut du Moyen Age Grec et Latin* 57, p. 81-147.

FRYE, NORTHROP 1983 *The Great Code. The Bible and Literature*. London, Melbourne & Henley.

FUNKENSTEIN, AMOS 1986 *Theology and the Scientific Imagination from the Middle Ages to the Seventeenth Century*. Princeton, N.J..

GANDILLAC, MAURICE DE 1992 *Genèses de la modernité. Les douze siècles où se fit notre Europe. De la "Cité de Dieu" à la "Nouvelle Atlantide"*. Paris.

GARCIA-VILLOSLADA, RICARDO 1975 *La Poesia ritmica de los goliardos medievales*. Publicaciones de la Fundacion Universitaria Espanola.

Monografias 16. Madrid.

GELLRICH, JESSE M. 1985 *The Idea of the Book in the Middle Ages. Language theory, mythology, and fiction*. Ithaca & London.

GENETTE, GÉRARD 1982 *Palimpsestes. La littérare au second degré*. Paris.

Geschichte der Universität in Europa. Bd. I: Mittelalter. Hrsg. von W. Rüegg. München 1993.

GILSON, ÉTIENNE 1944/1986 *La philosophie au moyen âge*. Paris.

GLAUCHE, GÜNTER 1970 Schullektüre im Mittelalter. Entstehung und Wandlungen des Lektürekanons bis 1200, nach den Quellen dargestellt. *Münchener Beiträge zur Mediävistik und Renaissance Forschung* 5. München.

GOMPF, LUDWIG 1973 Figmenta poetarum. In *Literatur und Sprache im Europäische Mittelalter. Festschrift für Karl Langosch*. Hrsg. von A. Önnerfors, J. Rothofer & F. Wagner. Darmstadt, p. 53-62.

GÖSSMANN, ELISABETH 1974 "Antiqui" und "moderni" 12. Jahrhundert. In *Antiqui und Moderni*, p. 40-57.

GREEN, DAVID L. Alieniloquium. Zur Begriffsbestimmung der mittelalterlichen Ironie. In *Verbum et Signum. Beiträge zur mediävistischen Bedeutungsforschung. Bd. 2: Studien zu Semantik und Sinntradition im Mittelalter*. München, p. 119-159.

GREGORY, TULLIO 1966 L'idea di natura nella filosofia medioevale prima dell'ingresso della fisica di Aristotele il secolo XII. In *La Filosofia della natura nel medioevo*. Atti del 3° congresso internazionale di filosofia medioevale 1964. Milano, p. 27-65.

- 1990 Forme di conoscenza e ideali di sapere nella cultura medievale. In *Knowledge and the Sciences in Medieval Philosophy*. Proceedings of the Eight International Congress of Medieval Philosophy (S.I.E.P.M.) Vol. I. Ed. by M. Asztalos, J.E. Murdoch and I. Niiniluoto. Acta Philosophica Fennica 48. Helsinki, p. 10-71.

GRUNDMANN, HERBERT 1958 Litteratus - illitteratus. Der Wandel einer Bildungsnorm vom Altertum zum Mittelalter. In *Archiv für Kulturgeschichte* 40, p. 1-65.

GUENÉE, BERNARD 1980 *Histoire et culture historique dans l'Occident médiéval*. Paris.

GUREVITCH, ARON 1970/1979 Feodalismens uppkomst i Västeuropa. Övers. M.-A. Sahlin. Stockholm.

- 1972/1983 *Les catégories de la culture médiévale*. Tr. par H. Courtin et N. Godneff. Paris.

HAAVIO, MARTTI 1959 The Upside-Down World. In *Essais Folkloriques par Martti*

Haavio. Publiés à l'occasion de son 60e anniversaire. Studia Fennica VIII. Helsinki, p. 209-221, 241.

HANFORD, JAMES HOLLY 1926 The Progenitors of Golias. In *Speculum* 1, p. 38-58.

HARDISON, O.B. 1970 The Place of Averroes' Commentary on the Poetics in the History of Medieval Criticism. In *Medieval and Renaissance Studies*. Ed. J.L. Lievsay, p. 57-81.

HÄRING, NIKOLAUS M. 1982 Commentary and Hermeneutics. In *Renaissance and Renewal in the Twelfth Century*, p. 173-200.

HASKINS, CHARLES HOMER 1928/1982 *The Renaissance of the Twelfth Century*. Cambridge, Mass. & London.

HEIMBUCHER, MAX 1933 *Die Orden und Kongregationen des katolischen Kirche*. I Bd. Paderborn.

HIETANIEMI, TAPANI 1992 Otto Brunner (1998-1982) ja herruuden maailma. In O. Brunner, *Euroopan keskiajan sosiaalihistoria*. Tr. T. Hietaniemi. Tampere, p. 145-173.

HILKA, ALFONS & SCHUMANN, OTTO 1930/1961 *Carmina Burana*. II Band: *Kommentar. Die moralisch-satirischen Dichtungen*. Zweite unveränderte Auflage. Heidelberg.

A History of Twelfth-Century Western Philosophy. Ed. by P. Dronke. Cambridge 1988/1992.

HÖFNER, ECKHARD 1988 Parodie und Lachen. Zu *Carmina Burana 222* und einem Lied des Raimbaut d'Arenga. In *Festschrift für Paul Klopsch*. Göppinger Arbeiten zur Germanistik 492. Hrsg. von U. Kindermann, W. Maaz und F. Wagner. Göppingen, p. 101-127.

HOOD, ALLAN B.E. 1994 The Golden Rose of Besançon: Ecclesiastical Politics and the Feast of Fools in a Poem of Walter of Châtillon. In *Studi Medievali* 3[a] serie. Anno XXXV, fasc. I, giugno 1994, p. 195-216.

HOROWITZ, JEANNINE & MENACHE, SOPHIA 1994 *L'humour en chaire. Le rire dans l'Église médiévale*. Histoire et société 28. Genève.

HUNT, RICHARD W. 1948/1980 The Introductions to the "Artes" in the Twelfth Century. Teoksessa R.W. Hunt, *The History of Grammar in the Middle Ages: Collected papers*. Ed. G.L. Bursill-Hall. Amsterdam, p. 117-144.

HUYGENS, R.B.C. 1970 Introduction. In *Accessus ad auctores etc.* p. 1-18.

IRVINE, M. 1987 Interpretation and the semiotics of allegory in Clement of Alexandria, Origen and Augustine. In *Semiotica* 63, p. 33-71.

JACKSON, B. DARRELL 1969 The Theory of Signs in Saint Augustine's *De doctrina christian*. In *Revue des études augustiniennes* 15, p. 9-49.

JACKSON, W. T. H. 1960 *The Literature of the Middle Ages*. New York.
- 1980a Introduction. In *The Interpretation of Medieval Lyric Poetry*. Ed. by W.T.H. Jackson. New York, p. 1-21.
- 1980b The Interpretation of Carmina Burana 62, 'Dum Diane vitrea'. *Ibid.*, p. 44-60.

JEAUNEAU, EDOUARD 1965 Introduction. Teoksessa Guillelmus de Conchis, *Glosae super Platonem*, p. 1-56.

KAJANTO, IIRO 1960 *Ovid's conception of Fate*. Turku.

KELLY, HENRY ANSGAR 1993 *Ideas and Forms of Tragedy from Aristotle to the Middle Ages*. Cambridge Studies in Medieval Literature 18. Cambridge.

KENNEDY, GEORGE 1980 *Classical Rhetoric and its Christian and Secular Tradition from Ancient to Modern Times*. London & Sydney.

KINDERMANN, UDO 1978 *Satyra: Die Theorie der Satire in Mittellateinischen*. Nürnberg.
- 1982 Gattungssysteme im Mittelalter. In *Kontinuität und Transformation der Antike im Mittelalter*. Veröffentlichung der Konfrensakten zum Freiburger Symposion des Mediävistenverbandes. Hrsg. von W. Erzgräber. Sigmaringen, p. 303-313.

KIRWAN, CHRISTOPHER 1989/1991 *Augustine*. London & New York.

KITZINGER, ERNST 1973 World Map and Fortune's Wheel: A Medieval Mosaic Floor in Turin. In *Proceedings of the American Philosophical Society* 117:5, p. 344-373.

KLOPSCH, PAUL 1980 *Einführung in die Dichtungslehren der lateinischen Mittelalter*. Darmstadt.

KNOX, DILWYN 1989 *Ironia: Medieval and Renaissance Ideas on Irony*. Columbia Studies in the Classical Tradition 16. Leiden.

KNUUTTILA, SIMO 1992 Selitykset. In Aristoteles, *Fysiikka. Teokset III*. Helsinki, p. 191-228.
- 1993 *Modalities in Medieval Philosophy*. London & New York 1993.

KOROLEC, J.B. 1982/1990 Free Will and Free Choice. In *The Cambridge History of Later Medieval Philosophy*. Ed. by N. Kretzmann, A. Kenny & J. Pinborg. Cambridge, p. 629-641.

KRETZMANN, NORMAN 1985 *Nos Ipsi Principia Sumus*: Boethius and the Basis of Contingency. In *Divine Omniscience and Omnipotence in Medieval Philosphy. Islamic, Jewish and Christian Perspectives*. Ed. by T. Rudavsky. Dordrecht - Boston - Lancaster, p. 23-50.

KRISTEVA, JULIA 1969/1978 Le mot, le dialogue et le roman. In *Semeiotike*.

Recherches pour une sémanalyse. Paris,
p. 82-112.

LANGOSCH, KARL 1963/1975 *Lateinisches
Mittelalter. Einleitung in Sprache und
Literatur*. Darmstadt.

- 1964 *Die deutsche Literatur des lateinischen
Mittelalters in ihrer geschichtlichen
Entwicklung*. Berlin.

LATZKE, THERESE 1968 Die Mantel-
gedichte des Primas Hugo von Orléans
und Martial. In *Mittellateinisches Jahrbuch 5*, p. 54-58.

- 1970 Der Topos Mantelgedicht. In
Mittellateinisches Jahrbuch 6, p. 109-131.

LAUSBERG, HEINRICH 1960 *Handbuch
der literarischen Rhetorik. Eine
Grundlegung der Literaturwissenschaft
I-II*. München.

LAWRENCE, C.H. 1984 *Medieval
Monasticism. Forms of religious life in
Western Europe in the Middle Ages*.
London & New York.

LE BRAS, GABRIEL 1959 *Institutions
ecclésiastiques de la Chrétienté
médiévale. Préliminaires & Iere partie.
Livre I. Histoire de l'Église depuis les
origines jusqu'à nos jours 12*. Paris -
Tournai.

LE GOFF, JACQUES 1957/1985 *Les
intellectuels au Môyen Age*. Paris.

- 1977/1984 *Le civilisation de l'Occident
médiéval*. Paris.

- 1985 *L'imaginaire médiévale*. Paris.

LEHMANN, PAUL 1922 *Mittellateinische
Verse in Distinctiones monasticae et
morales vom Anfang des 13.
Jahrhunderts*. Sitzungsberichte der
bayerischen Akademie der Wissenschaften, philos.-philol. und hist. Klasse,
Jhrg 1922, Abh. 2. München.

- 1922-23/1963 *Die Parodie im Mittelalter.
Mit 24 ausgewählteparodistischen Texten*.
2., neu bearbeitete und ergänzte Auflage.
Stuttgart.

LEHTINEN, ANJA-INKERI 1993 Poetiikka
ja retoriikka tieteiden järjestelmässä
sydänkeskiajalla. In *Keskusteluja profes-
sorin kanssa. Professori Veikko Litzenin
juhlakirja*. Ed. T. Tuhkanen, E. Pispala ja
K. Virtanen. Turun yliopiston historian
laitoksen julkaisuja 28. Turku, p.
123-148.

LEHTONEN, TUOMAS M. S. 1989 Tempus
adest floridum: Poems and Interpreta-
tions. From Literary Criticism to
Intellectual History. In Miscellanea. Ed.
A. Tammisto, K. Mustakallio & H.
Saarinen. Societas Historica Fennica:
Studia historica 33. Helsinki, p.47-75.

- 1990 Puhutusta kirjoitettuun. Keskiaikaisesta
merkkiteoriasta, kirjallisuudesta ja yhteis-
kunnasta. In *tiede & edistys 15:3*, p.
193-208.

- 1991 Metafora, allegoria ja tulkinta.
Retorisesta traditiosta Augustinuksen

hermeneutiikkaan. In *Kirjallisuuden tutkijain Seuran vuosikirja 45*. Helsinki, p.
11-27.

- 1992 Kadonneen avaimen arvoitus ja
kuunalainen maailma. Keskiaikaista ja
modernia teoriaa runoudesta. In *Kirjallisuuden tutkijain seuran vuosikirja 46*.
Helsinki, p. 47-63.

- 1993 Ethice subponitur. Runous ja tiedon-
alojen järjestelmä sydänkeskiajalla. In
Historian alku. Toim. T. Seppä, T.
Hietaniemi, H. Mikkeli & J. Sihvola.
Helsinki, p. 135-157.

- 1994 *Hopemarkkojen evankeliumi*: Parodia,
ironia ja vaihto. In *Kirjallisuuden tutkijain Seuran vuosikirja 48*. Helsinki, p.
128-145.

- 1996 The World Upside Down. Poetry as
Ethics and Carmina Burana (CB 142). In
Göppinger Arbeiten zur Germanistik.
Göppingen (forthcoming).

LEMOINE, MICHEL 1991 Introduction. In
Hugues de Saint-Victor, *L'Art de lire.
Didascalicon*. Trad. M. Lemoine. Paris, p.
7-58.

LIPPHARDT, WALTHER 1982 Zur Herkunft
der 'Carmina Burana'. In *Literatur und
Bildende Kunst im Tiroler Mittelalter*.
Innsbruker Beiträge zur Kultur-
wissenschaften. Germanistische Reihe 15.
Hrsg. von J. Holzer, E. Koller, H.-P.
Ortner und S. P. Scheichl. Innsbruck, p.
209-223.

LITTLE, LESTER K. 1978/1983 *Religious
Poverty and the Profit Economy in
Medieval Europe*. Ithaca, N.Y.

LOTMAN, YURIJ 1971 Teser till problemet
'Konstens plats bland de model-bildande
system'. Övers. av E. Adolfsson. In *Form
och struktur*. Red. av K. Aspelin och B.A.
Lundberg. Stockholm.

LOTTIN, ODON 1942/1957-1960
*Psychologie et morale aux XIIe et XIIIe
siècles I-VI*. Gembloux.

LUBAC, HENRI DE 1959-1963/1993
*Exégèse médiévale: Les Quatre sens de
l'Écriture I-IV*. Paris.

LUSCOMBE, D.E. 1971 Peter Abelard and
Twelfth-Century Ethics. In *Peter
Abelard's Ethics*. Ed. by D.E. Luscombe.
Oxford, p. xiii-xxxvii.

MCDONOUGH, C.J. 1984 Introduction. In
*The Oxford Poems of Hugh Primas and
the Arundel Lyrics*. Ed. by C.J.
McDonough. Toronto, p. 1-25.

MCGREGOR, JAMES H. 1978 Ovid at
School: From the Ninth to the Fifteenth
Century. In *Classical Folia 32*, p. 29-51.

MCKEON, R. 1945 Poetry and Philosophy in
the Twelfth Century: The Renaissance of
Rhetoric. In *Modern Philology 43*, p.
217-234.

MANITIUS, MAX 1931 *Geschichte der
lateinischen Literatur des Mittelalters.
Vom Ausbruch des Kirchenstreites bis*

zum ende des zwölften Jahrhunderts. Bd. 3. Unter Paul Lehmanns Mitwirkung. München.

MANN, JILL 1980 Satiric Subject and Satiric Object in Goliardic Literature. In *Mittellateinische Jahrbuch* 15, p. 63-86.

MARKS, CLAUDE 1975 *Pilgrims, Heretics and Lovers: A Medieval Journey*. New York.

MARX, KARL 1859/1903 *Zur Kritik der politischen Ökonomie*. Hrsg. von Karl Kautsky. Stuttgart.

MAUSS, MARCEL 1950/1993 *Sociologie et anthropologie*. Paris.

MEHTONEN, PÄIVI 1991 "Mentiri debemus probabiliter" (Valehdelkaamme todennäköisesti) In *Kirjallisuuden tutkijain seuran vuosikirja* 45. Helsinki, p. 127-137.

- 1992 *Totuudellisuuden taito: Sepitteiden asema 1100-luvun ja 1200-luvun alun latinankielisessä kirjallisuusteoriassa*. Tampereen yliopisto, yleinen kirjallisuustiede: Julkaisuja 26. Tampere.

- 1996 *Old Concepts and New Poetics*. Historia, Argumentum *and* Fabula *in the 12th and Early 13th Century Latin Poetics of Fiction*. Tampere (forthcoming).

MEIER, CHRISTEL 1977 Zum Problem der allegorischen Interpretation mittelalterlicher Dichtung. Über ein neues Buch zum 'Anticlaudianus' des Alan von Lille. In *Beiträge zur Geschichte der Deutschen Sprache und Literatur* 99:2, p. 250-296.

MICHAUD-QUANTIN, PIERRE 1966 Notes sur le hasard et la chance. In *La Filosofia della natura del medioevo*. Atti del 3° congresso internazionale di filosofia medioevale 1964. Milano, 156-163.

MIKKELI, HEIKKI 1992 *An Aristotelian Response to Renaissance Humanism. Jacopo Zabarella on the Nature of Arts and Sciences*. Societas Historica Finlandiae: Studia Historica 41. Helsinki.

MINNIS, A. J. 1984 *Medieval Theory of Authorship. Scholastic Literary Attitudes in the Later Middle Ages*. London.

MINNIS, A.J. & SCOTT, A.B. (eds.) 1988/1991 *Medieval Literary Theory and Criticism c. 1100- c. 1375. The Commentary Tradition*. Rev. ed. Oxford.

MORRIS, COLIN 1972 *The Discovery of the Individual 1050-1200*. Church History Outlines 5. London.

MORSE, RUTH 1991 *Truth and Convention in the Middle Ages. Rhetoric, Representation, and Reality*. Cambridge.

MOULIN, LEO 1991 *La vie des étudiants au Moyen Age*. Paris.

MUNDY, JOHN 1973/1980 *Europe in the High Middle Ages 1150-1309*. London.

MURPHY, JAMES J. 1974/1981 *Rhetoric in the Middle Ages. A History of Rhetorical Theory from Saint Augustine to the Renaissance*. Berkeley, Los Angeles & London.

MURRAY, ALEXANDER 1978/1990 *Reason and Society in the Middle Ages*. Oxford.

NEDERMANN, CARY J. 1990 Editor's Introduction. In John of Salisbury, *Policraticus*. Ed. & transl. by C.J. Nedermann. Cambridge, p. xv-xxix.

NICHOLS, STEPHEN G. 1991 The New Medievalism: Tradition and Discontinuity in Medieval Culture. In *The New Medievalism*. Ed. by M.S. Brownlee, K. Brownlee & S.G. Nichols. Baltimore & London, p. 1-26.

NIELSEN, LAUGE OLAF 1982 *Theology and Philosophy in the Twelfth Century. A Study of Gilbert Porreta's Thinking and the Theological Expositions of the Doctrine of the Incarnation during the Period 1130-1180*. Acta Theologica Danica XV. Leiden.

NUSSBAUM, MARTHA 1993 Poetry and the passions: two Stoic views. In *Passions and Perceptions. Studies in Hellenistic Philosophy of Mind*. Proceedings of the Fifth Symposium Hellenisticum. Ed. by J. Bruschwig & M.C. Nussbaum. Cambridge, p. 92-149.

OCHSENBEIN, P. 1975 *Studien zum Anticlaudianus des Alanus ab Insulis*. Frankfurt A.M. - Bern.

OLSEN, GLENDING 1982 *Literature as Recreation in the Later Middle Ages*. Ithaca & London 1982.

PARLETT, DAVID 1986/1988 Introduction and Notes. In *Selections from the Carmina Burana. A New Verse Translation, Introduction, and Notes by David Parlett*. Harmondsworth, p. 9-50, 202-242.

PATCH, H. R. 1927 *The Goddess Fortuna in Medieval Literature*. Cambridge, Mass.

PAULY-WISSOWA II.5 *Paulys Real-Encyclopädie der classischen Altertumswissenschaft*. Neue Bearbeitung. Zweite Reihe V Bd. Begonnen von G. Wissowa, hrsg. von W. Kroll & K. Mittelhaus. Stuttgart 1934.

PELEN, MARC M. 1988 *Latin Poetic Irony in the Roman de la Rose*. Viniver Studies in French 4. Liverpool.

PELIKAN, JAROSLAV 1978 *The Christian Tradition. A History of the Development of Doctrine 3: The Growth of Medieval Theology 600-1300*. Chicago & London.

PÉPIN, JEAN 1987 *La tradition de l'allégorie de Philon d'Alexandrie à Dante*. Paris.

PEPIN, RONALD E. 1988 *Literature of Satire in the Twelfth Century. A Neglected Mediaeval Genre*. Studies in Mediaeval Literature 2. Lewinston - Queenston - Lampeter.

PFISTER, MANFRED 1985 Konzepte der Intertextualität. In *Intertextualität, Formen, Funktionen, anglistische Fallstudien*. Hrsg. von U. Broich und M.

Pfister. Tübingen, p. 1-30.

PICKERING, FREDERICK P. 1966 *Literatur und darstellende Kunst im Mittelalter.* Grunlagen der Germanistik 4. Berlin.

- 1967 *Augustinus oder Boethius? Geschichtsschreibung und epische Dichtung im Mittelalter - und der Neuzeit I: Einführender Teil.* Philologische Studien und Quellen 39. Berlin.

- 1976 *Augustinus oder Boethius. Geschichtsschreibung und epische Dichtung im Mittelalter - und der Neuzeit II: Darstellender Teil.* Philologische Studien und Quellen 80. Berlin.

PREMINGER, ALEX 1972/1990 Goliardic Verse. In *Princeton Encyclopedia of Poetry and Poetics.* Enlarged edition. Ed. by A. Preminger, F.J. Warnke & O.B. Hardison Jr. Princeton.

QUAIN, EDWIN A. 1945/1986 *The Medieval Accessus ad auctores.* Repr. from *Traditio* 3 (1945). New York.

RABY, F. J. E. 1934 *A History of Secular Latin Poetry in the* Middle Ages II. Oxford.

Renaissance and Renewal in the Twelfth Century. Ed. by R. L. Benson & G. Constable. Cambridge, Mass. 1982.

RAPP, FRANCIS 1993 Rapport introductif. In *Le clerc séculier au moyen âge. XXII* Congrés de la S.H.M.E.S. (Amiens, juin 1991). Société des Historiens Médiévistes de l'Enseignement Public. Série Ancienne et Médiévale 27. Paris, p. 9-25.

RICOEUR, PAUL 1986 *Du texte à l'action. Essais d'herméneutique II.* Paris.

RIFFATERRE, MICHAEL 1978 *Semiotics of Poetry.* Bloomington.

- 1981 L'intertexte inconnu. In *Littérature* 41, p. 4-7.

- 1991 The Mind's Eye: Memory and Textuality. In *The New Medievalism.* See Nichols 1991, p. 29-45.

RIGG, A. G. 1977a Golias and other Pseudonyms. In *Studi Medievali* 3. ser. XVIII:1, p. 65-109.

- 1977b Medieval Latin Poetic Anthologies I. In *Mediaeval Studies* 39, p. 281-321.

RIIKONEN, HANNU K. 1987 *Menippean Satire as a Literary Genre with special reference to Seneca's Apocolocyntosis.* Commentationes Humanarum Litterarum 83. Helsinki.

ROBERTSON, D.W. 1980 Two Poems from the Carmina Burana. In *idem, Essays in Medieval Culture.* Princeton, p. 131-150.

ROBINSON, DAVID M. 1946 The Wheel of Fortune. In *Classical Philology* 61, p. 207-216.

ROBINSON, I.S. 1990/1993 *The Papacy 1073-1198. Continuity and Innovation.* Cambridge.

ROLLINSON, PHILIP 1981 *Classical Theories of Allegory and Christian Culture.* Duquesne Studies Vol. 3.

Pittsburgh, Pa. & London.

RÜEGG, WALTHER 1993 Vorwort and Themen, Probleme, Erkenntnisse. In *Geschichte der Universität in Europa I: Mittelalter.* Hrsg. von W. Rüegg. München, p. 13-48.

SAYCE, OLIVE 1992 *Plurilingualism in the Carmina Burana. A Study of the Linguistic and Literary Influences on the Codex.* Göppinger Arbeiten zur Germanistik 556. Göppingen.

SCHALLER, DIETRICH 1975 Bemerkungen zum Schlußband der kritischenEdition der 'Carmina Burana'. In *Mittellateinisches Jahrbuch* 10, p. 106-115.

SCHIEFFER, R. 1974 Marchiones. Steiermärker in den Carmina Burana. In *Mitteilungen des Instituts für österreichische Geschichtforschung* 82, p. 412-418.

SCHMIDT, PAUL GERHARD 1974/1990 The Quotation in Goliardic Poetry: The Feast of Fools and the Goliardic Strophe *cum auctoritate.* Tr. by P. Godman. In *Latin Poetry and the Classical Tradition. Essays in Medieval and Renaissance Literature.* Ed. by P. Godman & O. Murray. Oxford, p.39-55.

SCHUMANN, OTTO 1930/1961, Einleitung (die Handschrift der Carmina Burana). In Hilka & Schumann 1930/1961, p. 1*-95*.

SCHÜPPERT, HELGA 1972 *Kirchenkritik in der lateinischen Lyrik des 12. und 13. Jahrhunderts.* Medium Aevum. Philologischen Studien 23. München.

SHERIDAN, JAMES J. 1980 Introduction. In Alan of Lille, *The Plaint of Nature,* p. 1-64.

SICARD, PATRICE 1991 *Hugues de Saint-Victor et son École.* Turnhout.

SMALLEY, BERYL 1952/1984 *The Study of the Bible in the Middle Ages.* Oxford.

SMOLAK, KURT 1986 Die bacchusgemeinschaft. (Drei mittelalterliche Trinklieder). In *Wiener Studien* N.S. 20 (99), p. 260-286.

- 1987 Epicurus propheta. Eine Interpretation von Carmen Buranum 211. In *Wiener Studien* 100, p. 247-256.

SOUTHERN, RICHARD W. 1970/1983 *Western Society and the Church in the Middle Ages.* Harmondsworth.

SOWELL, MADISON U. 1991 Introduction. In *Dante and Ovid: Essays in Intertextuality.* Ed. by M.U. Sowell. Medieval & Renaissance Texts & Studies 82. Binghamton, N.Y. p. 1-15.

STEER, GEORG 1982 Das Fortuna-Bild der 'Carmina Burana'-Handschrift clm. 46660. Eine Darstellung der *Fortuna cesarea* Kaiser Friedrichs II? In *Literatur und Bildende Kunst im Tiroler Mittelalter.* Innsbrucker Beiträge zur Kultruwissenschaft. Germanistische Reihe Bd. 15. Hrsg. von J. Holzner, E.

Koller, H.-P. Ortner & S.P. Scherchl. Innsbruck, p. 182-208.
- 1983 'Carmina Burana' in Südtirol. Zur Herkunft des clm 4660. In *Zeitschrift für deutsches Altertum und deutsche Literatur* 112, p. 1-17.
STRECKER, KARL 1929 *Moralischsatirische Gedichte Walters von Châtillon aus deutschen, englischen, französischen und italienischen Handschriften*. Hrsg. von K. Strecker. Heidelberg.
STIEFFEL, TINA 1985 *The Intellectual Revolution in the Twelfth-Century Europe*. London & Sydney.
STOCK, BRIAN 1972 *Myth and Science in the Twelfth Century. A Study of Bernard Silvester*. Princeton, N.J.
- 1978 Science, Technology, and Economic Progress in the Early Middle Ages. In *Science in the Middle Ages*. Ed. by David C. Lindberg. Chicago & London, p. 1-51.
- 1979 *Antiqui* and *Moderni* as 'Giants' and 'Dwarfs': A Reflection of Popular Culture? In *Journal of Modern Philology* 76, p. 370-374.
- 1983 *The Implications of Literacy. Written Language and Models of Interpretation in the Eleventh and Twelfth Centuries*. Princeton, N.J.
- 1990 *Listening for the Text: On the Uses of the Past*. Baltimore, MD.
STRUBEL, ARMAND 1975 "Allegoria in factis" et "allegoria in verbis". In *Poétique* 23, p. 342-370.
STUMP, ELEONORE 1983/1986 Dialectic. In *The Seven Liberal Arts in the Middle Ages*. Ed. by D.L. Wagner. Bloomington, 125-146.
SULOWSKI, JAN 1966 La philosophie de la nature chez Raoul de Longchamp. In *La Filosofia della natura nel medioevo*. Atti del 3° congresso internazionale di filosofia medioevale 1964. Milano, p. 320-327.
- 1976 Introduction. In Ralph of Longchamp, *In Anticl. Al. comm.*, p. I-XXXIV.
SZÖVÉRFFY, JOSEPH 1992-1994 *Secular Latin Lyrics and Minor Poetic Forms of the Middle Ages: A Historical Survey and Literary Repertory from the Tenth to the Late Fifteenth Century* I-III. Classical Folia: Main Series 25-27. Concord, N.H.
TAYLOR, JEROME 1961/1991 Introduction. In *The Didascalicon of Hugh of St. Victor*. Transl. J.J. Taylor. New York, p. 3-39.
THOMSON, RODNEY M. 1978 The Origins of Latin Satire in Twelfth Century Europe. In *Mittellateinisches Jahrbuch* 13, p. 73-83.
TODOROV, TZVETAN 1978 *Symbolisme et interprétation*. Paris.
VANCE, EUGENE 1986 *Mervelous Signals. Poetics and Sign Theory in the Middle Ages*. Lincoln & London.
- 1987 *From Topic to Tale. Logic and Narrativity in the Middle Ages*. Theory and History of Literature, Vol. 47. Minneapolis.
VAUCHEZ, ANDRÉ 1982/1990 Une normalisation sévère. In R. Fossier, *Le Moyen Age. L'èveil de l'Europe 950-1250*. Paris, p. 375-422.
VICKERS, BRIAN 1988/1990 *In Defence of Rhetoric*. Oxford.
VIIKARI, AULI 1990 Lyriikan runousoppia. In M. Kantokorpi, P. Lyytikäinen & A. Viikari, *Runousopin perusteet*. Lahti, p. 37-102.
VIIKARI, MATTI 1985 Edistyksestä. In *Kronikka* 3/85. Kronoksen 40-vuotisjuhlanumero. Helsinki, 8-11.
- 1995 *Historiallinen ajattelu, edistys ja yhteiskunta*. Eds. T. Hietaniemi & T.M.S. Lehtonen & työryhmä. Helsinki.
WADDELL, HELEN 1927/1955 *The Wandering Scholars. The Life and Art of the Lyric Poets of the Latin Middle Ages*. Garden City, N.Y.
WAGNER, DAVID L. 1983/1986 The Seven Liberal Arts and Classical Scholarship. In *The Seven Liberal Arts in the Middle Ages*. Ed. by D.L. Wagner. Bloomington, Ind., p. 1-31.
WALSH, P.G. 1976 Introduction & Commentary. In *Thirty Poems from the Carmina Burana*. Ed. by P.G. Walsh. Reading, p. 1-8, 63-141.
- 1983 'Golias' and Goliardic Poetry. In *Medium Aevum* 52:1, p. 1-9.
WATENPUHL, HEINRICH & KREFELD, HEINRICH 1958 Einführung. In *Die Gedichte des Archipoeta*. Kritisch bearbeitet von H. Watenpuhl, herausgegeben von H. Krefeld. Heidelberg, p. 19-45.
WEHRLI, MAX 1985 Poeta ludens. Zum Spielelement der mittelalterlichen Literatur. In *Variorum munera florum. Latinität als prägende Kraft des mittelaltelichen Kultur*. Festschrift für Hans F. Haefele. Hrsg. von A. Reinle, C. Schmugge & P. Stotz. Sigmaringen, p. 193-203.
WEISHEIPL, J. A. 1965 Classification of the sciences in Medieval Thought. In *Mediaeval Studies* 27, p. 54-90.
- 1978 The Nature, Scope, and Classification of the Sciences. In *Science in the Middle Ages*. Ed. D. C. Lindberg. Chicago, p. 461-482.
WESTRA, HAIJO J. 1986 Introduction. In Bernard Silvester, *Comm. in Mart.*, p. 1-33.
WETHERBEE, WINTHROP 1972 *Platonism and Poetry in the Twelfth Century*. Princeton, N.J.
WHITMAN, JON 1987 *Allegory. The Dynamics of an Ancient and Medieval Technique*. Cambridge, Mass.
WILHELM, J.J. 1965 The Cruelest Month.

Spring, Nature, and Love in Classical and Medieval Lyrics. New Haven & London.

WIRTH, JEAN 1989 *L'image médiévale. Naissance et développements (VIe -XIe siècle)*. Paris.

WITKE, CHARLES 1970 *Latin Satire: The Structure of Persuasion*. Leiden.

WOLFF, ÉTIENNE 1995 Présentation. In *Carmina Burana*. Tr. par É. Wolff. Paris, 7-41.

YUNCK, JOHN A. 1961 Economic Conservatism, Papal Finance, and the Medieval Satires on Rome. In *Medieval Studies* 23, p. 334.351.

- 1963 *The Lineage of Lady Meed: The Development of Mediaeval Venality Satire*. Publications in Mediaeval Studies 17. Notre Dame, Ind.

ZUMTHOR, PAUL 1986 Y-a-t-il une 'littérature' médiévale? In *Poétique* 66, p. 131-140.

■ References to the poems of the *Carmina Burana*

■ Index